Paul Eggerman

Guilt and Desire

Guilt and Desire

*Religious Attitudes and Their
Pathological Derivatives*

Antoine Vergote

Translated by M. H. Wood

Yale University Press
New Haven and London

M. H. Wood wishes to acknowledge the assistance that she received from consulting Thomas Acklin's preliminary translation of this work.

Originally published in French as *Dette et désir: Deux axes chrétiens et la dérive pathologique,* © Editions du Seuil, 1978.
First published in English by Yale University Press, © 1988, Yale University.

Designed by Sujata Keshavan Guha and set in Baskerville type by Rainsford Type, Ridgefield, Connecticut.
Printed in the United States of America by Book Crafters, Inc., Chelsea, Michigan.

Library of Congress Cataloging-in-Publication Data

Vergote, Antoine.
  [Dette et désir. English]
  Guilt and desire: religious attitudes and their pathological
  derivatives/
  Antoine Vergote: translated by M. H. Wood.
  p.   cm.
  Translation of: Dette et désir.
  Includes index.
  ISBN 0–300–02938–1 (alk. paper)
  1. Psychology, Religious.   2. Guilt—Religious aspects.
3. Desire.   I. Title.
BL53.V37613 1988
200'.1'9—dc19   87–31615
                    CIP

The paper in this book meets the guidelines for permanence and durability of the Committee on Production Guidelines for Book Longevity of the Council on Library Resources.

10 9 8 7 6 5 4 3 2 1

• Contents

• Preface

Debt and desire: two words, both charged with an uncanny, disquieting familiarity. They subvert the very ground on which reason would confidently establish its empire. Although the ordinary connotations of these two words are known to everyone, they also evoke the strange, imaginary terrains inhabited by the rambling disorders of mind.

Man is a creature of unknown and distant origins. Neither the ground nor the source of his own being, every man receives his existence as a gift by which he is called forth to be, through the process of becoming. Whether or not he is a religious believer he is aware that he is the steward of his own life as well as the guardian of man's humanity. To silence the insistent reminders of his indebtedness he would have to be completely oblivious to all his origins, near, distant, and ultimate. Even were he to attain this state of innocence, he would still have to exile himself from the human community, and then he would have to erase the very memory of his flight into solitary freedom. For the word, the glance, the gaze of another, which travel through the innermost parts of his being, must inevitably remind him of his human, and eventually of his divine, heritage, a heritage of which he is the indebted recipient and pledged, obligated agent. Each and every individual must come to terms with this debt, or, in one way or another, guilt will in turn dictate its terms to him.

And when an individual attempts to seclude himself in serene harmony with himself, a secret pain needles his slumbering existence. Desire comes to hollow out a trench between what he is and what he is not. He may try to live in resignation or to lose himself in the varied pleasures that are offered him; but try as he will, he knows that the state of no desire, the obliteration of all desire, is an impossible dream. Beyond the horizon of objects which captivate his fascination and by means of which he attempts to compensate for what he is not, a certain presence solicits him: a presence close to the most intimate and yet incessantly receding experience he has of himself, a presence lingering at the extremity of his most obstinate dreams. From the moment of his first awakening, in fact, language has struck his being and, challenging his passions, deprives him of the interior stronghold in which he might find support when he turns in upon himself. Later in his life, words of love will speak promises that seem to hearken back to an indelible memory of a primal happiness. Desire launches an odyssey: propelled by the hope of returning to our native soil, it projects us forward toward a new future. It is in this desire that religious mysticism finds its spring.

Debt and desire represent two basic dimensions of existence. For this reason, these two themes are at the heart of both religion and psychoanalysis. In concrete existence these two dimensions intersect, whether on a specifically religious or a universally human plane. Nevertheless, they establish two different fields of manifestation that we must distinguish yet not separate.

Kant summed up the universal questions of mankind: What can one know? What must one do? What can one hope for? The first question springs from the theoretical interests of reason. The last two express the vital concern with which man regards his existence. Although Kant's formulation confers a certain philosophical serenity on these queries, the actual force of debt and desire in concrete experience makes them urgent, pressing questions, questions pertinent to the way men live their lives. Even before his first memories have taken full shape, an individual's particular experience of debt and desire has already left its mark in the fundamentally instinctual stratum of his being. Then later, both by disclosing the origins of life and by prompting him to a divine purpose, religious discourse deepens the sense of his indebtedness and quickens the force of his desire.

The mutually interacting networks of demands—those from outside the individual and those inscribed within the psychic system—constitute the two dimensions where the disciplines of psychoanalysis and religious studies can be brought together in a common field of inquiry. Measured against the vast scope of such an enterprise, this work is considerably limited. I have chosen here to concentrate on the internal tensions and unavoidable conflicts with which religion must grapple. These conflicts are inscribed in the very heart of religion, and it is these that propel and determine its progress. Moreover, the believer's standpoint is marked by a twofold excess: an excess of the unconscious significations that, in spite of man's intentions, assert themselves on him, and the excess of hidden significations he apprehends in manifestations of the divine. A truly authentic faith will assume these tensions, but no matter how legitimate the explicit intentions of belief may be, these conflicts, which touch the very roots of man's being, are fraught with snares and delusions, and the religious path remains a confused and risky one. Like any other human enterprise, faith can also fall into the helplessness and pathological binds that distort the best acts and intentions of religious men.

The analysis of different pathological forms occupies a central place in this work; throughout, my intention has been to approach these forms through an examination of the internal logic of the psychic apparatus, as psychoanalysis has elucidated it. Such an examination will, I hope, disclose the unconscious material that tends to obscure the aims of faith; it may also uncover the obstacles that prevent a believer from complying with the divine appeal that summons him. The detours I have taken through the various pathological forms of religious faith are prompted by one fundamental purpose: to disclose the structured significations that make up a healthfully lived religion. In order to specify my intention more fully, I would add that "words ought to be understood according to their lateral implications, not just their manifest and frontal meaning."[1] An interpretation of religious pathology clarifies especially those "lateral implications" that organize the life of faith. Thus, by examining these mentally obstructing conflicts we can better understand the import of impulses that appear arbitrary and confused but in fact concern the most profound depths of our being.

In the first part of this book I set forth the principles that inform my interpretations and try to demonstrate how the two discourses of psychoanalysis and faith can be articulated one with the other. It is not my purpose here to unify these disciplines or to examine their conjuncture in the theoretical field of inquiry; rather, my object is to legitimate the twofold process of analysis operating throughout this book: one having constant recourse to the theory and experience of psychoanalysis, the other to the religious set of meanings at work. I have already suggested that it is this very circularity linking unconscious representations and cultural and religious signifiers that guides our interpretive procedure. As this circularity raises some rather complex questions, however, I have attempted to pinpoint the basic issues.

The second and third parts examine the two dimensions evoked in the title of this book. Each carries its own set of pathological expressions, in everyday life, in culture, and in religion. It is not strictly by accident that man is beset by two basic forms of neurosis or that these are organized along the two basic registers of debt and desire. Man is easily subject to pathological forces: at that point in his being where *pathos* imposes its own necessity upon him, the point at which man is put to the test and—as Euripides reminds us—the test instructs him. An analysis of these tests and the setbacks they can offer man will contribute to our knowledge of the forces at play in our lives and in our faith. Even though a religious destiny breaks the bounds of other human endeavors, it still summons man to the place where his human destiny is forged. We must delve into the deep recesses of pathology if we are to redeem the words so silently mouthed there and the suffering that awaits its significance, or if we are to revive the body and the spirit by the power of those signs by which our destiny requests us.

PART ONE

Introduction

1 • Religion and Pathology: Guidelines

Historical Perspective

In cultures that have not yet been affected by modern Western rationality, the interpretation of mental pathology still remains a religious one. Although minds permeated by the medical concepts dominant today may find this peculiar or puerile, the fact nonetheless remains that beneath such "magical" and "superstitious" representations is the perception of a fundamentally human dimension in "mental" illness, for these cultures have a commonly shared and comprehensive symbolic system that allows religion to situate pathological anomalies within an integral vision of man. Since the rupture brought about by the scientific spirit, it is no longer a question of simply transposing a mythological language into our therapies. It is, rather, a question of recovering—against our positivistic narrowness—the human significance of these illnesses. In this respect, as the emergence of ethnopsychiatry has confirmed, archaic civilizations have an instructive value for us. And while the relationship between the religious life and mental illness is a far more subtle one than scientifically immature civilizations have yet conceived it to be, the close connection between these two domains must be recognized in any inquiry concerned with the human sciences.

Let us briefly recall the ancient religious interpretation of psychopathological phenomena. Because mental disturbance is both human and uncanny, it was understood as a form of possession by a divine, ancestral, or demonic spirit. Depending on the cultural climate and the forms of its expression, possession was considered either a sign of election or a punishment for an offense or fault.[1] Later, primitive Christianity revived the demonological notion of mental illness and, by submitting it to a monotheistic faith, reinterpreted and reinforced it. Because it is a message of salvation addressing man in his radical liberty and demanding from him a decision concerning his own being, monotheism demystifies the primitive universe peopled by propitious and injurious spirits and demons. The only supernatural powers that exert their influence on men are the spirit of God and the antagonistic spirit; and since the spirit of God illuminates, heals, and raises man's mind to the understanding of the mystery of salvation, the demonological explanation imputes all unreason to the activity of the devil.

The evangelical narratives support this interpretation. In fact, according to the evangelists, Christ himself adopted the Judaic belief of his time, which had reformulated the demonological explanation by a deepening of creationist faith. As the creature of the one and only God, man does not subsist by himself alone; for fear of finding himself given over to the undermining power of the Evil One, man must remain bound by faith to the vivifying power of the Creator. Now, observation of those who suffered disorders of mind revealed that they were not in harmony with the order of creation; from this it was concluded that a subversive, alien force had seized them, producing through them and in them acts of destructive violence. In the absence of a medical anthropology, a faith that concentrates on God as the creator of all life and order would necessarily relate any derangement of reason to the father of all monstrosity. Furthermore, the cures Christ performed became for his contemporaries a sign of the work He came to accomplish. The Gospels present Christ as having the divine power to liberate the "possessed" man, to restore his reason and health by binding him to God through faith—not with ritual exorcisms but simply by the authority of his word.[2]

All these religious interpretations tend to attribute possession by an evil spirit to some offense committed by the possessed or some fault in his surroundings. Curative rites always consist of the identification and confession of a transgression followed by an act of reparation.[3] Such an approach sometimes astonishes those who know to what extent freedom is entrenched in the body and in the unconscious; but an interpretation that regards the possessed as responsible agents at least does not treat their disorders as byproducts of a mechanical body but rather links mental alienation to a personal history. In this way exorcism acts as a form of therapy. (I will return to this point at the end of this work.)

The resurgence of the demonological explanation, however, resulted in the atrocious persecution of those believed to be secret allies of the devil. At the end of the Middle Ages and during the Renaissance, Christianity was convinced that the devil exercised his subversive activity through sorcerers as well as heretics, and because they were considered guilty, the most severe sentences were set aside for them. Divisions in the Church and the consequent oscillations in its representation of God the Father generally diffused the dread of the devil and of witchcraft, inciting the population to combat them.[4]

Since then science has demystified the demonological concept of mental alienation. The father of medicine, Hippocrates, who had already fought against this concept, proposed instead an organic explanation, which was sporadically taken up by isolated others. Yet it was not until the seventeenth century that a medical explanation arose—and it did not lead to a thoroughly humane treatment of the mentally ill. However, by demystifying the ancient religious interpretation, the sciences of psychiatry have also lost the specifically human significance of mental illness. It was left to Freud's genius to demonstrate the inadequacy of a strictly scientific explanation and to substitute an interpretation that restored the understanding concealed in ancient interpretations.[5] An individual who is mentally ill is in fact in the grip of forces that act upon him against his will, but these forces are specifically human—psychic, not supernatural. By translating primitive religious forms into psychological language it is possible to decipher the symbolic expression of psychic reality latent in demonology, a reality consisting of disguised wishes, anxieties, and the stratagems to slip by censorship. These demonological forms would constitute—in terms of religious imagery—a staggering psychiatric record. For example, the celebrated *Malleus Maleficarum* ("the sorcerer's hammer"), written toward the end of the fifteenth century, already compiled a number of psychiatric syndromes organized as different forms of diabolical possession.

The psychological interpretation established by Freud tends to be just as comprehensive as the ancient one. But if mental illness is a psychological phenomenon and not a religious one, could not the same be true for all aspects of religion? If mental disorders have taken the form of supernatural visitations, is it not because the belief in supernatural agencies belongs to the same order of psychological pathology? Thus religion, which treats mental pathology, itself becomes an object of interpretation for the new science of psychopathology. For this reason religious circles were wary of psychoanalysis: they were far more comfortable with an organicist psychiatry that permitted them to adopt the scientific explanation of the established forms of mental illness while retaining a "spiritualist" concept of man.

Freud's positivist convictions, repeatedly affirmed in his declaration that only science has the authority to speak on issues of truth, definitely determined his psychological interpretations of religion. But of greater importance is the fact that the psychoanalytic interpretation of religion has restored to the whole problematic of mental pathology the scope it had in the ancient religious interpretations. As Freud continued to develop his interpretations, through his clinical experience and his work in cultural anthropology, he became more clearly aware of the interplay between individual pathology and the cultural history of men and women. Thus it was possible to understand individual pathology as a manifestation of the general disorder characterizing humanity. For it is not only the ancient religious interpretation of established diseases that contains a hidden truth but religion itself that acts as the symbolic guardian of psychic events.

Let us illustrate this psychoanalytic perspective, for it is important to see how, by expanding the field of pathology, psychoanalysis has prepared the way for other inquiries concerning the relation between religion and mental health and, broadly speaking, between culture and pathology.

Religion, according to Freud, is the collective neurosis of humanity. This maxim is as well known as it is misunderstood. In order to grasp the problematic broached by this formula it should be confronted with another, less frequently quoted maxim: "Obsessional neurosis presents a travesty, half-comic and half-tragic, of a private religion."[6] Although the differences between neurosis and religion cannot be affirmed more clearly, this "analogy" between the two phenomena shows how, in Freud's view, both are ways of more or less successfully resolving one of the fundamental problems of mankind: the problem of guilt. Guilt is an unavoidable reality; it is a fact with which man must contend and which he cannot deny with impunity. This is why religion often spares men the necessity of taking unconscious recourse in one of its most painful simulations: obsessional neurosis.[7]

This is not the place to discuss either Freud's notion of civilization's discontents or the "scientific myth" by which he explains the universal wounding of man's nature by the parricide committed at the threshold of human history. It is important, however, to observe that, through the development of his theories of mental pathology, Freud was progressively led to identify the resolution of all the ills of humanity that culture has not been able to overcome with an ideal of sanity and well-being. It was not to signal a purely antireligious defiance that Freud represented himself as the new Moses who would lead the chosen into health through the initiation of analysis, but also to revive in all its fullness—now from a radically atheistic perspective—the quest for an impossible psychic integrity.

The problem of psychic health, then, goes beyond the question of individual neuroses. In order to summarize Freud's position one might take a modified version of Hegel's statement that man is a sick animal. In Freud's interpretive analysis of pathologies one finds more than one bargained for: the image is one of humanity overwhelmed by a strange destiny, held in its power and prevented from attaining the longed-for happiness and ideal of sanity. According to Freud's later work, Christianity elucidates this fundamental truth, but it does so in the religious language of sin and redemption—a language that, for Freud, remains only symbolic. Therefore it both reveals and obscures the dramatic plight of our culture and psyche by displacing it onto a celestial screen.

Since Freud, most of his adherents have taken a more pragmatic approach to the question. These new advocates of healthy sexual activity and neat adaptation to reality have scarcely troubled themselves to study his anthropological investigations into the foundations of mental illness. To present a reassuring humanist front they avoid any truly essential questions, and in the interest of displaying the benevolent face of science, the established Freudians of our day have chosen to shield themselves from Freud's troubling speculations. One even wonders if most Freudians have not preferred to neutralize the entire question of religion by invoking from the very start some principle of neutrality. As we know, Freud affirms that since psychoanalysis is not a world vision, it should remain neutral regarding the value of religious affirmations—this forms a part of the therapeutic canon governing every analyst.[8] But insofar as he was also a theorist of pathology, Freud was persuaded that the roots of pathology are deeply anchored in the sorts of event evoked by religious representations, and he believed that it is the task of psychoanalysis to disclose their real meaning.

Others since Freud have erased the vague boundaries he traced between psychoanalytic theory and a psychoanalysis of culture, between mental illness and the malaise of civilization. For these psychotherapists, no therapy can heal the roots of an illness if it does not reconcile the individual with the religious nature that is the universal source and origin of his desires and symbolic creations. They believe they are justified in reinstating mental health to its original religious context. Contrary to Freud, they attribute the abnormal derangements of man not to a latent, fundamental sense of guilt but rather to the mystical desire for an absolute meaning and an absolute participation in the divine spirit, a desire whose deprivation entails a fundamental and profound discontent. Freud interprets mysticism through a romantic vitalist perspective, identifying it with the desire for immediate contact with the raw being of the id. For him, the faith in one god, God the Father, is the essential factor of religion, stemming first from the guilt that ensues from the murder of the father. This is culturally "spiritualized" and then inevitably becomes the foundation of "cultural renunciations" and a more general sense of guilt. For those who in contradistinction to Freud would incorporate the entire legacy of religion into psychology, the essence of religion lies in the breach that mystical eruptions create in the apparently reassuring enclosures constructed by limited beings. How can man escape from what Kierkegaard calls "the sickness unto death" if he seeks to eradicate the cleavage at the very origin of his being? Where Freud refuses to grant the psyche any final totality, others hold that this desire for the absolute or the divine which grants the psychic apparatus a religious finality is at the heart of psychopathology. By this argument they justify the positive introduction of religion into the therapeutic endeavor.

Let us briefly mention some of those who have attempted to erase the boundaries between the domain of religion and that of mental health. Convinced that the beneficent presence of religious language and symbols profoundly structures the psyche, C. G. Jung, first a disciple of Freud and then a dissenter, assimilated them within an extended psychology. The individual in search of psychic integrity must incorporate into his life the archetypal religious productions that make up the web of his life. Paradoxically, this psychological transcription of religious language turns Jung's God into a psychic quality that few religious believers would recognize as the God of their prayers and worship. Jung's psychomysticism has often aroused the fervor of third-rate theologians and individuals looking for a revival of the great mystical spring. Others, such as Maeder, who is closer to Freud, are convinced that religious faith has a therapeutic value, which they introduce into their practice without translating it into psychological terms when the patients themselves expressly search for a faith to ground their existence and bring reconciliation into their lives.[9]

Recently certain tendencies in the "antipsychiatry" movement reaffirm the position that the religious dimension is not just an erratic step in the progression of those who seek some form of self-realization. Norman Brown finds sufficient support in Freud's works to criticize his rationalism as well as the technical rationalism of contemporary culture; Brown argues that both art and mystical religion ought to deploy the experience of play, of union and well-being, that prevails in the first figurations of man's psyche.[10] Close to Brown in this respect, R. Laing maintains that in many forms of schizophrenia a "transcendental experience" opens the mentally ill to a dimension of existence not available to most people.[11] In his view, psychosis imparts a mystical message whose significance is obscured by psychiatry and repressed by contemporary civilization. We might also recall that Abraham Maslow, the founder of "humanist psychology," considered the capacity to lend oneself to mystical experience a necessary characteristic of the fully realized personality and an indispensable force for psychic health.[12] In short, the invasion of Eastern mysticism and thought into the West has generally promoted a broader notion of mental health as well as prompted a number of psychotherapists to systematically incorporate into their practices various forms of religious experience.[13]

The general indictment brought by the older forms of psychiatry against the scientifically suspect irregularities of mysticism is no longer considered unanimous. Thus the mystical phenomenon, being congenial with religion as is guilt, lends itself to contradictory interpretations. Is mysticism the experience of an ineffable presence at once revealed and veiled both to the senses and to reason? Is it a figure of madness? Or is it, within the range of essentially human possibilities, actually the highest spiritual communication that man is capable of achieving? There is no point in shirking the question by claiming that the mystical phenomenon is confined to the phantasmagoric fringes of religion, because it is, in fact, at the vital center. In the prophetic message and in the evangelical narratives, supernatural visions and auditions are the means by which faith is expressed and disseminated.

This is not the place to judge either the religious authenticity or the psychological quality of mystical phenomena; these matters will be considered later and, where possible, their ambiguous connections to hysteria or schizophrenia will be untangled. Is schizophrenia, for instance, strictly a negative phenomenon, or does it conceal the affirmation of an absolute presence, a presence without which any existence stretched to the limits of its viability becomes difficult to sustain. For some a morbid phantasmagoria and for others a spiritual waking torn from the sleep of reason and the slumber of the senses, the psyche's proclivity for mystical experience confronts us with the problematic limits of the normal and the pathological.

That there is an exchange between religion and psychopathology cannot be denied. As soon as it recognizes the reality of the psyche, psychopathology discovers that far from being an isolated, residual anomaly, mental illness is an affliction that any individual may face. Mental health is a moving point that ranges from the clear-cut pathological case to the asymptotic ideal of a fully realized and reconciled life. And in the span between these two interdependent movements, between the search for an explanation of the origins of evil and the search for sanity, psychopathology encounters religious interpretations of existence.

Our survey of the historical affinities between psychopathology and religion will allow us to articulate fundamental questions raised by this rapport. In the remainder of this chapter we will explore these questions and so present the prolegomenon necessary for the studies that follow.

1. We have seen how the emergence of a psychopathology worthy of the name inaugurated the development of a plurality of perspectives on the rapport between psychopathology and religion. Various people have affirmed in many ways that religion is favorable, indeed necessary, to mental health. Despite the profound differences among them, the aim of all religions is to help man achieve his essential stature and to proffer remedies for his various wounds. Although informed by science now, Christianity continues to invoke the Holy Spirit as the power that heals what is wounded, straightens what is twisted, and renders fertile what is sterile. As this is a psychological and not a theological study, we are not obliged to judge the religious convictions we meet in our study.

2. If religious beliefs, representations, and ritual behavior are considered not as mediations of a divine activity but as a cultural fact and the matrix of subjective orientations, the question of religion's impact on psychic health remains pertinent for the human sciences. Let us simply recall here that according to Freud, religion has spared many an individual from a neurotic disorder; in the final analysis this clinical observation finds justification in the drama generated by the fundamental fissure traversing all cultures, which introduces an irremediable fault, as it were, into the human condition. Furthermore, Jung and certain spokesmen for the school of antipsychiatry consider that without a religious dimension, man remains inwardly incomplete. I do not intend to address this issue here.[14] The questions involved are too complex to allow for any final resolution; they are, strictly speaking, "undecidable." As they concern the specific individual, they are devoid of meaning, for it is evident that religion is not generally a necessary condition for mental health, and it does not universally serve to prevent individuals from becoming neurotic. The problem could be approached appropriately only by keeping in view the whole of society and by considering how it affects the individual involved.

   How does religion influence the quality of a civilization? Can it be proven that a radically desacralized culture can no longer find the means to regenerate and save itself from anomie? If the desire for mysticism is essential to man, to what extent does the failure to recognize this have a disturbing effect on him? These questions are posed by any psychopathology that takes seriously human desire and distress, and we must keep them constantly in view. But any answer must be necessarily conjectural and should be drawn from the point where cultural anthropology, sociology, and psychology meet, each discipline presupposing the instruction the others bring to bear on these issues.

3. Once the idea of mental health itself is tackled, an infinity of questions opens up. But however broad a scope one gives the concept of integral well-being and whatever the ultimate roots of evil may be, there are nevertheless some forms of existence that are manifestly morbid. It is with reference to these forms that psychopathology is progressively elaborated. However, if we take into account the fact that the term *collective neurosis* is simply an analogical transposition of the concept of individual neurosis, what then are the discernible limits and contours of pathology? Our first task, therefore, is to formulate a definite set of criteria that will enable us to differentiate between pathology and health. It may be noted that these criteria are no more simple than the reality to which they must apply. For example, after having eliminated as irrelevant any given canonical measure of normalcy that might be extrinsically imposed upon the subject, we will have to draw our criteria from man's expressive life itself.

4. In order to show how psychopathology is a corresponding negative of the psyche, it must be examined within the formative process of the psychic life that has been altered by the pathological condition. For psychic life develops according to the vicissitudes that prevail at its genesis, and the causes of psychic illness are themselves psychic. Consequently I accept the translation of a religious interpretation of psychopathology into a psychological language, and I am convinced that only a theory of psychic causality can account for the fact that the boundary between health and illness is not fixed and explain how an intervention of a therapeutic or existential order can transform the negative into its positive.

5. Can the pathological modalities of religion also be attributed to a psychic causality? To what extent is the psychological reinterpretation of religious pathology effective? I hope to demonstrate that either a global religious interpretation or an exhaustive psychological interpretation is imaginary. This will lead us, in turn, to broaden the notion of psychic causality by taking up the question of the link between the psychic and the religious—both considered as cultural facts. To claim that psychic causality is operative here does not exclude a causal relation between the psychic and the social. On the contrary, the interpretation of individual pathologies always leads us back to the family structure and the social milieu that make them possible and sometimes even provoke them. Religious representations and practices also belong to the cultural networks that can promote psychic

health or induce pathological conditions. This observation leads us to ask whether we can find in religion itself the principles that might permit us to identify its more nefarious forms. If so, we must then confront these principles with our psychological criteria.

The Illusion of Objective Measurements

By "objective measurements" I mean the use of concepts and instruments that would determine what is pathological by measuring the degree to which a particular symptom or phenomenon deviates from standard rules of functioning, rules extraneously imposed. Take, for example, the following concepts, which seem to bracket a purely subjective standard and to promise an objective ground for diagnosis: the concept of a social norm; the concept of adaptation, corollary to the first; and the concept of reality as an empirically verifiable entity. The individual whose behavior does not conform to that approved by the group to which he belongs, the one who does not adapt to his society, and the one who cannot distinguish what is real from what is not—these are the individuals who would be considered ill according to these criteria. And yet these spontaneous judgments on what is pathological are in fact conceptual traps. They always presuppose an underlying and unavowed anthropology that shifts incessantly according to the needs and ends of whoever employs them; moreover, they impose an alienating repression upon the psychic life of man.

The term *abnormal* implies a value judgment made in reference to a given situation. So if the norm invoked is extraneous to the psyche, its source can be found only in the laws society has set for itself—those laws, in other words, that furnish the models according to which individuals regulate their relationships and pattern their lives and activities. But where can we find a social norm that would allow us to define what is pathological? If we take recourse in a statistical mean of behavior, we reduce an individual's singularity to pathology. Such an approach is clearly absurd. What is more, any creative initiative shown by individuals—a clear sign of psychic health and a contribution to the good of society—is statistically and even socially "deviant." Individual initiative opens up unforeseen possibilities, but it also fosters an insecurity that makes it suspect to common sense.[15]

The same kind of ambiguity hampers the concept of adaptation. Because it is dependent on the idea of a social norm, the notion of adaptation promotes conformity to social demands as the standard of mental health and, in the long run, proposes a rigid model as an ideal of sanity. The term *deviance*, which some have recently chosen in lieu of "mental illness," brings into relief, under the guise of apparent respect and decency, the qualitative differences of value judgments largely influenced by specific social conditions and political orientations. In this context it is impossible not to evoke the specter of totalitarian regimes that reject differences of opinion as anomalies and treat them by psychiatric techniques of brainwashing. Nevertheless, the term *adaptation* still has meaning and use for psychopathology, provided that it is qualified by keeping it in dialectical relation to creativity.[16] Any evaluation of mental health or sanity inevitably takes into account the individual's recognition or failure to recognize social realities. A positive adaptation is signaled by the subject's knowing how to observe these realities and to operate with them so as to draw new experience from them.

To distinguish pathology according to an idea of reality that takes it as an objectively given entity remains a rather summary procedure; for what ultimately anchors the certitude of what is real and unreal, probable and improbable? Many individuals have experienced a transformation of reality at a given moment. A reality that was previously invisible, objectively unverifiable, and until that rich moment improbable, takes on density, transforming ordinary reality and investing it with another sense. A similarly surreal irruption takes place in delirium, but it occurs also in religious conversion, philosophical illumination, and poetic inspiration. With his exemplary lucidity, Freud concluded *The Future of an Illusion* with the qualification that religion is an illusion, not hallucination, for religion does not deny the fact of common reality but rather reaffirms by the force of its desire a reality that science can neither prove nor refute. In Freud's view, then, religion, insofar as it is an illusion of desire, does not fall within the scope of psychopathology in the proper sense of the term. His positivism tends to flatten out and reduce the notion of reality to the single dimension of scientific knowledge, relegating both art and religion to the status of oneiric consolation; still, he refused himself the right to judge as pathological a belief that did not happen to agree with his own philosophy of reality.

The distinction between illusion and hallucination is considerably more problematic when one is faced with specific religious experiences than it is when one analyzes religion as a cultural and institutional phenomenon. Struck by a religious calling, fascinated and disturbed by the oracular force of certain words, an individual's certitude may desert him. A different view of life, never perceived before, may subvert his previously acquired perception of reality; at times he may even find himself threatened by a profound spiritual disorder. A feeling of religious shame, the intensification of the common religious sense of modesty, frequently follows; it is, in fact, the expression of an underlying fear of surrendering to phantasmagorical visions. This confusion inevitably produces a profound conflict concerning the criteria that orient reality. The external signs of a commonly shared belief do not guarantee the consistency of an experience as singular and individualized as this, where the uncertain boundaries between the imaginary, the illusory, the spiritual vision, and the irruption of madness are blurred. It would be pointless to appeal to some conventional or epistemological principle of reality to differentiate between the normal and the pathological here.

The variations among cultures alert us to the inadequacy of criteria based on principles of adaptation and reality. For example, signing a pact with the devil to buy power and thus to escape the material and affective calamities of life would, in our culture, be considered a psychotic delusion. But in an era when diabolical interference was a widespread belief, such a pact was seen as a religious transgression of a neurotic sort, and not necessarily understood as the sign of madness. In "A Seventeenth-Century Demonological Neurosis," Freud takes into account the religious context of the age in which Haitzmann lived and does not consider him mad.[17] Similarly, one cannot take shamanistic ritual or the strangeness of its belief as signs of pathology, because it evolves from a precise cultural context.[18] However, if an individual were to invent such a construct outside of any institutional context, the same system of beliefs would be aberrant.[19] For the same reason, we do not give St. Paul's visions of being transported to heaven (whether in or outside of his body, he could not tell)[20] a pathological diagnosis. It would be convenient here to distinguish between two levels: the beliefs of a society and the system of beliefs that organizes the interior life of the individual. Viewed from the outside, some forms of behavior appear bizarre or even overtly pathological, even though they can be situated within the symbolic system of the given culture.

Must we conclude, then, that the criteria of pathology are irremediably relative? Actually they are far more universal than they appear to be at a superficial glance. Even if the concept of madness varies according to a society's notion of the forces at work, the fact that every culture provides therapeutic means for remedying the various disorders of the spirit indicates that it has some way of distinguishing sanity from madness according to its own rules of order. It makes no fundamental difference whether one interprets madness as an invasion by evil spirits or as a spirit's wish to possess the subject in order to confer upon him a lost or not yet attained identity; a sick person is so judged because his life and behavior do not conform to the essential symbols governing the community.[21]

Therefore we see that a certain notion of adaptation to reality is always operative—the notion that situates a given form of behavior within its cultural context. Vision, possessions, rituals, and beliefs that strike the stranger as bizarre must be evaluated according to the community's system of beliefs. Cultural systems, however, are not simply rigid entities, and if one considers the possibilities for transformation they offer, it becomes evident that the notions of adaptation and reality do not provide sufficient criteria to distinguish between mental illness and health. Often only in retrospect does it become clear that individual deviations have their own life. As Hegel said, the history of the world constitutes its own judgment. William James regarded primary religious experiences as the effervescence of a spiritual fever containing pathological traits; since it was impossible to characterize these experiences accurately, he suggested that the tree be judged by its fruits.[22] We might recall in this connection the odd impression Jesus made upon certain members of his family; because he did not assume the familial duties prescribed by his milieu but proceeded, instead, like an inspired prophet, to proclaim a strange and previously unheard message, some of them regarded him as being "beside himself" and sought to bring him home by force.[23] It is clear, then, that if we take into account the initiatives that inaugurate new meanings and establish new forms of order, we cannot identify one norm ethereally posed beyond and above the process of history that will dictate whether in a particular case a specific norm of behavior is "normal" or "abnormal."

All things considered, the notions of adaptation and reality must be constantly referred to the actual moment of existence and the concrete forms of culture that establish them, not simply reduced to factitious social rules and empirically verifiable facts. What matters is the style of the relationship to reality and to society. It is precisely this element of style that contains the qualitative excess that evades objective rules.

Psychological Criteria

It is essential, then, to summon psychological criteria to our aid—that is, criteria intrinsic to the psychic apparatus itself. Psychology, as a science of the psyche, is an objectification, but it expresses conceptually the rapport man establishes with himself as he attempts to realize his nature through his relations to others and to the world.

Let us bear in mind the transmutation effected by the arrival of psychopathology into the realm of knowledge. Whereas the religious interpretation considered pathology the result of external evil powers acting upon the individual, psychology contends that man is a system more or less favorably organized into various configurations. The psychic apparatus is, of course, a system open to external influences, but psychology's particular contribution consisted in revealing the internal connections governing both the psyche's constitutive elements and their transformations. Thus psychology translates what was previously conceived as relations to a reality beyond the human universe into relations between forces and systems of meaning within the human domain. This implies a recognition of the law governing these psychic ensembles. I share these fundamental assumptions and I reject Thomas Szasz's position, which reduces psychology to a mere game of medical language and simply offers a modern substitute for the religious version of pathology prevalent in the middle ages.[24] Szasz is correct in stating that hysteria is a form of communication that takes the place of an impossible word. This is in fact the very interpretation Freud proposed. But psychoanalysis tries to understand in precise terms the meaning of hysterical behavior, the word it replaces, and what makes that word impossible to begin with.

Once we admit the reality of the psyche, we can proceed to specify the principles that govern the psyche, conceived as a configuration of various subtending systems. Two concepts that suggest themselves are frequently invoked as criteria for mental health: integration and autonomy. Integration designates the architectonic order that organizes these subtending systems in a hierarchical manner. Accordingly, all pathology can be seen as a form of disintegration in which some essential element evades the control of the directive power that characterizes psychic life.[25] Autonomy is that quality of the psyche that maintains it as a living unity in the midst of influences exerted upon it by the environment. One will find some form of alienating dependency in all psychic illness.

Nevertheless, taken abstractly, the criteria of integration and autonomy are profoundly ambiguous. A perfectly integrated balance of the psychic components would result in a stable but rigidly static system, and a perfect autonomy would preclude all exchange with one's surroundings, hence with life itself. A healthy psychic life requires the "metabolization" and regulated transformation of contributions from the outside. Autonomy and integration are primarily formal principles that characterize the tensions and exchanges between the milieu and the various functional elements that constitute psychic life. Now, in concrete experience we can distinguish four essential activities through which man assumes and elaborates an existence conditioned by his body and his culture: work, communication by language, love, and pleasure or joy. These four basic functions characterize human life, and the incapacitation or serious psychic inhibition of any of these is a sign of mental illness.[26] Each of these concepts implies a whole anthropology whose development would provide the frame of reference necessary for a cogent account of psychopathology. Thus a certain margin of indeterminacy will necessarily inhere in any formulation of integration and autonomy. Furthermore, one will find in these concepts variations depending on the cultural context. Here, however, I will simply point out the repercussions this type of anthropology has upon the criteria of mental health.

Through work man transforms his natural surroundings, primarily in order to meet his own needs; so work is one of the activities by which man preserves his life. Through work one overcomes the child's dependence, thus confirming his psychological autonomy with regard to others. It is immediately evident that the psychic incapacity to work opposes the natural tendency toward self-preservation and autonomy that one has a right to expect of a psychologically and intellectually mature individual. And yet because of the exchange that takes place between the human spirit and matter through work, the significance of work exceeds its function as a mere satisfaction of elementary needs. Man conceives projects that anticipate conditions not yet in existence, and, realizing these projects by means of his natural gifts, he humanizes the cosmos and gives actuality to his own ideas. A certain fervor enters into this process precisely because work engages the two passions of mastery and possession. These passions can take hold of one to such an extent that they consume one's best energies. At what point do these passions become a form of alienation? The answer to this question can be formulated from two points of view. If we identify psychic health with the balanced development of all our human possibilities, the passion for work should be considered a sickness. I prefer, however, to limit the term *pathological* to the specific disorders resulting from an overwhelming passion for work. If the repression of certain other desires fails, indirectly interfering with one's capacity to work, then we have a disintegration of personality that signals mental illness.

Under the two rubrics of integration and autonomy we should also include the capacity to work as a general criterion for distinguishing the pathological manifestations of religion. If an individual is so absorbed by his religious quest that he no longer has the freedom necessary to do his work, then his commitment must be seen as suspect. On the other hand, it would be a mistake to characterize as pathological the kind of passion for work that represses or eliminates all religious aspiration, for religious desire does not stem from that category of instincts that will not suffer repression without demanding compensatory satisfaction. However, the complete disavowal of religious interest can be pathological if it results in a depressive inhibition.

It is not surprising that language can be symptomatic. Nor does it suffice to say that language expresses the psyche, for it is only by access to the properly symbolic function of language that a person becomes present both to the world of things around him and to others. Through the intervention of cultural signs man shapes the space and articulates the play of distance and presence in which the world of things and other people come to be in their own specificity. With regard to these he situates himself as a subject and expresses himself in his own voice. An extravagant, contorted style of language indicates a certain loss of access to the world of intersubjective communion. An analysis of such language could reveal the delirious nature of mystical experiences. On the other hand, the reduction of language to a one-dimensional utilitarian function indicates an affective impoverishment that results from defensive and repressive mechanisms. Mental illness often manifests itself in language by two forms of usage that are to some extent contradictory: on the one hand, a rupture from the ordinary use of language; on the other, a rigid conformity to conventional linguistic codes. In order to exercise the properly articulative force of words the instinctual life of man must indeed be shaped and structured by the laws of language, but it is also important that as a subject of language man inject his own imaginative and driving force into the linguistic system. If the play of language collapses or if the subject ceases to be engaged in this play, then language becomes little more than a spoken symptom.

In the domain of religion it is equally important that, beyond its strictly formal characteristics, language should comply with the intentions that derive from the context in which the speaker supposes himself to be. Take for example an individual who explicitly adheres to a Christian frame of reference but whose language is severed from the specific context of the faith he allegedly affirms, so that it is clearly not simply an intellectually acknowledged discrepancy; instead we discern an unconscious rupture of an essentially psychic nature. The study of language places at our disposal diverse resources; we can draw on these to judge whether one's language corresponds to the religious reality it is meant to signify. Now, this reality may impart its own particular meaning to language, but as it is, in principle, a universal and hence communicable reality, it also respects the laws of language. So if a religious language fails to hold a possible meaning for others, or if it radically shatters the structure of language, or if it is no longer consonant with the reality envisioned, we may justifiably identify it as a pathological product of a religious consciousness.

The capacity to love is another distinguishing sign of psychic health, as Freud remarked. The range of meanings covered by the word *love*, a word that cannot be reduced to a simple definition, indicates the multiplicity of components that make up the possible experiences of love. We can agree that one basic and constant characteristic of love is the desire for communication and union; yet each of these words evades simple or lucid definition. Ever since Plato's *Symposium*, philosophers have tried to unearth the mystery of love and to propose an ideal image for it, but ultimately and paradoxically, love is as impossible as it is fundamental to human existence—a paradox it shares with the ideals of ethical probity and the attainment of truth. This is because love, like the desire for communication and union, is marked by the same infinity that characterizes desire, and like desire it is thrown back upon itself—becoming the desire to love and thereby instilling a void within itself. Love is a desire to love and to be loved, and insofar as it is marked by desire, love is a movement deprived of any final certainty or perfection on which it could fall back.[27] In spite of the element of suffering due to its uncertainty and imperfection, love is the power to maintain union and communication, to regenerate these when they fail—thereby finding enjoyment in them—then giving, in turn, joy to the other.

Although any consideration of love can do little more than trace a general direction that one might follow, the incapacity to love, which manifests itself by negative characteristics, is more easily identified. The suffering attached to the incapacity to love is different from that connected to the desirous nature of love; they are the torments of love's perversion, of its sterile conflicts and destructive doubts. The desire to love can deceive the subject: a passionate attachment can deceptively conceal a distorted and twisted love, and the noblest, most charitable intentions can mask, even from the subject himself, a jealous hatred. In order to perceive one's capacity to establish affective bonds, what we call love must be examined within the context of one's relations to other people, and this is not a capacity that good will alone can supply. An authoritarian intolerance for the peculiarities of the other, the ever-unsatisfied claim for his attention, a constantly suspicious mistrust, the insurmountable oscillation between an imaginary aggrandizement of the other and the subsequent disappointment provoked by his actual presence—all these are signs that the necessary elements have not converged to create the capacity to love. The subject himself can become aware of the contradiction between his desire for communication and union and its actual realization by certain oblique signs that therapy can trace back to the domain of love. As a matter of fact, there is no complaint concerning any intolerable form of suffering that cannot be traced to some disturbance in the capacity to love.

An analysis of the development of love, like that elaborated first by Freud and then by others, would justify our adopting this distinct criterion for mental health and illness. For however natural and universal the desire to love may be, love itself is not just the product of corporeal spontaneity or any affective impulse. It is reached after a series of both conscious and unconscious vicissitudes. This is not the place to outline the hard apprenticeship by which the psyche is transformed, but we may recall Freud's thesis that love is not an instinct but rather the assumption of the sexual instincts into the total ego (*Gesamt-Ich*).[28] This implies that a psychology of love would involve a study of the instincts and their various derivatives and offshoots and an examination of the nature and formation of subjectivity. So it is clear that the development of the power to love, like any psychological study that may attempt to encompass it, is a never-ending task. But it is not the purpose of this inquiry to lay upon others the burden of an impossible demand for perfect love. We propose, then, to orient ourselves in the field of mental pathology by taking as distinct signs of disturbance the various ruptures that emerge in relationships to others, ruptures that counteract the desire for communication and union.

The fourth criterion, the capacity for the enjoyment of pleasure, has to be approached with more delicacy. It is an essential capacity, for man is an affective being endowed with a body disposed to pleasure, a being who draws natural enjoyment from his activities, intellectual, volitional, and spiritual. The happy companions of good health, comparable, Aristotle said, to the flower of youth itself, joy and pleasure are diffuse, omnipresent, and yet constantly struggling with effort and counterbalanced by suffering; they are both difficult to circumscribe and yet inherent in man's nature and necessary to his existence. So great is the variety of forms pleasure takes that it is impossible to delineate any one ideal image. Pleasure is such a fundamental aspect of man's life that he always looks for means to increase it in his pursuit of happiness, which, according to Aristotle, is the final aim of all human endeavor. Although we are neither so ingenuous nor so optimistic as to suppose that the realization of happiness can serve as a criterion of mental health, its opposite, the inability to enjoy, does provide incontestable evidence of pathology. Man must find some form of enjoyment in his activities, whatever they may be, in order to make them truly his own and to discover something of himself through them. The principle of enjoyment does not necessarily imply a hedonistic view of life, because enjoyment itself takes different forms depending on the particular type of activity involved, for example, the bodily functions, thinking, sexual love, work, religion.[29] Man can renounce certain forms of pleasure in order to intensify others or to attain a higher quality of joy. Far from being pathological, renunciation is necessary for the cultivation of enjoyment, and the ability to tolerate the suffering that renunciation and effort imply actually plays an important part in psychic health. But a suffering that precludes all possibility of joy indicates that the psychic system is seriously disturbed; this, in turn, will manifest itself by a significant inhibition of those activities from which the quality of pleasure has been withdrawn.

Having the capacity to enjoy does not imply that one is always explicitly seeking pleasure. Joy and pleasure often accompany health, for example, and health is precisely the ability to welcome these gifts as freely given to the person who can abandon himself to them. A driven pursuit of pleasure in concentrated forms prevents one from receiving other, gratuitous visitations of joy.

In the religious domain, this criterion applies to one's rapport with the world as well as to the strictly religious relation. When religious life is devoid of joy there is no doubt that it has undergone some sort of psychic wound. A religion dominated by a sense of obligation and duty seems, moreover, to be contradictory to the specific aim of religion, which is to expand the range of existence by regenerating it with the divine source of life. Christianity, in any case, explicitly proclaims a message of salvation and liberation, but this is a principle I would extend to all forms of religious belief, for it appears to me that they all aim to integrate man into a larger, beneficent mystery.

Nevertheless, on both the religious and the psychological level, an excessive fascination with enjoyment and the exclusive quest of pleasure betray an unfortunate tendency: they pose an obstacle to the self-abandonment necessary for the experience of authentic joy. For example, certain forms of mystical rapture, which appear strange or unusual because they combine the deliberate quest of suffering with an exalted sense of joy, definitely call for a psychopathological diagnosis.

As these comments have shown, we are not dealing with qualities that can be separated from one another, but with four dimensions of human existence that constantly merge into one another. As a desire that actualizes itself, love is marked by a specific sense of joy that is connected to both the loving presence of the other and the pleasure of loving itself. When it is not paralyzed by an impassioned and spellbound fascination, love can contribute to the accomplishment of one's work by the supplementary meaning and self-confidence it confers. As for work itself, it requires a solidarity with others that is rooted in a libidinal bond.[30] On the other hand, because this is basically a decentered bond, it prevents the entire being from falling captive to an exacerbated amorous passion.

Each of these distinctive traits of psychic health represents only a segment of psychic life, and any judgment as to their quality must be suspended until the whole ensemble has been considered. In these four fields of existence the instincts intersect and make their ramifications felt; there they project and realize their "I can" and "I want"—affirmations first originating, then fashioned, in the wake of cultural signifiers. Work combines hard necessity and creative pleasure, so it can accomplish itself within a community defined and united by a common language. Love, in turn, accomplishes its purpose: the union and joy that are anticipated by libidinal instincts but are then structured into identifiable relationships by language. Religion too must hold to the expectations raised by instinctual life, but religious signs open new fields of possibility that can actually anticipate instinctual aims and finally fulfill them through a fundamental transformation.

Psychic Causality

The criteria of normality imply that the psyche is shaped in the juncture between the instincts and the symbolic forms and meanings of culture. Although it appears to be relatively independent from the instinctual body, religion is nonetheless rooted in it, insofar as it draws from the experience of suffering and contingency, or finds itself implicated in the meaning of life and death, or is mobilized by the desire for happiness and seeks to control or transform men's passions. Signs operative in religious rituals leave their seal upon the body, while metaphors derived from corporeal instincts—rebirth, union, the quenching of thirst, the sacrificial meal, illumination—are in turn deployed throughout religious discourse.

The psychic conjunction of the instinctual body and cultural significations comprises a cumulative history that leads back to the very origins of each individual. Because of the nature of its formation the psyche forgets the source of its history. Reason, seeking an explanation for psychic anomalies, readily attributes them to the discernible causes seized by man's will, thus spontaneously granting little importance to the psyche's archeology. In a society heavily marked by the discovery of organic functions, one in which, moreover, a philosophical dualism aggravated and vulgarized by medicine is still largely pervasive, it is believed that psychic aberrations can be understood as the effects of organic causes. Indeed, the beneficial effect of certain drugs used to treat delirium, mental confusion, and some types of depression proves the influence of organic deficiencies in these cases. But these are not the only factors involved. They should be seen as an interactive spiral of both organic and psychic causes.

The failure of a purely organic psychiatry to explain mental illness and the increasing awareness of a dimension of meaning that cannot be reduced to obvious degenerative processes have recently oriented investigation toward sociological explanations. Thus we have seen a number of previously confirmed organicist psychiatrists convert to the sociological school of antipsychiatry. The social influences on the formation and deformation of man's character are indeed clear. Man's concrete situation is inevitably a social one, and from the moment he begins his life it is his cultural system that will largely prescribe the spectrum of roles available to him and determine the possibilities open to him. There is no vector of existence, whether it be work, sexuality, communication with others, or religion, in which the range of meanings and possibilities is not largely oriented to and limited by the institutional networks and conflicting interests of society.

Does it follow that the individual dramas of mental pathology are just the crystallization of larger societal dramas? One may ask, how then can we understand society without bringing into play the conflicting forces within the being that establish it to begin with? To reduce all psychopathology to sociological causality is to repeat the same simplistic and linear causality implied in the direct transposition of psychopathology onto social reality. The misfortunes of society are not simply an amplification of individual dramas, just as the latter are not simply a result of the former. Besides, the same social conditions produce men who are capable of modifying society effectively and those who are psychologically disturbed.

Within his cultural history and the broader societal sphere surrounding him, the individual encounters a historical private community that allows him, by various convergent or discordant actions, to appropriate its means, decipher its significations, and confront its gaps and contradictions. The child is caught in this small social field, traversed by multiple lines of force and fire, himself besieged by conflicting forces and tendencies that no natural harmony will felicitously integrate. This history, which brings him to his actual present, is primarily a singular one, composed of his particular relationship to his particular parents, his particular pleasures and sufferings, his triumphs and his failures, his loves, his deceptions. And to these events that constitute first his slumbering, then his vigilant history, to these events he reacts according to his impulses, thus preparing, without his awareness, his perception of future encounters and events—all following a continuous process of appeal and response, acceptance and defense. The result of this chain of events is the formation of his singular individuality. So the real psyche is indeed the consequence of an "initiation," in both the active and the passive sense of the term; the infant's precocious "I" and the subjectivities that shape his universe exert their mutual influence upon each other.

The psychic reality composed by the individual's prehistory constitutes the element of contingency that—inherent in the human condition—characterizes his entire progression through life. Because it is more comfortable with the enumeration of objective facts, theoretical reason cannot easily assimilate the profound contingency implied in man's specific historicity. This historicity, moreover, delivers a blow to his pride inasmuch as he is interested primarily in promoting his mastery over his natural circumstances, both physical and social. Because of their very nature and interests, both theoretical and practical reason tend to grant psychic reality small recognition.

We call this determination of the psyche by our archaic history "psychic causality" because the historical past present within us circumscribes the actual possibilities open to us as well as the limits that bind us.

One need only examine the different forms of psychotherapy in order to see that all of them operate at the level of our representations: representations of the body, of the ideal, of pleasure, of prohibitions, of danger, of human destiny, of intersubjective space. Whether its status is historically elaborated or not, the psyche presents itself as an affective body on which previous experience records its various impressions. Certain therapeutic approaches prefer to suspend past history and concentrate rather on the experience of the present, even though the present is actually composed of representations whose sources reach far into the past and govern the subject without his awareness. Although these "ideas" remain at the edge of our consciousness, they still form a part of the subject's innermost experience. One cannot reduce them to messages received strictly from one's present surroundings because these messages, however particular the actual circumstances from which they arise, are overdetermined in such a way that the subject will unwittingly read into them the meanings and associations he is predisposed to receive. Man takes from the discourses that surround him, and the institutional rapports that define his relationships to others, those elements elicited by the deep structure of his particular subjectivity. This subjective disposition, this combination of mind scanning for signs of meaning and clues to deciphering them, is not, however, a mechanical psychological apparatus of innate "needs and drives" but rather the memorial of the long history of experiences that have fashioned the specific sensibility, the feats and desires of the psyche's present. To deny the weight and influence of past events upon the present is to fail to recognize the interrogatory activity and perceptual range of the child. These approaches suppose, moreover, the fantastic, futile, and absurd task of trying to commence an individual's history from the point of an omnipotent and transparent self, a self that is nothing but a preposterous embodiment of the dream for a pure subject, one, in other words, without history or destiny.

The psyche's deep roots in its history and in the causal effects it produces by means of durably inscribed dynamic representations do not themselves constitute a mental pathology. Psychic causality asserts itself in creative activities as well as inhibitions; in the capacity, or loss of capacity, for enjoyment; in undertakings that proceed smoothly and projects that meet obstacles; in a bond of love or in its impossibility; in a religion that enlarges life or in one that belittles it. The pathological, as such, depends on the way particular representations have been linked together by their constitutive history, and no one formula can account for its cause and origin. All pathologies can be understood in terms of repressions, but not all repression is pathological. One can find frustration in all forms of pathology, but frustration itself is a part of all existence. And if excessive frustration seems a discernible cause in a specific case, one would still have to account for this excess relative to that particular subject's experience of it and his ability to contend with it. In any case, excessive pleasure can be as pathogenic as excessive suffering; but here again it is a matter of intensity, which is both subjective and conditioned by the context.

Because of the very nature of psychic reality, the causes of pathology tend to be evasive. Each pathological instance participates in a whole network of recorded experiences that have led up to the traumatic moment; this trauma, in turn, then confirms the entire network and consolidates it into one of the points of view already available to the subject. Every illness entails a complex history where the knots of pathology are tied and untied, then tied again and reinforced as a result of the insurmountable and conflictual hold they exert on experience.

To understand pathology with reference to psychic causality does not imply an exclusion of conflicts in the subject's present circumstances. There is nothing more misleading than the fixed alternative between past and present. The past remains active upon the present, and the present modulates itself according to the past. This is why transference is a universal phenomenon in the psychoanalytic cure: everything that takes place in transference is a reenactment of the past through its actualization in the present—thus psychoanalytic transference becomes a paradigm of psychic life in general. And yet it does not follow that the transferential nature of love or of a religious bond renders either of them pathological, for, as Freud pointed out, the transference-love at work in the psychoanalytic process is a real love.[31] Indeed, what conceivable love or desire does not shape itself according to the models established by previous affective experience?

This is not, however, to suggest that transference love is the same thing as repetition compulsion, unless the former is trapped in a fantasy that precludes the two desiring subjects from appealing and responding to each other. The term *repetition compulsion* characterizes the pathological point at which a psychic history has somehow become blocked and is prevented from finding a creative adaptation to the conflicts and demands of the present. Except in the extreme cases where the subject is paralyzed by doubt, trapped by phobic confinement, plagued by delusions of persecution, or incapacitated by serious depression, he continues to live out his story. But the price he pays is a heavy one, and the dead-ends and failures are painfully borne. Usually he knows he is caught in a subjective and solitary fatality that he must learn to articulate in order to free himself or give it meaning, for meaning is a directing of meaning, a taking charge of it. But the psychologically ill individual who cannot express himself knows from experience that his attempts to do so repeatedly go over the same experience, whose source and meaning are hidden from him. The real words that must be spoken remain unsaid, lost and hidden in pathology's monument to the obliterated memories of the past.

In pathology the same conflict repeats itself incessantly. It can take several forms: a passive resignation to a certain order of things interrupted by bursts of rage; the impression of being subjected to absurd internal injunctions and the accompanying sense that one is powerless to release oneself from them; the desire for pleasure and a subsequent insurmountable aversion to it. In all cases one is haunted by an erratic and intrusive component that governs one's actions and forces itself upon the mind, and even thrusts itself on the body, causing a pain words cannot convey.

The absence of conflict is not, however, a sign of psychic health. All personal suffering can be avoided by evading troublesome demands, but in doing so one will extinguish the vital force of all personal desire as well. It may happen, then, that an individual will seek out illness in order to reopen a history he had closed; this is one reason that some people become ill after too much success. Just like the life of the mind or that of society, psychic life can retain its vitality only if it exercises itself in the margin of difference between what man is and what he wants to be, between what he does and what he wants to accomplish. I do not identify the kind of interior peace that indicates mental health with the gloomy tranquility of stifled conflicts; in fact I would go so far as to denounce the morbid complacency of any religion that defends itself so well that it entrenches itself in a fallacious sense of its own harmony. Mental health is constantly troubled by antagonisms that it manages to conquer but to which psychic illness succumbs. Religion too moves between internal oppositions out of which a living faith emerges as an incessantly renewed response.

The psyche's conflictual nature makes it prone to illness. In whatever domain human beings unfold their activity—in sexuality, in an ethical consciousness, in relation to others, in religion—they will not find an orbit where their evolution is harmoniously regulated. From the moment he begins his life the child must learn to take for granted tribulations like the loss of love, blows to his pride, his bodily deficiencies. His ability to move on to new experiences requires that he renounce pleasures of excessive intensity; deceptions will test his confidence in other people;

he must learn to affirm himself in the arena of competitive jealousy and risk alienation in order to establish with his fellowman a bond he simultaneously tends to undermine. Through the experience of both normal and abnormal patients in psychoanalysis, we can follow with more detail and precision than we can through external observation of children the vicissitudes a child undergoes as he progressively shapes his identity, his relations to others and to the world.

Sociologist Emile Durkheim emphasized the need to impose constraints on presocial man in order to socialize what he conceived as a biological, egotistic, and anarchic being. Freud then went on to show that repression is not simply a mechanism imposed from without but that contradictions arising from within the psyche itself force it to initiate transformations through which man finally bestows a form upon himself. If he fails in this, in order to survive he mutilates some part of his psychic being. Pathology is the mutilation the psyche carries out upon itself for defensive purposes. In its way it accomplishes the evangelical injunction: if your hand causes you scandal, cut it off, for it is better to enter life with only one hand than to be cast into death with two. But the self-mutilation that inaugurates pathology is real and not symbolic; it takes place at the earliest stages of psychic life, before the subject's self can acknowledge it or give it meaning.

Psychic illness is therefore a negative phenomenon, but it is not caused simply by an organic deficiency, as the medical men would have it. Nor is it the result of social repression, even though a repressive culture is favorable to it. The subject himself brings about this self-mutilation, and as it acquires significance for him he becomes attached to it and sustains it. Any therapist will have experienced that the subject's resistance to healing is as fervent as his desire to be free from his illness. The self-mutilating subject is not a consciousness transparently existing for itself but is rather the psyche in its totality, comprising various mutually opposing passions and tendencies that establish links with their surroundings and that, once introduced into the domain of language, give rise to the various psychic agencies such as the ego, the ego ideal, the superego, and finally, ethical conscience. An obscure intention supports this pathological self-mutilation, and this intention becomes intelligible not if we refer it to the conscious "I," but rather if we place it within the transformations of the psyche taken as a whole system—in other words, as a moving totality whose elements operate in reciprocal relation to one another. It is precisely this active effectuation of the psychic system's own mutilation that gives the term *psychic causality* its full significance: the psyche itself causes its own illness. Its instinctual forces are motivated by the wish to protect and maintain a certain level of unity in the subject and to sustain the form of pleasure that it considers best or most available to it. Consequently, pathological suffering, like dreams, is motivated by wish fulfillment.

The actual nature of psychic pathology makes it apparent that its negative value should be attributed to a positive one. As a psychic system the subject performs this mutilation upon itself with the end of assuring its ultimate well-being. As it actively subjects itself to its own suffering, in some manner it is capable of controlling it and to some extent of redefining its own historical process of becoming by tracing it back through the successive junctures where it performed and repeated its own mutilation. The technical method of psychoanalytic treatment works systematically to unbind this knot of repetitions. Other forms of therapy also operate upon the psychic representations that govern the psyche's self-mutilation, but none of these goes so far as to mobilize all the historical inscriptions engraved, like a palimpsest, on the psyche. It is not my purpose here to pursue the analysis of theoretical procedures. It suffices to mention the double aspect of pathology: self-mutilation and the latent persistency of those psychic possibilities that have been eliminated.

Interpretation of Religious Pathologies

Do religious meanings imprinted upon the psyche furnish us with particular criteria for determining "normality"? Is the type of causality involved here of a religious or psychical order? Or is this perhaps a false alternative? Can religious representations have a disturbing effect upon the psyche? Or, on the contrary, can the influence of religious representations have a healing effect? And then we may ask more generally, should a psychotherapy appeal to the representations and spiritual forces invoked by religion?

When we examined the distinctive signs of sanity and morbidity we suggested that they have equal validity for both religious life and the psyche in general. I am aware of the decision this conviction implies— clearly, it is one that I cannot entirely justify by objective reasons. If we affirm a similarity between those criteria we apply to psychic life and those used to distinguish between the various forms and figures of religion, this implies that religion participates in the psyche and that, as well as conferring a new meaning upon it, religion must itself be judged according to the relation it has developed with the psyche's internal organization. We must, therefore, submit religion to the logic of the psyche (to psycho-logy) as well as reject the discontinuity that would disrupt the cohesion faith is called to establish between the human and the divine. This will then lead us to take a clinical look at various forms of religion, including certain sects that reject the very principle we adhere to. One thing, in any case, is certain: the very notion of a religious psychopathology involves a critique of any religious form that does not open human reality to new possibilities. To open new possibilities does not mean, however, that religion is simply a dim reflection of a positive mystical faculty latent in the psyche. My refusal to entangle the bonds between religion and the psychic system is as firm as my refusal to sever them.

The grounds on which I justify extending my psychological criteria to religion necessarily entail a specific concept of religion. Insofar as it presents itself as the link to the source of all life, religion cannot be conceived as something externally thrust upon and opposite to earthly reality, as if it could shatter both the historical conditions and the psychological laws to which human beings are subject. Religion offers a content and dynamism of its own, but it also addresses itself to man's reason, heart, and will, thus presupposing a concept of humanity. Religion, through faith, urges man to go beyond this humanity, since man on his own account lacks what religion may offer him; but his humanity is itself the premise necessary for opening up a new relationship, coherent with the life of man. Religious psychopathology consists precisely in examining to what degree this agreement of principle between religion and human existence fails. Religion is no more immune to decadence than are other forms of life. Therefore its sources must be suitable, or else religion as such must be subjected to psychopathological analysis. Even if we disagree about the ultimate source of religion, we have to consider both the whole set of characteristics it presents and the mode of life it proposes.

As far as Christianity is concerned, we would best approach it by grounding any articulation of its supernatural aspects on the actual nature of the psychic systems, as St. Paul has done. There is a striking analogy between the characteristics of mental health and the conditions that, according to St. Paul, a genuine faith must fulfill. Paul urges those who are idly waiting for the eschatological coming of Christ to work;[32] although many during that period believed the end of time was imminent, Paul warned that any faith that leads men to live at the expense of others, indifferent to their lot, betrays a profound falsehood. Paul also instructed the Corinthians who had been fervently taken by the fire of prophetic inspiration that any inspiration proceeding from the Holy Spirit must be capable of being translated into an intelligible language and should edify the community.[33] If language loses its power to communicate and the signs produced through inspiration have no universal import, it is because the occult forces in the guise of inspired faith have taken possession of the individual. We cannot but recognize in Paul's pronouncements the correspondence between the capacity for love and joy, on the one hand, and the "fruits of the Spirit"—peace, joy, and benign love (*agape*)—on the other.[34] Peace is attained when the diverse tendencies in one's interior affective life are unified in acquiescence to a divine presence. It is equivalent to the integration of the psychic forces that threaten to tear man apart. Joy is the perception, on the affective order, of a profound harmony with oneself, with the world, and with the source of existence. By allowing the spirit of God to inhabit man, faith gives him a foretaste of that divine quality whose diffuse presence in the world is but the herald of its full manifestation. Faith guarantees its authenticity, then, by the quality of joy it makes possible. Finally, there is also a concurrence between, on the one hand, the quality of benign love through which man participates in the essential attribute of the revealed God and, on the other hand, the capacity to love, which Freud specified as a sign of psychic health and in which he saw the mark of Eros, the mythical life force at war with the power of death.

This correspondence between the criteria of mental health and the characteristics of faith does not, however, imply that I simply equate inauthentic faith with pathology. The distinction between the two, however, raises a serious problem, the most difficult problem, in fact, to be clarified in the course of this work. Odd behavior and self-delusion on the level of faith often have their origins in a cultural context. The fascination that mystery religions held for the Corinthians, for example, led most Christians to aspire to ecstatic inspiration. Likewise, the irruption of the irrational, as a counter to the ideal of technical efficacy in our times, has been widely propagated in the churches, stirring all sorts of pentecostal fervor, sometimes at the expense of that communicability that St. Paul tells us is a sign of genuine faith.

What is considered divergent behavior according to the norms of faith is not necessarily the sign of a real pathology. To the extent that the distinctive characteristics of genuine faith coincide with the criteria of mental health, any divergency from the intrinsic norms of faith obliges us to examine its pathological bent. Naturally, we will not consider in this light divergencies regarding intellectual interpretations. Even if theological differences are inseparable from the anthropological elements on which they are grounded and which they comprise, the question of pathology is clearly not pertinent here. Beyond such differences of reason there are two other possibilities: it might be a question of a collective phenomenon or of an individual peculiarity. If a local or historical collectivity manifests a style of religious life or experience that clashes with the internal norms of its religion, then the question of its pathological nature should be posited within the framework of that particular cultural context. But any judgment to be formulated should refer to the psychological criteria outlined here. It follows that if it applies to a collective unit, the term *pathological* must be taken analogically, meaning that the cultural and religious climate diminishes its members' opportunity to realize their human potential and favors individual pathologies. The same principle applies to individual divergencies from the proper religious norm. Only when religious differences are accompanied by specific psychological disturbances have we the right to judge a case to be pathological.

Psychic Causality and Symbolic Efficacy

How do the psychic and religious dimensions relate to each other, in sickness and in health? Some people, convinced that religion is the fundamental truth guiding a believer's life, maintain that since the essence of religious pathology is indeed religious, its cure falls upon religious agencies, who bring it about by a spiritual guidance—a sort of religious orthopedagogy in fact—which relies on the saving power of a divine spirit.[35] Interpreting the religious explanation of mental illness in light of the Judeo-Christian context, they claim that the use of psychological techniques demonstrates a lack of faith in God. This unilateral position is often found in the fundamentalist churches that interpret Scripture in the most literal sense and exclude as a matter of principle the autonomy of different dimensions of human reality. The same unilateral spiritualism is evident in the mistrust shown by some Catholic milieus toward the practice of psychology and science in general.

Yet others, following anthropological principles, posit that concrete existence is the inseparable unity of the psyche and various natural religious tendencies. Psychic illness would therefore always have a religious context, whether it is recognized or repressed, and psychic health would necessarily proceed through the clarification and assumption of one's religious destiny. Moreover, in order to be fully effective all therapy must operate simultaneously on psychic processes and on the religious representations that are a part of the psyche's fabric. The tasks of therapist and religious guide coincide in the same person. These two orders of activity, although distinct, become so closely related that one can say of this type of psychology what St. Augustine said about philosophy: true religion is true psychology, and true psychology, in turn, is true religion. In their various ways, C. G. Jung and religious existentialists like W. Daim, I. A. Caruso, and V. Frankl can be considered representatives of this notion.[36]

It is my conviction that religion is so intimately enmeshed in the web of psychological circumstances that religious pathology is always an effect of psychic causality. This conviction is based on clinical experience, and it is justified by theological reasons as well as by the theoretical elucidation built on the basis of this experience.

My position neither divorces nor equates the psychological and "spiritual" dimensions. It conforms neither to a dualism nor to a monism that might affirm either the psychological or the spiritual. I do affirm a standpoint that both maintains and articulates the difference between the two.

If we take psychic reality as our starting point, we see that it has two facets: an instinctual and a cultural aspect. As Freud aptly put it, the dynamism of the instincts imposes a certain labor upon the psyche: by somehow satisfying the internal demands of the instincts man must find the means to reduce the tension they create. But for man the path of satisfaction cannot be one of brute discharge, for from the start of his life the child is caught in a mediated network of culturally determined objects, significations, and intersubjective relations, the coordinates of which are designated by language. It is impossible then to conceive of a human instinct whose course is not marked by the cultural references that define it. Whether it be the instincts of sex, mastery, or attachment, they are never merely natural forces; the strata of meanings deposited in them invariably condition the strategies of satisfaction as well as the pitfalls of suffering and discontent. So along with the psychic labor that the tensive energy of the instincts exacts we should also include the labor that culture imposes on the psyche by virtue of the bonds forged between the instincts and the cultural repository of significations. This twofold labor leads the psychic apparatus through the paths and processes by which the subject transforms and constitutes himself, processes such as the formation of a bodily schema and system of identifications, the disengaging of primal bonds and fantasies, the control of instincts, the development of a moral conscience. Through these processes new meanings emerge and old interests are transformed. Aesthetic works, social aspirations, love ideals, nationalist movements, all of these contribute their specific values. All these domains are rooted in the instinctual formations from which they draw their energy, thus elaborating new directions in meaning and modulating the sources of satisfaction. Religious orientations are also inscribed into psychic life and, like all cultural realities, exact the labor of spiritualization and sublimation that organizes the joys and pleasures in which the instincts seek satisfaction.

If we approach the issue from the other end we see that to deny the psychic ground in which religion is planted is to reduce religion to an arbitrarily erected system of ideas, as if it were nothing more than an isolated series of ritual acts completely dissociated from the life of man. Even a superficial examination of any religion will reveal the profoundly human realism that animates religious rituals. They bring into play extensive systems of elementary corporal symbols, which leave, in turn, their own seals of meaning upon the body. And it is with reason that men often use the expression "religious feelings," feelings such as those of dependence and protection, of guilt and reconciliation, of mystical fervor and the experience of the sacred; for religion evokes and motivates the expressive power of the psyche and provides access to the greater range of being that links it to the divine. The whole psyche is as much a part of religion as it is of work or of love.[37]

The effect of psychotherapy upon religious faith and the action of religion upon the psyche's formation both attest to the fact that the boundaries between religion and the psyche are indefinite. As Freud observed in "The Wolf-Man":

> Apart from these pathological phenomena [exaggerated obsessional religious ceremonials], it may be said that in the present case religion achieved all the aims for the sake of which it is included in the education of the individual. It put a restraint on his sexual impulses by affording them a sublimation and a safe mooring; it lowered the importance of his family relationships, and thus protected him from the threat of isolation by giving him access to the great community of mankind. The untamed and fear-ridden child became social, well-behaved, and amenable to education.[38]

We should note, though, that God was so strictly a substitute for the father in this case that when the child came under the influence of a nonbelieving schoolmaster who became himself the father's substitute, "the child's piety sank away along with his dependence upon his father."[39] One need only survey the characteristics that make up a religion to realize that it does not consist simply of the sum of its articulated beliefs but it also organizes and refashions the forms, objects, and coordinates of instinctual life. It is understandable that psychoanalysts like Ernest Jones, on discovering the constant mutual encroachment of the two, believed that psychoanalysis could entirely explain religion, leaving it to the particular judgment of believers to decide upon the "philosophical" truth of religious meaning.[40] The incursion of religion into the psyche and the correlative manifestations of the psyche's genetic development upon religion are both analogies to the function of "metabolization" that religion serves to bring about among groups that are in the process of acculturation.[41]

Still, one cannot conclude on the basis of this conjunction between religion and the psyche that religion alone—even when its true value is restored to it—can, by the signs and messages appropriate to it, free men from illness. It does have this sort of healing efficacy at moments when new conflictual experiences reawaken antagonisms from the past, but this is not surprising if one considers that even artistic forms of expression are of help in overcoming psychic adversities.[42] Experience has shown, however, that religion is not effective in undoing disturbances accumulated in the course of an extended history. What is more, there are cases in which religion not only repeats these distortions but even polarizes and confirms them. Yet, at the same time, it is necessary to add that illness is always a form, albeit an unfortunate one, of the only healing process available to the subject in light of threatening disaster.

Like the interpretations of mental illness to which they were connected, the early forms of therapy were religious ones. This mutual interdependence of the psyche and religion explains the efficacy of these therapies that we, following Lévi-Strauss, would also call "symbolic" therapies.[43] Through the polysemous process Freud first called condensation, anthropological discourse mobilizes the energies and representations of the body, the past, and the subject's feelings; it restructures them according to an order of cosmic and religious significations. But the course of civilization radically and irreversibly modifies this primitive situation to the extent that our present society cannot be seen as a simple cultural variation of those civilizations we call archaic. A whole new way of thinking, the Christian religion's upheaval, and the subsequent changes in man's relationship to language and to the body have all produced a different type of man. This entire cumulative history clings to and leaves its mark in the depths of man's being, without his awareness. A striking consequence of this is the birth of clinical psychology at the turn of the century.

I am convinced this was not simply a consequence of discovering an aspect of human reality that had always been present; rather, an actual modification of man's relation to himself and the world brought the psyche to crystallize itself as a more autonomous reality. This is an undoubtedly risky idea, but it is difficult to contest the fact that, now more than in previous times, man experiences himself more particularly as a subjectivity; he has become more attentive to himself, and more prone, therefore, to strive to lose this consciousness of himself, yearning for the oblivion that might distract him from his interior void. Besides, is it conceivable that the same type of man is responsible for the creation of such contrasting works as the *Iliad*, the dramas of Sophocles or Shakespeare, and the works of Dostoevski?

Some readers will probably not find this historical and psychological interpretation of religious pathology particularly convincing, but experience has shown that such pathologies are indeed *psycho*-pathological, that the mode of causality operative in them is a psychic one, and that any treatment of them must depend on therapeutic techniques that operate on the structures and representations underlying these religious aberrations.

It follows that although it respects the various religious or secular options, the therapeutic process must implicate faith. But to believe that religious faith emerges, fully invigorated and released, from a psychic substratum that has just undergone a process of healing is still to posit the relationship between faith and the psychic in dualistic terms. For it is the nature of man not so much that he possesses a psyche as that he is a psychic being, inasmuch as his psyche is an outline of his relations with the real world and inasmuch as his activity is a self-reflexive activity that modifies these relations. Moreover, the religious signs according to which men direct their lives always contain more meanings than they may emotionally perceive or experience, and in these signs, which precede and anticipate man's evolution, he may discover a large reserve of unexpected meanings. Thus therapy often results in a renewed commitment to faith; or inversely, it may lead to a patient's suspending former religious convictions; or—and this will occur independently of the therapist's convictions—it may even lead to a complete abandonment of beliefs that were previously very firmly held.

The complexity of the elements at play prevents any prediction of the outcome and makes it impossible to draw, even after the fact, any exhaustive explanation of the processes that took place. Sometimes analysis allows the patient to overcome a hostility to religion that was an obscure negative form of a passionate attachment to it. At other times it dissolves a form of religious obedience that harbors a growing revolt and whose roots are anchored in fear. If a therapy is, as it should be, a progression in freedom and truth, then it is not possible for a believer to relegate his faith, in all honesty, to some extraterrestrial domain completely divorced from the larger aims of the human endeavor. On the other hand, religious faith should not be considered so subject to, or determined by, psychological laws that it becomes nothing more than a superstructure of them. First of all, I do not suggest that mental illness invades the patient's religious life in every case, invariably, and to the same degree of intensity; I do not, at any rate, know of any research that has proven such a deterministic link between the two. Furthermore, and I have already stressed this point, religious references have as much autonomous coherence as signifiers in other fields of existence. It is precisely this autonomy of use preserved in the significations circulating through our common world that makes social or verbal therapy functional.

We may also wonder whether therapists' silence as regards the religious interests of patients is not in fact a failure on their part to recognize a fundamental aspect of their patients' lives. If sickness often intensifies the essential questions man poses on the nature of good and evil, on his destiny and origin, how could he avoid being preoccupied by religious questions? Besides, studies have shown that even apparently nonreligious patients are concerned with such questions and are often astonished that they are encouraged in therapy to speak of every intimate aspect of their lives except religion.[44]

There are reasons, of course, to justify this silence: unbelieving therapists either wish to avoid transmitting their skepticism to their patients or simply take no interest in ideas that to them are only phantasmagoric reflections of purely psychological problems. Religious therapists, on the other hand, prefer not to give the impression that they want to influence their patients. In a pluralistic society where therapy must acknowledge and observe the individual's right to his personal convictions it requires considerable delicacy on the therapist's part to both respect this essential right and avoid excluding, by his well-meaning neutrality, this most important part of the patient's life, as if it were no more than a hollow form. Beyond that, however, anything resembling an appeal to the patient's will, inducing him to opt for any particular form of life, is antitherapeutic. But because the analytic cure encourages the patient to speak freely about everything that crosses his mind, this difficulty is not often encountered in psychoanalytic therapy.

Individual Lives and Psychological Patterns

It is within the conjunction between psychic and religious life that we will find the principle and categories that will guide our analysis.

In order to understand the forms of religious pathology we must proceed to interpret them according to the double set of references that delimit the field. On the one hand we must consider the context of religious expressions. The actions of the subject and the content of his experience should be interpreted within the whole context of his religious system, and all religions do in fact present a network structured by the signs and linguistic sequences that constitute the signifying life of their participants. It is in reference to this structural network that pathology manifests its deviance, precisely because pathology eliminates one of the foundations of the intended signification. This is why pathological forms of religion often manifest the quality of being private religions. Naturally, any form of religious adherence will appear somewhat peculiar because of the unfathomable play of representations that animates it, but "normally" it is the total movement of the objective religious signifiers belonging to the community of faith that urges the individual to work through his particular representations, to adjust and balance himself according to the general system of religious signs, and to participate in the communal life that the play among these signs puts at his disposal.

The interpretation of religious pathology operates, then, according to a system of double reference. One point of reference is based on the signifiers that mediate and found religious life. An examination of the internal relationships between these signifiers reveals how man personally organizes the elements of the religious universe he appropriates. The other is based on the private character of the pathological phenomena, and these must be interpreted according to the particular intentions that constitute the pathology. It is important to emphasize that this aspect must be deciphered by elucidating the particular movement that produced it as a particular and individual pathology. Because it is actuated by a subject, the apparent nonsense of pathological symptoms conceals a meaning for him, and although this meaning is not at his immediate disposal, he nevertheless feels bound and compelled by it. We might therefore understand it as a misconstruction that has availed itself of an element of religious signification in order to operate as an instrument of self-mutilation inside the psychic system.

"To understand is not therefore simply to observe; it is to grasp a necessary reason within the very heart of contingency."[45] In its pathological form, a religious intent tries in principle to submit to the meanings made available by objective signs, but in fact this intent remains a prisoner of more powerfully binding reasons that misconstrue it. It is impossible in these circumstances to determine to what extent a faith can maintain its integrity. It is certain, though, that religious representations lose a major part of their intentional and articulatory force, becoming to a great extent functional substitutions of unconscious representation. Religious psychopathology is a religious self-mutilation supported by a psychological self-mutilation that becomes, in turn, motivated by the first.

Because religious pathology is determined by a limited number of necessary conditions, it is possible to enumerate the categories of pathological phenomena. As a matter of fact they correspond to the major syndromes of general psychopathology, a correlation that is not surprising since religious meanings are inevitably linked to psychological motivations.

This work limits itself to a study of the incidence within the religious domain of the two major neuroses, obsession and hysteria, each of which affects a basic dimension of both existence and religion. It is my view that neurosis is inscribed into the very heart of man's destiny and consequently into his religious history as well. Neuroses are the counterpart of those impending truths that the subject apprehends only obliquely; hence an analysis of the modifications they produce enables us to understand more fully the process and instances through which religious intentions actualize themselves. This is the fundamental perspective that guides and coordinates my analyses. Thus, for example, morbid guilt and the assumption of one's indebtedness become psychological instances that clarify each other. In the same way I will attempt to determine what makes ritual revert to ritualism, symbolic defilement to imaginary defilement, the sacrificial act that binds to the sacrificial act that mutilates. The third section, which is dedicated to a study of desire, will combine an elucidation of the repressed material that reemerges in pathological distortions of mysticism with a study of the works accomplished by the process of sublimation. This will lead to an examination of a type of phenomena, marginally related to mystical experience, in which human and religious fantasy and experiences intermingle: phenomena such as visions, possession, belief in demons.

Even though pathological typology can give us only an abstract picture of the field, it does allow us to identify the elements of meaning and the major processes that recur in specific cases, thus giving rise to a certain logic of types. Each individual is indeterminately complex and atypical, and there is no type of pathology or psychic life in general that does not cover, at certain moments and under certain conditions, the whole repertory of pathological formation. Again I stress that the concept of psychic causality does not allow us to attribute pathology to one primary cause. As a result, any concrete interpretation must necessarily remain analytic and conjectural. Nevertheless, through analysis we can trace the various paths a subject has taken and the ones he has regularly retraced and will continue indefinitely to retrace—even against his own will; this gives an identifiable shape to his particular psychic itinerary. The pattern that analysis imposes on polymorphous realities reveals the outline of the subject's multiple relations.

The therapist concentrates on his patient's word, his discourse; he is attentive to its ramifications and overdeterminations, but he forbears from imposing his theoretical preconceptions on it. Through this commotion of language, however, psychological patterns allow him to pick up elements that would otherwise escape the notice of those who have not received the necessary conceptual formation and theoretical training. It is the therapist's art to combine an ability to construct models with an ingenuous curiosity for concrete connections. Let us consider this well; the psyche is not a heap of haphazard accidents. Fortuitous events leave traces that are arranged according to an order of meaning. I will attempt to reveal the human and religious aspect of psychopathological aberrations by picking out the typical, explanatory fragments of the subject's particular history. Psychopathology undoubtedly makes judgments, but this in no way implies that they are made in a spirit of accusation or suspicion. On the contrary, psychopathology demystifies that revolutionary fanaticism that constantly seeks to unmask false consciousness only for the purpose of settling accounts. By untying the knots of useless suffering, therapy also shows how the same conflicts that bring about the destruction of some also form a part of the destiny of others. The passions, the elements of meaning, the processes are universal. By this excursion into the field of religious psychopathology I hope to show the work religion has yet to accomplish in order to become a true source of healing for men and women living today. The unhappy destiny of the less fortunate throws a necessary light on the various vectors and coordinates that make up both a human and a religious life, as well as those that threaten to mutilate it.

PART TWO

The Consciousness of Evil and the
Labyrinth of Culpability

• Introduction

 The pathology of the uneasy conscience is certainly not a problem unique to Christianity. Although Christianity does provide a fertile soil for guilt, it also purports to provide the means for overcoming guilt. Therefore an understanding of a pathological sense of transgression in the Christian religion presupposes that one situate it within the context of Christian meanings.

Christianity presents itself as a religion that offers salvation: even the etymology of the word (*salvus*) indicates that salvation is not only a matter of promising an ultimate happiness but of restoring present existence to its full powers. The promise of salvation implies, then, that a wound inflicted upon man and society has diminished and demeaned them both. In biblical religion this wound is called sin. As a transgression against man and God, sin infects the individual and the community like a disease. In the Germanic languages, the term *salvation* very explicitly connotes not only a healing of man's soul but a more general healing (*heilen, helen*). We noted in chapter 1 that for primitive Christianity the idea of salvation encompassed the restoration of psychic well-being and even, to some extent, physical healing. As a result of sin, destructive and chaotic forces invade man and society. And yet biblical thought does not locate these forces in the cosmos, nor in the body, nor in the passions; here no dualistic explanation is evoked. This discourse on the power of evil remains a mythical discourse; it uses symbolic means to speak about the fundamental reality of evil without attributing it to identifiable beings. Even the notion of the demonic tempter works to preserve the natural cosmos from the contempt inherent in dualistic explanations; it also serves to avoid making man the sole agent of the radical sin for which he otherwise would be wholly responsible.

But the Christian message of salvation is not limited to proclaiming man's liberation from sin and restoration through his bond with God. God's manifestation through the word of Christ gives man the means to reach beyond himself and to receive an abundance of life that tradition calls the divinization of man by the Holy Spirit. Nevertheless, the concept of redemption still implies redemption from sin.

It is the paradox of Christianity that in proclaiming freedom from sin and deliverance from the law it accentuates the demands of the law and sharpens the sense of sin. Thus the call to salvation also invokes a call to conversion. Man then actively responds to this appeal from an absolute authority who does not judge according to appearances or the illusion of high reputation but scrutinizes "truth in the inward parts" and separates evil from good, as if with a sword. Insofar as it posits man as a full being, responsible for the decisions he makes concerning his own existence, Christianity, as Hegel forcefully argued, is the origin of the modern age.[1] Liberty cannot be achieved either by an external force that would violently abolish evil or by any inherently effective ritualized technique. God liberates those who liberate themselves, and in this way divine power joins forces with human powers without substituting itself for them.

By claiming that the confession of sin is a necessary condition for liberation from sin, Christianity exposes man to a morbid sense of guilt or, in clinical terms, to obsessional neurosis—even sometimes to the most extreme form of mental illness, an obsession with evil that manifests itself as a psychotic form of guilt. The pathology of the fault is, in fact, one of the sicknesses congenital to Christianity.

However, clinical experience, on the one hand, convincingly shows that the pathological sense of fault is not limited to believers, while interpretation, on the other, reveals that obsession, even in its religious form, is structured according to universal psychological laws. It is precisely the specifically psychic nature of pathology that allows us to understand how it insinuates itself into religious conscience and thus attaches the Christian avowal of guilt to unconscious representations.

Of course, the word *sin* is more heavily charged than the word *fault*; it implies the unavoidable personal responsibility one must bear before an Other that cannot be mystified or misled. It is this that gives the religious form of neurotic guilt a semblance of being lucid, of not being a result of repression. It is understandable that some people have thought that substituting the concept of fault for that of sin would deliver man from a burden and teach him to "correct" and "surpass" himself. Formulated in this way the opposition is clearly only a verbal one, for Christianity also urges the individual to surpass himself through his involvement in the course of human history. It calls on man to establish a new relationship with God, which might also be thought of in terms of "surpassing," except that in light of the personal bond of faith the sense of fault takes on a dimension of its own: it is to one's deepest self as well as to God that one must answer for one's existence. If the term *sin* then takes on a more serious connotation, the demand—written into man's destiny—that the individual strive to surpass himself in turn implies an ethical responsibility. This responsibility lies at the very heart of our being-for-others, and consequently man will always have to confront and contend with the judgment made on his life.

Sometimes, spurred by a dream of blissful innocence, people will accuse all accusation, interdict every interdiction, and legislate against all law, but in the long run only an anarchist can put himself beyond good and evil and avoid the dangers of a pathological conscience. Even so, he would have to be capable of renouncing all desire, for, as Jacques Lacan has aptly observed, that one take enjoyment from life is one of the imperatives of the superego. Perhaps only Buddhism is in a position to eliminate even the question of an uneasy conscience, as it teaches the renunciation of all desire. In any case, in these times, when ideologies of humanism are so prevalent and discourse on man's liberation so widespread, it is difficult to avoid the issue of an uneasy conscience. Never has the attitude to moral accusation been so pervasively clamorous. Unless he manages to divest himself of a bad conscience by self-righteously blaming others for all the evil in society, an individual can scarcely find the peace of mind to enjoy the leisure moments of his life.

The term *sin*, however, evokes the idea of an internalized censure far more formidable than any accusation a person may bring against another. It is true that the notion of sin may encourage the projective attitude that allows one to displace onto others the burden of his own bad conscience. But by testifying to the reality of sin, religion also claims that before God man is an open book whose text can never be obfuscated or erased by man's lies. How could man, summoned to stand before such a radical justice, avoid a feeling of "fear and trembling"? Freud has stressed it often enough: it is the most pious of believers who have the sharpest sense of sin. Even though the final aim of religion is basically to triumph over this particular evil that plagues mankind, Freud concluded that even religion cannot release man from guilt.[2]

If we consider the whole range of meanings covered by the Christian religious scheme, we see that it establishes a delicate balance between good and bad conscience, indictment and exoneration, censure and permissiveness, renunciation and enjoyment. But achieving this balance is not a matter of finding a middle way between the various extremes but of maintaining in complex unity all the elements that structure the history of relations between God and man. This experience, lived through history, explodes in a hymn of the Easter vigil, dense with meaning: "Oh blessed fault!"

Morbid guilt takes different forms according to the context prescribing the ethical conscience and desires of a culture, for guilt is provoked not solely by the sense of duty but by the demands of the superego as well. We can illustrate this by the tensive unity created between duty and permissiveness. If God does not exist, concludes Dostoevski, then everything is allowed. On the contrary, replies Lacan, if God does not exist then nothing is allowed. This apparent contradiction outlines two possibilities in a field whose complexities are difficult to circumscribe. For some the death of God promises a blissful state divested of every interdiction; for others it announces the savagery of a lawless, faithless world. Authors such as Nietzsche and Solzhenitsyn have explored these dreams and nightmares. Left to himself, an orphan of existence, the individual seeks authority within himself; nothing is then forbidden him by a greater authority that grounds the judgment of good and evil, but nothing is allowed him by an authority that could authenticate his desire or enjoyment.

Prohibition and permission are necessary correlatives. Permission is a letting be; it delegates a right and confirms an autonomy on the subject. One could analyze the effects of uncertainty following the abolition of a religious referent. The absence of an anchoring word to ground the instances of "yes" and "no" can give rise to a pathological distortion of the moral conscience just as easily—though in a different fashion—as the sense of one's responsibility before God. We can see the development of this distortion in two opposite directions that can sometimes join to create an oppressive contradiction. Required, on the one hand, to surpass himself by measuring up to a utopian ideal of humanity, man risks crumbling beneath the Sisyphean task imposed on him by the ideological discourse defining the duties that shape his life. If, on the other hand, he claims his right to happiness as one of the realizable possibilities on the human horizon, he is exposed to a constant discourse inciting him to an exaggerated expectation of pleasure. This in turn subjects him to a state of constant erethism accompanied by the sense that he is a diminished being inadequately meeting his expectations.

Religious faith, too, is a double-edged sword. It comprises a number of elements favorable to interior freedom and to the pacification of one's conscience. God's forgiveness, the manifestation of his humanity in Jesus

Christ, his promise of a faithful love, his modest expectations, his attention to the slightest acts of human kindness (a proffered glass of water ...), all these reassure the believer. Inspired by God's magnanimous tolerance, he learns to endure himself. There are men more censorious than God himself, men who lay upon others the burden of a heavy conscience. But there are other elements in the Christian message that encourage an uneasy conscience. God's judgment looks down on the individual's destiny as well as human history in general; he penetrates the secret heart where the monster of hatred and destructive violence takes cover. Between the two coordinates of God's divine manifestation—his reassuring kindness and his exacting holiness—no conceptual synthesis is possible; in biblical terms, the justice by which he justifies man is the same as that by which he judges him. I do not intend to elaborate here this mobile tension in the relation between God and man; I mention it as a frame of reference in which to place the pathological religious conscience.

2 • The Religious Neurosis of Culpability

Its Manifestations

In both medical and psychological pathology, any description of symptoms always groups together very diverse phenomena according to our understanding of their etiology and hence of the latent structure that engenders these symptoms. The mental state that Freud first specified as obsessional neurosis will guide my interpretation of the symptoms and my analysis of their mechanisms in the instance I will presently consider. The German term *Zwangsneurose*, by which Freud identified this mental state, designates the pathological entity more adequately than does the English translation. "Obsessional neurosis" is immediately associated with the ideas that "haunt" the patient—doubt, a sense of inferiority, the fear of hurting others—whereas the term *Zwang*, compulsion, characterizes the whole psychic life of such a patient. He finds that he is subject to a coercion at once internal and yet foreign to his consciousness. Not only is he obsessively besieged by unwanted thoughts, but he also finds himself forced to perform, under threat of a mounting anxiety, certain odd, compulsive (*compellere* in Latin) actions. He also experiences uncanny feelings, disproportionate to or altogether taken out of their proper context, feelings that something unidentifiable forces him to undergo against his will.

The feeling of guilt—the sense of being at fault—is not always present. On the contrary, in most cases of obsessional neurosis it comes to light only in the course of treatment—a fact that led Freud to explain this neurosis as a feeling of unconscious guilt. This expression serves as a theoretical abbreviation whose inadequacy he later recognized, for by its very nature feeling must be perceived by consciousness. However, when obsession takes a religious form, it crystallizes primarily as an inexorable sense of guilt before God. This fundamental difference in morbid manifestations already indicates that the neurotic sense of religious guilt draws its resources from an underlying problematic.[1] God then becomes the signifier by which a conflict raging elsewhere—on the hither side of the bond between God and man—is radically polarized. By the same token this insurmountable guilt before God has something in common with a monothematic delirium that absorbs and triggers all sorts of other psychic ramifications, unknown to the subject. Like the delirium, the subsisting guilt represents both an attempt at cure and an obfuscation of the representations at work.

The term *delirium*, as used here, has, of course, only a metaphorical value, but religious obsession is close to it and often, in the more serious cases of malignant obsession, actually lapses into delirium. Religious scrupulosity, too, gives the impression of being quasi-delirium, which no doubt explains why it often provokes laughter. The half-comical, half-lamentable aspects that Freud notices in religious obsession make it similar to the incongruous deliria whose themes call to mind scenes of tragicomedy. And yet, as one listens to these patients, one is aware that they are in the grip of intense anxiety.

Let's start with a case of particularly great scrupulosity. X is a man of 40, a university graduate, single, who leads an active, even too active, professional life. If he develops a passion for something he has chosen to do, he finds, intermittently, that it becomes completely devoid of meaning. He suffers from migraines and intestinal troubles and has been treated by the best specialists. It was finally decided that his troubles were psychosomatic, but, judged to be too psychologically disturbed, he was dissuaded from psychoanalysis. He nevertheless persisted and subsequently emerged from treatment quite well.

For years he had been tormented by the anxiety of committing "mortal sins." At certain times he went to confession every day, sometimes twice a day. Fortunately his priest saw clearly into the matter and encouraged him to seek out a psychotherapist. Every incident became for him an occasion for torturous doubts of conscience, the themes of which were predominantly sexual. For example, he walks into a store where he meets the wife of a colleague, a woman whom he appreciates for her beauty, sweet voice, and welcoming smile, and he cannot help finding her desirable. If he looks at her he desires her, so it follows that he looks at her in order to desire her—which is, according to Christ's words, sinning in one's heart. How can he assure himself that he doesn't desire her? He knows that if he looks at her he will desire her, so he wants to look at her in order to desire her, and this he does, in full knowledge and consent. . . . But aren't women's fashions designed to make women desirable and therefore provocative? How can he avoid undressing them with his eyes when their clothing covers their form only in order to make it more suggestive? One would have to be asexual, without penis or vagina, to stop desiring. But then words themselves impose upon him an obsessive rhythm: "pubis-mother," spinning around in his head, turning indefinitely like a ring of light. Just isolated images, but nonetheless scandalous words. He realizes the absurdity of his ruminations; he knows better than to believe that God would condemn him for eternity on account of a single transgressive desire. And yet how can he rely on his own judgment, since he is bound to be an advocate, pleading in his own interest? Shouldn't he trust his anxiety instead, leaving it the sole voice of his conscience?

There is only one logical alternative: either everything is sinful, or nothing is. He must decide whether he is "a pig or a fool." Once in a while, when he compulsively "commits a sin" by seeking pleasure in an imaginary desire or in masturbation, he finds momentary peace and a vestige of human respect. Even as he rebels against the nonsensical demands of Christian morality (which he considers in other respects to correspond to his personal interpretation of things), he still feels himself to be too much of a believer to disobey them, so he forces himself to recognize and confess his sins. However, if he doesn't keep an account of them from day to day, by the end of the week he cannot remember them. Moreover, if he doesn't rush directly from the confessional to communion, he cannot be sure he hasn't committed a sin in the meantime. Even the brief interval between them is very dangerous.

This small sample of the vertiginous reasonings that raged in his mind for years shows us only a part of the anxiety that ravaged his soul and body. It does at least portray the fantastic compulsion that dominates the obsessional's imagination and affectivity. It also reveals the clamor of sexual instincts that constantly assail those who would seek to be pure of all sexual desire. X had been free of his problems of conscience only during his military service, when he had derived great pleasure from shooting off the company machine gun and plunging his bayonet into a straw dummy. Through the breach opened by the obligatory process of "free" association in psychoanalysis, a flood of all sorts of sexual representations poured forth. And as a trained listener might have expected, his expressions of explosive violence, of murderous rage and sadistic torture, quickly revealed the nature of the demons stirring behind the anxiety of conscience he had erected as a bulwark against them.

Where religious interest is lacking, obsessional neurosis clearly takes on a different cast. Take the following case as an example. Z made a recording of a lecture she could not attend, the subject of which she wished to study in depth. When she began to listen and take notes on the lecture, she couldn't make up her mind to summarize it as she didn't want to miss any of the details. After trying a number of times to note down the truly important facts she resigned herself to the impossible task of transcribing everything, anguished by her awareness that she would not be able to memorize it. Has she understood everything correctly? Hasn't she missed certain words? She listens to the same phrases innumerable times without being certain of what she has heard. But this repeated process of verification imperceptibly transports her into a dreamlike state, which is nevertheless disquieting because she cannot be sure of having heard correctly. Into this state an agreeable image introduces itself: that of caressing, with her ears, the recording and the voice speaking from it. The classic obsessional symptoms are recognizable here: doubt and verification, a ritualized behavior that wards off the doubt, and, finally, the masked and displaced pleasure that appears through the symptom itself. Especially noticeable is the absence of guilt.

It is pointless to prolong a description of the symptoms accompanying obsessional neurosis. The reader will find in the classic textbooks an ample harvest of clinical observations on the mental ruminations, the indecisiveness, the need to verify, the apparently insignificant rituals, the tics, the obsequious character, the mannered speech and gesture, the haunting fear of committing criminal acts. For our purposes it is important to retain the point that obsession can take a religious form. In these cases it is guilt that obsesses the individual. Its doubts and ruminations are of an immediately moral order; his fears relate to the defiances hurled against God; his tics are the filthy words that interrupt his prayers; his means of verification or his ritualism takes the form of religious rites. In other cases guilt is not the major symptom; it may even be entirely absent from conscious life, becoming manifest only in the course of therapy. This difference in symptomatology can be deceptive, leading us to suppose we are dealing with a specifically religious problematic. Its religious aspect is, in fact, indisputably present. But that the discourse on salvation has no effect on the illness indicates to us that this form of obsessive religiosity does not derive from a strictly religious conflict but rather that religion here serves as a means of displacing and expressing the conflict in an indirect way. Religion, however, could not divert the conflict if it did not share with the unconscious conflict certain analogies of context and structure.

This analogy has a twofold importance: on the one hand, as a pathological form obsessional neurosis poses a universal question for man; on the other hand, religion has some kinship with psychic illness. Because of this analogy, religion tends to take a position against psychiatry, while psychiatry, in turn, tends to "psychiatrize" religion.

Its Genesis and Structure

An Unconscious Knowing

The excessively scrupulous conscience of the obsessional neurotic is not appeased by the confession of guilt that takes place in religious rituals of penance and reconciliation. Even when he gives a rigorous account of his slightest transgressions, he has the feeling of not having confessed everything. He also feels that his confession is never quite sincere because he knows he is incapable of amending his habits. Although he makes a truthful confession he knows himself to be a liar, and any confessor who tries to convince him of his sound disposition becomes for him a deceitful figure in connivance with his lies.

This "half-comical, half-lamentable" behavior is in every way similar to that of the obsessional who is not tormented by a divine judgment. Consider for a moment such symptoms as the inability to finish a task or the necessity—usually perceived as proceeding from an uncanny source—to carry it out to the end even if it no longer serves any purpose. So, for example, some people keep rereading a text because they wish to grasp each and every meaning distinctly; others are incapable of interrupting the process of reading, yet others of reading a book through to its end. In all these cases an unknown necessity, one foreign to the individual's own will, governs his behavior and finds it always falling short of the mark. In cases of moral-religious anxiety, the sense of fault predominates, whereas in the other cases everything revolves around a duty the subject must fulfill, but the projected omission of this duty is not felt as a fault.

From where does the compulsive obligation to read a book through to the last word derive? And why does the scrupulous individual feel guilt for a sin that he might have left out of account? In both instances we are faced with a nonsensical form of behavior that nevertheless points to the same elements of meaning: the fault and the law. Clinicians who reject Freudian concepts concentrate on the nonsensical character of this mental condition, explaining it as an imbalance between the biological and the psychical or as a psychic incapacity caused by an organic deficiency. In my judgment only psychoanalytic theory can account for all the factors involved. As a matter of fact, the nonsensical aspect of the neurosis operates against a background of interrelated elements of meaning. The symptoms of weakness and impotence are only the reverse side of a compulsive power; the obsessive, affectively neutral ideas are never in fact indifferent. If the neurosis is allowed free expression through analysis the full chain of associations that lies behind these apparently nonsensical manifestations becomes progressively uncovered. These affectively neutral ideas also begin to appear as they originally were—that is, so emotionally and instinctually charged that they had to be neutralized, keeping only the compulsive aspect of the dangerous force that drives them.

The person whom no confession can pacify knows he is somehow at fault, but he does not know this consciously, and he remains unaware of the guilt that haunts him. He is conscious of lying, and this contradicts what he consciously knows to be true, but his anxiety about lying protects him from the counter-truth deeply rooted in his unconscious.

Lacan's analysis of the enunciation "I am lying"—absurd from a logical or linguistic point of view—does justice to the morbid sense of guilt.[2] The subject who does the acknowledging does not entirely co-incide with the subject of the statement of facts—the one who figures in the phrases of the acknowledgment. The subject is split: the word of avowal that proceeds from his unconscious is betrayed, he feels, by his conscious pronouncement. The scrupulous man whose case I briefly de-scribed earlier experienced this splitting from time to time, both before and during analysis. When he tried to force himself "to be conscious of what he really was" he then "became unconscious" and "felt himself slip into nothingness." He considered these to be the most excruciating ex-periences he knew; he never quite understood them and had never spoken to anyone about them. How was it that at the very moment he sought to collect himself, the abrupt sensation came over him that " 'I' is another," someone he could not identify? Is this not the other who, in possession of his self, knows he is lying? The question that animated his active engagement in the cure—"who am I?"—had nothing of the philosophical tone that could have assimilated it to a rational exercise. The question obtruded upon him from a source outside himself—an unconscious form of knowing. Consequently no religious message or philosophical reflection could have provided him with a comforting answer.

I do not intend to give a full exposition of the psychoanalytic theory of obsessional neurosis. A whole chapter could not contain it, and a complete justification of my interpretation would require a detailed ac-count of the entire course of an analytic cure. Those who have not retraced the process of discovery involved in psychoanalytic explana-tion—through their own experience, their reading, their practice, or by a combination of the three—will undoubtedly have difficulty acknowl-edging the power and significance psychoanalysis grants the unconscious. I hope, however, that this exposition will cast some light on the differences, the analogies, and the system of exchange between a pathologically guilty conscience and the avowal of sin.

Unconscious Fault

The neurotically guilty conscience exemplifies Bergson's observation that the "remembrance of the forbidden fruit is the earliest thing in the memory of each of us, as it is in that of mankind. We should notice this, were not this recollection overlaid by others that we are more inclined to dwell upon.... We did not fully realize this, but behind our parents and our teachers we had an inkling of some enormous or rather some shadowy thing that exerted pressure on us through them."[3] The obsessional's life evolves under the shadow cast by this memory, although the memory itself has been lost because it has been repressed. But it is not a question of somehow recovering the memory of any particular offense he has committed. Whatever serious or minor offenses the neurotic may remember, these will simply reiterate an incessant, invincible, and unavoidable transgression: the spontaneous instinctual force that pushes man to transgress the interdict.

To use the words *interdict* and *transgression*, however, risks introducing a twofold misunderstanding: first, the misunderstanding implicit in that garrulous type of psychoanalytic cure that tracks down infantile anecdotes and takes them as explanatory causes; and second, the misunderstanding implicit in sociologies of Rousseauian inspiration that propose the repressive hypothesis and pretend to understand the sense of transgression by imputing it to the severity of the prohibitive power. It is clear that the same conflicts and the same prohibitive interventions do not have the same effects in different instances, and the absence of prohibition is as likely to induce neurosis as an excessive prohibition. It is the child's very situation that is inherently conflictual; it is the savagery of his own instinctual agitation that actually does him violence. The affective relationships in which he finds himself caught are invariably crossed by ruptures and discontinuities. The alternating absence and presence of his mother holds no reason or logic for him; he attributes it to abandonment and rejection. His parents include him in their intimacy, yet at the same time he is excluded from it. His accession to the world of language installs him in the significative order, but it always inflicts a measure of violence on him, for he cannot reconcile the various representations he is still unable to formulate. His universe is riddled with contradictions stemming essentially from the affective desires awakened in him by the presence of those he loves and desires.

Although every child must pass through the same crises, not every child resolves them by neurotic constructions. There is no point in trying to look for *the* cause of a neurosis; there are too many interactive factors at play to allow us to isolate the decisive element. But we can apprehend the insistent unresolved and hidden conflict that moves behind the various neuroses, such as, for example, morbid guilt. Every analysis of obsessional neurosis shows that an unconscious interdict stamped on the sexual instincts later continues to censor them. This is not to imply that sexuality has been reduced to silence or even that the patient's compulsion exerts itself primarily in the domain of sexuality: because of the network of unconscious representations associated with the compulsion, it is more likely that his work and daily tasks will undergo inhibition. The strategy behind neurosis works, in fact, to displace the conflict away from its explosive center and onto ideas and actions that remain sexually neutral. Religious neurosis is less successful on this point because it carries the conflict onto open ground, where sexuality and a supposedly divine law confront each other; consequently this kind of neurosis can produce far more anxiety than the other.

The interdict is written into the child's very situation. As his body awakens to a variety of scattered pleasures, the signs of desire that transpire between his parents and between them and him implant in him a desire that he then addresses toward them. His identification with the parent of his own sex causes him to direct himself libidinally toward that parent's partner; however, his very position in regard to the parents precludes an attachment as intimate and exclusive as the model they present to him. It is not as if he had a conscious representation of what is taking place, but his representations of his conflictual position become deeply inscribed in him, leaving indelible traces of a systematic organization. He has an experience of affective and emotional incidents, as well as of his representation of them, and he also has an experience of the interdict, but these experiences are not yet formulated in linguistic terms, even though they do find an indirect voice in the words spoken, as it were, beside, rather than within, his understanding. These things are passively felt by the child; he does not actively speak them out and does not represent his feelings to himself. Therefore he can repress those representations of desire and prohibition that he is not yet able to assume as a part of his own person.

Now, what happens in the case of the obsessive is that the repression of antagonistic representations fails, so that he continues to work in vain to deal with them. Neurosis thus becomes an incessant struggle against both repressed desires and the repressed representations that effectuate the censorship. In 1924, when Freud introduced the concept of the superego, he clearly noted his observation that a part of the ego constitutes itself as an unconscious agency whose purpose is to prohibit, command, observe, and defend itself from the instincts. The instincts of preservation and narcissism then contribute their share by creating a protection against a breakthrough by instincts that are too violent. The superego takes its form and content from the models it encounters and the discourses it hears. The ego then transfers the thus-constituted superego onto persons who seem to lend themselves to it by their character or physical traits. But it is the subject himself who invests the other with the power to dominate him; it is he who projects onto the other the whole set of censorious and demanding repressions that are in fact recorded in the archive of his own unconscious. In the case of religious neurosis we mentioned, God became the figure of the judge, introjected at the time of the patient's archaic conflicts.

An Affective Antinomy

An ambivalence of affect brought about by an alloy of love and hatred forms the nucleus of obsessional neurosis. The conflict is interiorized as an affective antinomy and conceals itself by repressing the hatred. Genuine affective ambivalence does not consist in the normal coexistence of love and hate but in their topical separation. In order to preserve itself, love keeps hate repressed, causing it to burn on, as it were, underground. Even the very stirrings of love tend to reawaken hate, which then makes vain attempts to triumph over love. The popularized oedipal scheme of the rival parent accounts only for that aspect of this conflict that can be assimilated by the most elementary social psychology; the scheme does not allow us to understand the repression of hatred and the extent of its infiltration into love itself. In order to account for the obsessive's attachment to a harsh superego we must analyze the complex relationship between love and hatred.

Love is demanding. By the desire implanted in the child as a response to their desire, the parents trigger in him a jealousy so powerful that it demands the gift of their unrestricted presence. Because he lives in symbiosis with his parents, all the child's painful experiences—his parents' absence, the necessity of having to share with other children, all his physical sufferings and discomforts—seem to him to proceed from their lack of love. Even when they are happy, children experience this lack of love. As the infant develops libidinally, the pleasure accompanying his bodily functions takes on a sexual character that, originally deriving from the vital functions (anaclysis), progressively becomes an autonomous pleasure, sought for itself.[4] Through oedipal identifications, his desire becomes polarized onto the parent of opposite sex. Now his love redoubles the hatred it already carries within itself, and parental refusal then takes the shape of a prohibition that consequently adheres to all the libidinal representations accompanying love. The parent of the opposite sex is already forbidden because of his or her bond to the other parent. So then, if as a result of his or her very position in the oedipal triangle, the parent of the same sex becomes a rival and evokes a special sort of hostility, it is basically secondary hostility in the oedipal conflict. But the prohibition that is built into the very affective structure of the family gives this parental refusal to respond to the child's desire the quality of a law or a right.

Thus a love whose initial demands know no limit progressively undergoes a series of refusals and setbacks. These become stamped in the child in the form of a law; for the same language that gives individuals their identity and defines their relations ultimately gives these vicissitudes in the child's life the form and force that must shape them according to the human order. This law protects the child's personal life, orienting him toward a future and toward freely chosen bonds of love. His experience of the distance introduced into his attachments, and particularly the prohibition of an incestual relationship, are the vehicles by which the child delivers himself from the oedipal conflict.

Affective ambivalence, therefore, is a response to an actual situation, but it develops in light of the psyche's recognition of the legal order that shapes the relations between people as specifically human relations and not simply the reproductive biological responses of strictly instinctual creatures. In this way the child is induced to become what he perceives mankind expects him to be: he interiorizes the "law." This term designates under an abstract heading factors such as the necessity for renunciation, the prohibition of those relations inconsistent with the established human order, the models that serve as guideposts, and the promises that invite our affirmation. This interiorization of prohibitions and demands gives rise to affective relations of a particular quality; for example, when as an adult an individual tries to remember a feeling that he could not name as a child, he often refers to it as a sense of the sacred. Women often claim to experience it particularly with regard to their fathers, who were like sacred persons to them, and men speak of the affection they remember feeling toward their mothers in the same terms. Like Freud, I trace the origin of the sense of the sacred back to this archaic feeling.[5]

The internal appropriation of the law does not prevent exorbitant and subsequently frustrated desires from opposing the law, and this opposition gives rise to a hatred that continues to permeate the child's affective attachments. Thus the conflictual elements that bring about a neurosis can be found in anyone, but what is certain is that neurosis arises from an aggravated conflict between love and hate. A number of factors can exacerbate this conflict, and generally several factors will be found working together—factors such as a lack or an excess of tenderness, a strong constitutional propensity toward aggressiveness, family circumstances such as the individual's position among his brothers and sisters or the death of a sibling, excessive parental severity or permissiveness. Consider in particular the parental prohibition against all aggression, a prohibition that intensifies hatred in two ways: it unnecessarily frustrates the instinct for mastery, and it prevents the moderation of hatred by establishing a rapport where love is stronger than hate. In this way, a sense of guilt for every moment of hatred is instilled in the child. Thus the notion that hatred will be received by rejection and a loss of love is reinforced, and this in turn increases feelings of hatred. Now, since intense hate is as destructive to the subject as it is to his love relations, in order to survive he represses it. When it erupts in the course of a cure, sometimes after long resistance, one realizes the devastation it threatens to create; it then becomes evident that in fact the power of psychic health brought about the repression, even at the risk of producing a neurosis.

Strictly speaking, it is this simultaneous presence of repressed hate and a love accentuated by defense mechanisms that constitutes affective ambivalence. In every case this ambivalence forms the nucleus of obsessional neurosis and consumes the subject's energy in the incessant internal struggle between love and hate.

In order to understand how the subject becomes captive to the very prohibitions he unwittingly rebels against, we must see that he does not receive these interdicts as if he were an empty black box; rather, he has vested in them his passionate interest and love. The neurotic transfers onto prohibitions the instinctual energy for which he can find no other suitable form of expression. In this way, then, a boy who intensely desires his mother can channel the force of that desire into a defensive reaction against his dangerous desires; this consequently increases the internal demands he makes of himself in proportion to his love for his mother. He actually loves his superego with the same force that attached him to the first object of his love. The desire for a moral purity grows so absolute that it threatens to devour him with the same avidity with which his love once devoured him.

My analysis will not encompass all the processes in the formation of neurotic obsession; the reader can find descriptions and examples of these in numerous clinical and theoretical studies. I limit this study to the clarification of those points necessary to an understanding of religious neurosis.

Religious Ambivalence

In the religious form of obsessional neurosis, affective ambivalence is ponderously transferred onto God and the institution of religion. The subject expresses his aggression indirectly by ridiculous behavior and unwonted, disquieting ideas that he does not know what to do with but that others, much to his surprise, treat humorously. While gazing at a crucifix, for example, he might imagine Christ completely nude and with an erection; or during communion he might imagine that he bites off Christ's sex. The man whose ruminations we described earlier used to refrain from breaking wind because he could not shake off the idea that he was hurling it in the face of God or the Virgin Mary. The word *sacrilege*, learned from the catechism, fascinated and struck terror into him; without quite understanding why, he believed it involved some frightful crime, which he attempted to imagine and stage for himself in concrete terms by bizarre representations.

In all these phenomena we recognize the secret enjoyment of inflicting suffering on others, reminiscent of sadism. I would not characterize this form of behavior as perverse, however, for the repression that allows this small spark of pleasure to slip by is not geared toward exciting pleasure. These moments of turmoil, moreover, also lose their aura of horror later in the course of the cure. But once this pleasure in aggressivity is acknowledged, it triggers in the subject a murderous hatred that truly takes possession of him as he articulates it.

Even if they remain profound believers in other respects, these patients will either fearfully whisper or explosively vociferate their revolt against an iniquitous God. Religion becomes a yoke that they must throw off, and sin a ruse invented by avid priests eager to exert their power over other people's consciences. Through their bitter remarks these patients seem to echo Nietzsche, even when they have not read him: " 'Sin' ... constituted the greatest event in the entire history of the sick soul, the most dangerous sleight of hand of religious interpretation."[6] Thus, like a man posing nude before the mirror, penis raised toward the divine gaze behind his own reflected image, some imagine themselves to be the personification of wrath itself against a God whose existence they deny even as they take pleasure in defying him—a gesture strangely reminiscent of the ambivalent behavior of Freud's "Rat-man."

At the start of treatment, it often happens that this revolt is acknowledged only indirectly, through the wish to rage against God and church. But this wish betrays the hope for a quick cure by a form of brute emotional discharge, such as primal scream therapy. When the initial resistances are dismantled the patient may take this freedom, and he can take it all the more easily if the therapist, who is known to have a respect for religion, can accept such "sacrileges" without being shocked but also without taking a complicitous pleasure in them. Although these savage cries can bring the patient relief, they cannot liberate him. Along the path worn by hate, he must toil to disentangle his affective ambivalence; for if love sustains the hatred that it would vanquish, then hate is also the passionate attachment through which love in turn sustains itself.

The obsessive's attitude to the law indicates the measure of his ambivalence as well as its underlying significance. He passionately attaches himself to a concept of divine law that penalizes all sexual emotions and any representation not explicitly legitimized. By pushing obedience to the law to the extreme and adopting an excessive submissiveness to it, he lays bare its arbitrary tyranny and ridicules it. This process resembles that of masochism as Gilles Deleuze analyzes it: "By a scrupulous application of the law [the masochist] hopes to bring out its absurdity and produce the very disorder it is meant to prohibit and ward off. The law is taken literally, at its word; neither its primacy nor its finality are actually contested but he acts as if it were the nature of the law to keep for itself the pleasure it forbids us."[7] Unlike the masochist, the obsessional neurotic does not use the law to gratify his pleasure for punishment. More particularly, he does not elaborate a philosophical reasoning or contrive a rational strategy to procure a transgressive pleasure. The ironic gesture that subverts the law by exposing its absurd consequences has already achieved a measure of therapeutic distance, thus relieving his effort to comply with an obstinate and meticulous obedience. It also expresses the unconscious revolt brewing behind an apparently accepted bondage. Through this irony the notion eventually dawns that this absurd law is only the monstrous figment of a morbid imagination, and at the moment of this realization, the chimerical hold of the law dissolves. To be sure, there are transitional moments between the night and the day of this realization, when the indefinite limits excite the perverse pleasure of playing with a law paradoxically maintained for the sheer satisfaction of transgressing it. Conscious ambivalence then becomes the stage for a sadomasochistic gratification. But the essence of the obsessional neurotic's attitude is not to be found in the sadomasochistic structure of behavior. On the contrary, the obsessive has formed—by virtue of all the love he has transferred to it—a powerful attachment to the law. From it he derives the longed-for, but never quite attained, satisfaction of being the perfectly lovable and perfect lover. And yet, by the same token, the law subjugates him, imposing on him the same exigent demands he imposes on it.

In our analysis of the ambivalence produced by the trammeling of the instincts we saw that the aggressivity generally inherent in love is reinforced by a form of love that has taken the shape of an internalized prohibition. As a result of a massive repression, this aggressivity is then transformed to hatred for the parent situated in the position symbolically representing the order of law. In an attempt to dominate hate, love desperately resists every representation of a withdrawal of love that might be brought about by any insubordination to the law. Then, in order to silence the least movement of a dangerous freedom and prove, by a rigorous submission, that love is absolute, it becomes necessary to push the law's demands to their extreme. The subject is subsequently led by this unconscious dialectic to badger the lawmaker for meticulous explanations as to what is and is not licit—a rigorous codification of the law, a trap in which the moralistic theologian may be often caught if he loves censure for its own sake. (I will come back to this issue in my analysis of collective religious neurosis.)

From the moment the subject's first liberty is won, the lawmaker is willfully attacked and drawn into a labyrinth of ratiocinations. A morbid anxiety concerning one's guilt and the insistent feeling that one has not sincerely repented both have their explanation: the subject unconsciously knows that he has kept within himself his hate, his rebellion, and his desire to transgress the law. Perpetually watchful, he is always ready to confess—to something he has not even actually recognized.

The Transfer onto God

The excessively scrupulous individual lives under the constant gaze of a God who pries out his transgressive inclinations, especially sexual ones, tracks down his least escapades, and probes into his natural desires. The same words sung in jubilation by the author of Psalm 139 are whispered in terror by the obsessive with a neurotic sense of guilt: "O Lord, thou has searched me and known me. Thou knowest my downsitting and mine uprising . . . and hast laid thine hand upon me." For the obsessive divine knowledge is not benevolent intimacy with God, and God's hand catches culprits in the act. He knows that he ought to celebrate a God who brings life-giving goodness and light to the spirit, but this act of witness remains for him a duty, and an impossible one at that. He must first be capable of walking into the light, and he must learn to love without a guilty conscience.

What is it that causes God to freeze into the figure of a pitiless judge, notwithstanding a conviction to the contrary, every bit as strongly affirmed? The problem might be easily resolvable if the obsessional neurotic had but one notion of God, that is, as a despotic judge; but in point of fact he maintains two contradictory views and cannot refrain from testifying to both. Up to this point I have been analyzing the unconscious ambivalence that constitutes the core of obsession in general, as well as its particular character as a form of religious neurosis. But now we must understand why God becomes the agency that polarizes this neurosis.

We may note, first of all, that the signifier "God" is capable of drawing upon itself the obsessive's illicit love as well as his love for the law. In religious discourse, in fact, God becomes the point where the two different modes of loving distinguished by psychoanalysis converge: an object love with a tendency to unite with others in order to widen the subject's existence by the process of participation; and love through identification that magnifies the ego by transforming it according to the models, the desire, or the prohibitions proposed to it. If primary attachment to the mother is particularly intense it may give rise to the mystical quest for God as the absolute object of desire. This transference onto God occurs because the bond with the primordial object (the mother) is always experienced as something that has been cut off from the subject, and because the intensity of the bond is dangerous to him. But in this case the intense attachment also becomes invested in the law under two aspects: the law enables the subject to break off this first attachment, and at the same time it allows him to maintain it by transforming it into the process and duty of coming-to-be projected by the parent's will. The inability of some people to tolerate either physical or emotional suffering is often a sign that this primordial attachment was once strong and demanding for them. It also often betrays the existence of what Leopold Szondi has called a pleasure syndrome (*Lustsyndrom*), one that has been violently repressed.[8]

But this process of transference, with its power of metaphorical transformation, does not explain why God should become the object onto which is transposed this monstrous superego that devours life instead of transforming it. This process, after all, is a part of the normal formation of a religious bond; one function of religion is to overcome the oedipal complex by leading the subject out of an imaginary conflict and into a symbolically structured order. So the process I have described is a necessary but not sufficient condition for the formation of a religious obsession. On the basis of various observations I propose the following as a hypothesis: The emergence of the terrible God is often explained by the absence of a symbolic father, and this for two reasons. An effaced and humiliated father cannot become a support for the symbolic law he is meant to make present. Because this space remains void, the subject then appeals to an all-powerful father to assume the function written into the family constellation. Then, instead of presenting the model of a man who recognizes himself as having been granted by God the right to enjoy pleasure, this figure of an emasculated father, mere shadow of a deadened desire, communicates a message commanding the renunciation of desire. Moreover, if the prevailing religious milieu generally diffuses a mistrust of sexuality, then conscious representations also come to reinforce the transferring of the function of the superego onto God. Together, this unconscious transfer of the superego onto God and unconscious identification with a dead father figure both support the notion of a judging and persecuting God against whom reason and religion struggle in vain.

It is unusual for the religious transference to become suddenly concentrated in the superego's exaltation of God. Neurosis usually announces itself during childhood and then progressively reasserts itself during puberty and adulthood. A number of particularly pronounced representations and certain forms of ritualized behavior indicate that obsession has left a print on the child's practice of religion. Nevertheless, the benefits of religion are more frequently prevalent, bringing about a partial and temporary resolution of the infant's obsessional neurosis—as the improvement of his character and his socialization will both attest. An example is the case of the "Wolf-Man."[9]

As a result of a subsequent rejection of religion, this tactical displacement of neurosis onto religion can often open up in some subjects a partial path to freedom from illness. These individuals are especially demanding with regard to the representatives of religion and do not easily tolerate the fact that even the peripheral doctrines of the church remain uncertain. Changes in ritual or doctrinal formulations seem like sacrilege to them, testifying to a doubt and a lack of faith on the part of those chiefly responsible. Because they become so closely attached to the most minute truths and beliefs of the law, any break in the system leaves them exposed to their own repressed doubts. Their own lack of assurance makes them excessively sensitive to the narcissistic wounds an environment scornful of religion inflicts upon believers. The unconscious hate they have accumulated in the name of religion plays into the hands of its adversaries when, with a bitter sense of having been cheated, they break all their bonds with their faith. It seems to me that the hatred some people heap upon religion is but a substitute for their obstinate struggle against a superego whose power they have not yet managed to defuse. I have even heard one person confess to a fear of God's vengeance in the world beyond even though he no longer believed in either God or an afterlife.

Valid Questions That Border on the Irrational

Although they may be somewhat confused by transference, the neurotic sense of guilt raises a number of fundamental questions for religion. In the course of a therapy, they often emerge from a swarm of phantasmagorical representations. The imperious demand for truth and righteousness that imposes itself on the subject leads me to suppose that obsessional neurosis is also the site of the failure to make life conform to these demands.

The compulsive wish to give a fully truthful account of oneself leads back to the fundamental choices the subject has made throughout his life. He would have his life be wholly consistent, and yet he is acutely aware that his conduct and his choices are inevitably tainted. Whatever the conscious motives that haunt his desires with ambiguity, the wish for purity takes on the voice of a religious and moral imperative. Thus Christians justify their disavowal of themselves by invoking Christ's paradigm: the purest of the pure. Isn't this the ideal man must attain? Here we see raised to the level of personal choice one of the great themes of cultural anthropology: the theme of defilement. Although the wish for purity never ceases to haunt him, the obsessive never quite manages to formulate it truthfully to himself. The absolute purity of his contentions becomes an obtrusively commanding obligation; it begins to seem an attainable ideal, as if man were not an instinctual being making progress only by oblique means, allowing himself to be taught by the spontaneity of his body and his desires, incapable of totalizing his existence in the instance of one decision. The obsessional subject cannot accept simply making his way toward his desired purity because he would, instead, go straight to it. The splitting of the ego produced by the repression of unconscious desires and of their correlative, hatred, also brings about a refusal of this splitting into an ego governed by intentions and one governed by passions. The implacable vigilance of his unconscious causes him to become so absorbed in regretting the purity of the past that he is no longer open to seeking the purity that lies ahead.

Another great religious theme that preoccupies the obsessive is the concept of debt. As his chaotic representations are unraveled and his anxiety progressively yields up its meaning, a certain idea—against which all rational arguments are useless—emerges: the idea that all enjoyment and pleasure are stolen from God. Other reasonable people, theologians, or staunch believers may consider such a conception of God absurd, but to the obsessive it becomes an imperative that places him in a binding dilemma: either one must opt for the purely human plenitude promised by the enjoyment of pleasure or one must love God, the only reality that really matters. In moments of intense pleasure, God scarcely seems to count; in moments of the affirmation of one's faith, God alone gives meaning to existence. Since everything man receives comes from God he remains infinitely indebted, but in order to enjoy the pleasures of his life one must be able to forget his debt. Thus pleasure naturally tends to forget its divine origin and makes man turn in upon himself, recalling what believers often admit: when they are happy, they do not spontaneously think of God.

These two themes, then, the yearning for purity and the sense of an insolvent debt, are essential to the religious query. When the obsessive begins to penetrate into the core of his questionings, he finds himself faced with the antinomies of purity and defilement, pleasure and indebtedness. These antinomies plunge him into a confusion even more profound than the torments of his neurosis and so oblige him to work through an elucidation of his religious convictions in conjunction with a modification of his personal life and character. I have often confirmed the fact, mentioned in chapter 1, that through the progress of a therapy the patient's previous religious frame of reference does not remain intact. Therapy shakes up those convictions that have long participated in the neurosis by furnishing a ground for their displacement and vague arguments for sustaining the repression and its resistance. Therapy, I may add, not only unmasks the unconscious use of religious signifiers; it also reveals the basic antinomies that form the structure of religion, antinomies that religion must surmount if it is to achieve a truly viable relationship with God.

With regard to the morbid sense of guilt, therapy offers a twofold progress toward truth. On the one hand it releases the grip that binds the subject's representations of pleasure and desires to repression, thereby disengaging the movement of murderous hatred that accompanies them. It also forces him to confront his world of religious meanings, to open them up and infuse them with a new mobility by examining their function within the entire structure of his personal context—a task that must be carried out without any guarantee of absolute lucidity. In neurosis, religious meanings usually mask unconscious conflicts, and unconscious conflicts tend, in turn, to obscure the truth of religious meanings.

It would be wrong, however, to equate the rule to talk about everything in therapy to the act of confession in the rite of penance, for the confession of sins is a repentance based on a specific pact between the individual and God. In neurosis, this pact is yet to be established; it can take place at the end, after disengaging the strands of religious meanings from their unconscious representations. To see psychoanalysis as an act of confession, as Michel Foucault does, is to conceive of the unconscious representation as knowledge the subject refuses to admit, like the avoidance of truth in bad faith.[10] Moreover, the discursive articulation of sexuality in therapy is not simply another form of control exercised by the reigning medical authority. On the contrary, therapy delivers sexuality from the control that the neurosis itself—unconsciously and for motives unknown to the subject—exerts upon him. Neither is it a form of seeking out knowledge, for neurosis erases the very existence of the instincts by unconsciously willing to know nothing about them. Nor is it a matter of exposing through language the secrets used to compile some sort of *scientia sexualis*; in neurosis both sexuality and murderous violence exert their destructive power from afar precisely because language does not give them recognition as a part of the subject's existence. As far as religious language itself is concerned, if its power is used to maintain the instincts' exclusion from the domain of signification, it loses the power it has to bestow meaning by differentiating man's fundamental debt from his transgressions, a just God who judges in truth from a wicked one who persecutes man.

In order to be complete an analysis of religious obsession should consider characteristics that, although belonging to all forms of obsessional neurosis, here take on a specifically religious connotation: characteristics such as unconscious perfectionism, moral masochism, and ritualism. I will treat these in the account of collective neurosis, for, situated as they are at the border between conscious and unconscious formations, these traits predominate in the morbid guilt of certain religious milieus.

An Afterword on Malignant Obsession

The term *malignant obsession* designates a form of illness in which symptoms of an obsessional nature cover over but also manifest a mental structure that is basically psychotic. The following case will illustrate the difference between a neurosis and a malignant obsession: it concerns a contemplative nun who was admitted into a psychiatric clinic because of her insistently repeated doubts and strange behavior.

The rigidity of her body and the dull fixity of her gaze were immediately striking. She made her problem known at once: although she sought to live her life according to the absolute word of Scripture, she simply did not see how this was possible; at no time had she practiced total poverty, obedience, or mortification. Moreover, she did not have a true vocation, for her choice was haphazardly made and she could just as easily have chosen marriage. The proof of this, she felt, was that before entering the convent she had met a man she was drawn to and would probably have married if she had been asked.

She thought her doubts about her vocation began while she was a missionary. One day after communion she heard the word "Carmel." Except for a few vague memories about the life of St. Theresa of Lisieux, whose work she had read years earlier, she knew almost nothing about Carmel. So, since the word did not proceed from her, it must have been a formal command proceeding from God. Her opting for Carmelite life was not her own decision and therefore corresponded to a real vocation. And still it seemed to her that to live her life in perfect accordance with the gospel was in every way an impossible task. Besides, the demands

66

made by the gospel were contradictory. How can one reconcile obedience with fidelity to one's commitment? or practice complete poverty and charity when one's superiors will not allow it? And how would she be able to appear at the last judgment without being afraid? She knew she had done a poor job in the missions; she had to be sent home because of her negligence and her strange behavior. This she attributed partly to laziness but primarily to the insoluble conflicts provoked by the contradictions in the gospel. She also told how she had had, before entering the convent, an "affectionate" relationship with a girlfriend. It was not until the third year of her novitiate that she learned, during a course on morality, that this relationship was sinful. Then, feeling troubled about it, she spoke of it in confession but continued afterward to accuse herself of it each time she went to confession. Now, however, it no longer troubled her.

In considering this case we must of course immediately dismiss every commonsense or ideological point of view that would see in this account nothing more than a sentimental escapism into a religious fiction. We could hypothetically propose that we are dealing with neurotic behavior. The symptoms are the same as those of obsessional neurosis:mental ruminations, excessive scrupulosity, indecision, anguish at the idea of God's judgment. The idea that God had directly pointed her toward her vocation by an oracular word naturally leads us to think this might be the kernel of a religious delirium. But if we remain attentive to the psychic context, this typical obsessional tableau takes on a more specific significance.

The woman in question is inaccessible in presence and demeanor; she has no sense of herself as being mentally ill. In a strained and monotonous voice she incessantly repeats her doubts as to her vocation and reiterates her perplexity before the contradictory demands that she finds impossible to fulfill completely. She appears to ask for help so that she will be able to see more clearly, but in fact she remains wrapped up in her own thoughts, beyond time and place, forever absorbed in the haze of her indecision, cut off from others and indifferent to everything that concerns them. There is no variation in her mental or affective state, no warmth in her contact with others, no accentuation in tone modulating her discourse, no expressive gesture, no vestige of dramatic movement within her. The extreme rigidity of her body reveals so intense an anxiety that she seems almost like a corpse. It is significant that before the more serious illness set in she had manifested obsessional symptoms, such as her anxious concern to confess, long after the fact, her homosexual rapport, to expose it in full detail, and to compulsively repeat her confession. Afterward, the overwhelming feeling that she was base and powerless took over her perception of herself. An evil fatality had penetrated the order of the world because of the contradictory commands of the gospel. We do not find here the kind of affective ambivalence that may drive an individual to blame God for making impossible demands. Nor is there any flexibility in her ruminations about the law—only perplexity at not being able to avoid its judgment.

The nucleus of this illness was undeniably schizophrenia, with its two opposing poles: narcissism and radical abjectness. Psychotic narcissism marked every aspect of her demeanor. Although she was apparently obsessed by the duty to be charitable and serve the poor, in fact all her intent was invested in her preoccupation with a radical poverty—to such a point that she completely withdrew her interest from the work entrusted to her and was no longer available or open to anything but her own ruminations. The kernel of religious delirium clearly indicates that behind her prostrate silence and one-track ruminations she held to a vague notion of her sublime destiny. But in contrast to this privileged vocation she saw her life sinking into an abject egoism. To possess nothing, not even one's own will, to give up both body and soul to the point of feeling that they have been annihilated—such a radical desire for nondesire no longer involves the struggle of one's personal will; it is an imposed necessity that she must undergo. The rigidity of her whole being, meant to exclude the body, testified to this. For her the body must have been the infected source of pollution and evil, the carrier of death. This brings to mind the analytic works of V. E. von Gebsattel and E. Strauss.[11]

The universe of the body must have been for her the very stuff of horror and disgust, a counterworld of cadaveric putrefaction and sordid crime, the essence of defilement. In the only thing she still reproached herself for, her laziness, we see her rejection of a humiliating schizophrenic passivity. She spoke of her laziness, an apparently moral term, with no real sense of guilt; it was primarily an attempt to bestow some subjective meaning on this state of impotent passivity, and since for her the body was death itself, she lived in a constant state of introverted passivity.

Her obsessional symptoms—her ruminating over the contradictory injunctions of the gospel, the ritualism with which she performed her religious exercises—were a means of clutching onto a few signifiers that preserved the shreds of a collapsed reality. It is correct to diagnose cases such as these by stating that obsession is no more than a cover for schizophrenia, for in spite of the apparent symptoms, we are no longer dealing with neurosis here. Attempts to treat these cases by therapies appropriate for neuroses will inevitably fail; perhaps for this reason obsession is often said to be the most obstinate of mental illnesses. If one were to take on these symptoms through therapy, it would precipitate a delirium, for the "cover of obsession" is the means by which the patient, through his symptoms, retrieves some part of reality and preserves it from a complete derealization. Here the function of obsession differs radically from the function it has in neurosis.

In neurosis, as we have seen, the symptom is a strategy used to maintain the repressed instincts: obsessional behavior exercises an organized mastery over these instincts by availing itself of the secondary processes taken from the order of language: the metonymic displacement of affect onto less threatening representations, the polarization of symptom onto details, and the ritualization of life. In malignant obsession the same processes of mastery are used to protect the ego against a far more agonizing and radical danger, that of lapsing into a complete derealization. This patient's sterile ruminations were her way of restoring and protecting the few scraps left of her demolished universe. She clung to a number of isolated words—poverty, charity, obedience—because when taken absolutely these words became for her signs of an existence with a possible meaning. These signs, to be sure, had been emptied of their real significance, and, no longer having any bearing on the real world, they consequently forced themselves upon her in the form of impossible injunctions. In this way they reenacted a primordial rejection and maintained her split from a corporal reality whose horror she could not bear. But their repetition, by availing itself of abstract signs, served to defend the patient against what was now a more menacing anxiety: the total eclipse of a completely unanchored ego. Beneath the somewhat absurd cover of an apparently sad, egocentric, religious discourse, a drama unfolds, one that penetrates to the roots of being itself and touches the religious dimension of life: the haunted obsession with absolute purity and the obscene horror of the world. This is the question finally posed by the process of neurotic interrogation unfolding and elucidating itself here. This schizophrenic had lived and experienced this question too precociously and had been able to respond to it only by instituting a radical split between the absolute signifiers of purity and her accursed body.

In order to make more comprehensible what must have taken place in the early stages of an existence such as this I can relate the case of the temporary collapse of a woman after she saw a documentary that unexpectedly depicted a scene of torture. During a film on the "cruelty of animals" the sequence of a hunt for Indians in the Amazon was suddenly projected onto the screen. After a number of Indians had been slain, one was captured alive and tortured in various ways: he was impaled and pinned to the ground with a bayonet, his tongue was cut out, and he was castrated . . . all this, and more, carried out in the midst of shouts and laughter. This witness received the impression of an evil so radical that no psychological interpretation could suffice to account for it. A universal sense of obscenity pervaded the world and polluted all of humanity, for the hunters, having perhaps their own wives and children, looked no different from anyone else and, after their crime, moved about freely, protected by Brazilian law. Staggered and numbed, she found she was unable to flee from the theater until after the full scene had been shown, and she was for several days afterward unable to eat, sleep, or receive any form of embrace.

She spoke about this episode for hours, holding desperately onto a few sequences of words. She was overcome by a feeling of intense moral disgust and felt as if her body had been torn apart into disassociated bits. Certain words with which culture defiles itself, words such as *desire*, became disgusting, empty, superfluous masks. Although she was not a believer, she came to the conclusion that what she had witnessed *could not but* have a profoundly religious significance. It took a slow process of psychological labor to reconstruct her fragmented body. But she did not want to forget this hideous reality in the world, though she knew that life would eventually deaden the memory of an evil too unbearable to remain conscious. As we all know, mankind would prefer to live in a world of self-deception. Believers think that such events can be redeemed by the meaning forgiveness might bestow upon them, just as he who at the extremity of torture once prayed, "Father, forgive them for they know not what they do." Yet, if this forgiveness is not recognized as such, how can it possibly redeem such evil? We can only hope that some day forgiveness will be recognized.

A passage of another kind, to another genus, has taken place here: *metabasis eis allo genos*, as Aristotle once said of the metaphor. However, contrary to meaning, which can be articulated, evil is an incomprehensible and radical nonmeaning that cannot be articulated. Abruptly revealed in the banally human countenance, it suddenly seemed to be the hidden face of visible reality, the very substance of an abject world that insidiously penetrated all bodies and objects. Words that otherwise carried meaning lost their metaphorical power and value; the body was experienced as dismembered and language betrayed its inherent treachery.

This witness is not a schizophrenic and will therefore be able to reestablish a bond of communication with the world, but it is doubtful that this experience, which caused the ordinary world to collapse and made her border upon suicide, will pass without leaving some effects in its wake. As for the schizophrenic obsessional, there is good reason to suppose that some analogous phantasmagorical revelation, too precociously experienced, must have definitely dispossessed her of the expressive use of language.

The transformation of religion into a malignant obsession is the result of a process that took place long before. For a certain period of time a religious discourse allowed the patient to retain a measure of coherence, but these religious signifiers did not have the power to realign her corporal reality to the signifying level of existence. On the contrary, they were taken by her as messages sent from beyond to condemn her. Thus thrown out of their proper orbit by this profound rupture, they became no more than pure celestial signs, flickering indefinitely, darting their command for an impossible purity.

3 • The Collective Neurosis of Culpability

In both recent and ancient times certain Christian milieus have been so obsessed with sinfulness, particularly of a sexual nature, that one is led to posit an analogy between this exacerbated sense of sin and obsessional neurosis. For this reason I have adopted the analogical term *collective neurosis*. We may recall that Freud himself—for reasons already mentioned, to be discussed more fully at the end of this chapter—considered religion as such to be a collective neurosis of humanity. I give this term a more restricted sense, however, using it to refer specifically to the religious and pathological deviations caused by a form of Christianity whose message becomes concentrated on the consciousness of sin and whose larger aims are reduced to the constant struggle against sin.

This disposition to guilt throws the entire order of Christian values and meanings out of balance: it stifles the very life of faith and, by a surreptitious reemergence of passions that have been disregarded, ultimately alters the fundamental attitudes that govern faith. Even according to religious criteria, an exaggerated sense of guilt represents a distortion. In terms of the psychological criteria outlined earlier, this phenomenon is linked to the pathological formations of obsessional neurosis. It is easy to conceive, in fact, how such an acute and anxiety-ridden suppression of the instincts would be determined by an unconscious repression that makes use of the motives supplied to it by religion. How otherwise can we account for religion's failure to recognize man as he really is, or for its overemphasis of some aspects of its message to the detriment of others that are every bit as essential? This subjugation of faith to an obsessive sense of sin does not, strictly speaking, constitute a neurosis. One can conform to this pattern without the repressed material's taking its revenge in the form of the symptoms previously analyzed. Nevertheless, it remains true that, aside from the useless and sterile suffering it causes, the morbidity of such cultural and religious formations tends to induce neurosis in some individuals.

On this point our judgments and analyses will perhaps be received with more misgiving. An opposing interpretation of Christianity, legitimizing what we consider deviant, might be offered. When we are not dealing with clear-cut illness, we do not have the points of reference necessary to trace a sure boundary between a faith that transforms life and the formation of a sickness. It is necessary to examine the connections between the elements that constitute what we call collective neurosis and to avail ourselves of the religious and psychological apparatus with which to evaluate and interpret them.

Instincts, Suspected and Repressed

Books and memories keep the record of a religious education that holds sexuality in abeyance, represses all violence, and exalts the idea of self-mastery. Sexuality in particular is looked upon with distrust. The examination of conscience, which is a practice of wisdom and sincerity in faith, becomes displaced and becomes largely an exercise of self-observation for the purpose of ousting erotic fantasies and other demonstrations of carnal spontaneity. In certain milieus, the idea held by a number of moralists that in such matters there is no such thing as a venial sin takes authoritative hold of a theological tradition and becomes rigorously applied. Any imaginary acquiescence is heavily taxed as sin. One can imagine the torment of conscience experienced by those who want to decide at what point they become accomplices of an erotic image.

This massive culpabilization of sexuality acts as a paradoxical double bind, producing doubt and anxiety if not *genuine* neurosis. A contradiction between two attitudes and two discourses entraps the subject in a dilemma whose only solution is a guilty compromise. On the one hand educators understand that any discourse on sexuality conjures it up and invests it with meaning, so they deliberately deny its existence by virtually refusing to name it. Consequently a child's curiosity goes unsatisfied and his questions unanswered; if a certain amount of instruction becomes necessary, things are not directly named. On the other hand, in contrast to this negating silence, a moral discourse encouraging a minute examination of these matters is maintained. Thus, like some great enigma, sex haunts the conscience as if it were the nocturnal figure of an insidious power called "sin."[1]

Various influences were responsible for this obsession with sexuality in particular Christian epochs.[2] Monastic traditions spread an ideal of virginity among the whole community of believers, and moral thought became infused with a juridical mentality that pushed communities to a rigorous codification of prohibitions. Undoubtedly, rationalist philosophies that espoused the dualism of body and soul favored the idea of the body-as-instrument, which the spirit must subdue in the service of socially useful functions such as, in this case, procreation. A certain cultural refinement also contributed to the body's disgrace and tended to place a guard over its natural expressions.[3] These factors visibly inscribed on the face of all culture also borrow their effective force from the unconscious. Thus sexuality is formed and transformed through the early conflicts and repressions that have left their traces in the unconscious memory. No prophet proclaiming a garden of innocent delights will ever make possible a sexuality that can unfold without the shadow of an uneasy conscience.

This massive culpabilization of sexuality has some particularly pathogenic effects precisely because it is bound up with and reactivates unconscious representations. If the parents have themselves been mutilated or scarred in the history of their desire, and if their injunctions and prohibitions intensify a religious climate of guilt, the conditions favoring their offspring's development of neurosis converge. A heavy and suspicious sense of guilt generally impoverishes all affective life; it smothers creative forces and casts a shadow over life as a whole. What concerns us particularly here is that it produces a fearful and evasive style of religion, separating religion from the actual culture around it.

The repression and denial of sexuality are closely linked to a restrictive attitude with regard to all the instincts. In this context, for example, aggressivity is stamped by an equally radical exclusion. The watchful guard set over sexuality is more eloquent and its discourse more striking to the imagination, but the forms of education that reprove all aggressivity are no less productive of a mutilating sense of guilt.[4] This reprobation attacks the very source of the psyche because it injures one of the forces necessary to the development of all human activities: man's instinct for mastery.

The guilt cast over sexuality and aggressivity involves the very notion of the instincts; in collective neurosis the instincts themselves are suspect. Because they are spontaneously savage, dangerous, and obscure, an entire apparatus for correcting and curbing them is constructed around them. Around the violence and the pleasures of the instincts, guilt constructs a moral cage to strangle them at the source rather than putting them to use in the work of culture. It is my opinion that this suspicion aims at sexuality only insofar as it is the clearest demonstration of the positing of self that has its source in the instincts. Insofar as it is libidinal desiring for pleasure, sexuality involves the affirmation of the self's existing for itself. At base, guilt tends to repress the individual's passion for autonomy in all domains: sexuality, aggressivity, or freedom of thought. It is at this point that the repression of sexuality and the repression of aggressivity converge. But it is to the extent that it becomes the locus of a transgression—thus of an aggression—that sexuality lends itself to the interiorization of guilt.[5] The guilty conscience is produced by turning onto the self an aggressivity originally directed toward the external world and felt by the individual to be destructive to the bonds of love and friendship. For this reason, the twofold repression of both sexuality and aggressivity is all the more harmful; it brings the psyche to a condemnation of all instinctual life.

Education is a delicate process. In themselves, the instincts are anarchical and—because of their inordinate demands—stubbornly resistant to the requirements of social life. Thus all civilization must pay the price of what Freud calls "cultural renunciations."[6] Man's participation in language already implies the internal distance introduced by renunciation as well as the subjection of the instincts to regulatory principles: man's accession to the order of universal signs imposes on him a complex psychic labor. A respect for others and his engagement in the work of truth and humanization will then require an even more profound transformation of his instincts.

Being generally aware of the demands of truth and of man's relation to others, philosophers have often shown a certain distrust of the passions, although some, like Plato, have recognized the force and courage that the passions (*thumos*) impart to reason.[7] In this precisely consists the instincts' disquieting enigma. The libido and the instinct for mastery are both vital forces necessary to link human beings together, exert them to conquer hostile forces, and urge them to produce cultural works. But the instincts are also antagonistic to both culture and love. As a frequent witness of this contradiction against which man's dream of happiness runs aground, Freud eventually introduced the theory of a death instinct that stood in opposition to the large group of life instincts: "But man's natural aggressive instinct, the hostility of each against all and all against each, opposes this program of civilization. This aggressive instinct is the derivative and the main representative of the death instinct which we have found alongside of Eros, and which shares world-dominion with it."[8] The silent and insidious death instinct never appears in its raw form or shows its true face but instead insinuates and conceals itself in the life instincts. This accounts for the fact that Freud's standpoint is not one of optimistic humanism. Despite his lucid analysis of the power of death to perturb and supplant life, Freud nevertheless wanted to bring man to a positive recognition of his instincts, since it is from these that he must fashion his life and his work.

Freud's ambivalent evaluation of religion is directly linked to the various positions he held regarding the difficult marriage between culture and the instincts. The notion of divine paternity and the interdict against any representation of God, even the enunciation of his name, are the most powerful factors of renunciation on behalf of culture.[9] But the ensuing guilt and man's obedience to God diminishes man and implies a devaluation of life.[10] On the other hand, the religious sublimation of love allows some men to achieve the aim of civilization, the attainment of happiness by a transformation of the instincts: "The pleasure principle has often been brought into connection with religion; this connection may lie in the remote regions where the distinction between the ego and objects or between objects themselves is neglected."[11] Freud recognized that through religion man participates in the forces of life, but the consequences of this sublimation, the gospel's command to love one's enemies, constitute a limit Freud could not cross. He found this commandment absurd and dangerous because man was not worthy of this love, precisely because the death instinct makes him a wolf with regard to others.[12] Ultimately, this commandment corrodes the very life instinct that religion initially appears to affirm. Freud alternated, then, between positive and negative evaluations of religion, depending on whether he affirmed the importance of sublimation and cultural renunciation or spoke up for the instincts necessary for the preservation of life.

An insurmountable ambivalence governs instinctual life: as a force of life and unity it becomes the source of cultural works and religion, but it also contains within itself the potential for evil. The transformation of the instincts necessary for the maintenance of culture always remains ambiguous and full of risks. The danger of religion is that by wanting to triumph over death it can wind up depreciating life. With reference to religion's distrust of the instincts, psychological experience has taught us that one of the strategies often used by the death instinct is to enlist for its own ends the fear of death itself. On this point psychopathology and the wisdom of the gospel concur. By the same token, in the parable of the wheat and the darnel, which illustrates how both are randomly scattered over the field of history, Jesus condemns religious puritanism, exemplifying instead the importance of respecting the ambiguous mixture of good and evil contained in all man's endeavors.[13]

The culpabilization of the instincts tends to exalt the passive virtues of obedience, renunciation, and humility—all of them ambiguous terms. Of course pride is universally abhorrent, but a heavy emphasis on obedience deadens initiative, just as an exaggerated idealization of renunciation poisons joy and an insistence on humility paralyzes man's creative forces. By holding the passions responsible for all moral inversion and accusing them of opposing faith, collective neurosis also inhibits their accomplishments. In contrast to this deadly, morbid form of guilt we might consider the parable of the crafty steward, which extols with considerable humor the very active virtue of shrewd foresight.[14]

The Narcissistic Paradox of Perfection

A constant theme in obsessional neurosis is the patient's complaint that he suffers from perfectionism. Such patients wear themselves out because they feel compelled to accomplish every task to perfection; then, because they never achieve that goal, they find themselves in a constant state of uneasiness and dissatisfaction. An obscure and internal sense of duty demands that they always do more and better. They feel the constant presence of some anonymous spectator watching over their shoulder, always ready to observe their slightest faults and errors. The obsessional patient may not always be consciously aware that he finds himself perpetually called to stand before this internal and this external magistrate. On the contrary, he avoids facing any judgment that might be delivered by diverting his attention onto some conscious element or detail that might explain his state of uneasiness. Thus, for example, a patient who wants to express himself in a perfectly modulated and articulate manner will explain that it is precisely because he wishes to concentrate on speaking well that he hesitates or speaks poorly. He needs to be able to forget his own will, which, he claims, is the mysterious cause of all his misfortunes. Although he is not aware of it as the source of this implacable will there is another, more fundamental concern actually controlling his actions: he would like to hear the echo of a beautifully accomplished discourse proceeding from himself and then see admiration on the faces of those listening to him. In light of such demanding perfectionism he feels like a nobleman who has fallen to the rank of a vagabond.

The repressed libido makes its return by way of this exalted self-image, which the individual keeps before his eyes, rather like a sacred trust, and through which he perceives himself in the approving gaze of others—thereby holding up to himself a mirror that would reflect a purportedly integral image of his own ego.

By introducing a conscious element into this tyrannical and nar-cissistic perfectionism, the sense of guilt reinforces it as well as more effectively concealing it. Thus, in the collective obsessional neurosis the struggle against evil falls under the general rubric of the evangelical command to be "perfect as your heavenly father is perfect." The ac-knowledgment that "only God is good" only accentuates the staggering severity of the demand for perfection. In its specific biblical context, the idea of perfection aims for a decentering of the subject, inasmuch as the divine ideals that are proposed are those of a benevolent forgiveness and a form of generosity that goes far beyond the circuit of reciprocal exchange.[15] By taking the command to strive for perfection out of its proper context and understanding it in an absolute manner, the sense of guilt uses it to serve its own obsessive aims: to attain perfection by means of an internal struggle against all desires, joys, or pleasures. Meas-uring himself against the pure and splendid example that he seeks to emulate, the obsessive will inevitably fail and condemn himself for his own impurity and deception. But underneath his grievances and his relentless efforts, he is in fact a prisoner of his fantasized dedication to the way of perfection. In this way, the commandment whose original purpose is to break down the walls between an individual and his fellow beings is used to reinforce—for purportedly sublime motives—what is in fact an unconscious narcissism.

The great spiritual masters have long denounced the religious pit-falls of perfectionism, and clinical psychology has shown that narcissism is but the other side of religious presumption. The ideal of perfection exerts a paradoxical constraint that increasingly perplexes the patient as he becomes conscious of it during the course of therapy. Much to their surprise, obsessive perfectionists find that in addition to the laby-rinth of imperfections and faults of which they accuse themselves, there is yet another with which they must contend: the labyrinth of pharisaism, so called in reference to the parable of the pharisee and the publican. Isn't the desire for perfection (as they conceive of it) a way of clinging to one's own pride—even through the process of self-accusation? How can one escape the contradiction of the publican, who wants to recognize his sins so as not to be a pharisee and who, by that very fact, asserts that he is more perfect than the pharisee? The pursuit of perfection seems to be not only an impossible but a contradictory task. It condemns the individual to self-torture. And yet it becomes apparent that the suffering caused by one's imperfections is accompanied by the satisfaction received from a superior sense of one's perfection. The perfectionist sees only that the other sees that he sees himself as a publican. This logic inevitably leads to another reflective "doubling" in which one sees himself as the publican who distinguishes himself from the pharisee, thereby becoming himself a pharisee. When the process reaches this critical moment of lucidity the only solution is to jump directly out of this paradoxical double bind. If the bind appears inseparable from the entire order of religion, the subject will withdraw from religion itself in order to extricate himself from its restraints. This process can be illustrated by what Pierre Klossowski writes about Nietzsche: "When Nietzsche proclaims that God is dead it implies that Nietzsche necessarily loses his own identity.... Thus the absolute guarantor of his identity as a responsible ego disappears from Nietzsche's conscience, which, in turn, is also implicated in the disappearance."[16]

Anyone who wishes to go to the limit of his own possibilities must risk being entrapped in this circular dialectic of perfection, and those who seek God will often be caught in this trap. But faith can release them from this prison if they can renounce the desire to represent an absolute and certain identity, both in their own eyes and in those of God. When the contradictions of the religious message seem to dissolve the power of his language they will often feel that God is a traitor; nevertheless, the silent wisdom of faith can help guide them through this desert. Faith alone, however, will not suffice to bring about deliverance unless it is sustained by a certain degree of psychic health. If the religious conflict becomes the conscious scene onto which an unconscious psychic conflict has been transposed—as is the case with neurotic guilt—it then becomes necessary to work it out on a specifically psychological level in order to solve the religious conflict set up to screen the unconscious one.

Psychoanalysis uncovers the specific representations that underlie the snares of obsessive perfectionism and apprises us of the conditions necessary for man to break out of this imaginary imprisonment. The ideal of perfection is in fact a twofold desire, the desire to satisfy the desire of the other and the desire to eradicate every failing in oneself. (We cannot determine which of these two takes causal priority over the other; they correspond to, and sustain, each other.) The subject supposes that the other desires him to be faultless, but it is because the subject wants to see himself as perfect that he attributes this desire to the other.

Let us briefly analyze the subject's desire in relation to himself. This desire becomes stratified in the representation engendered through the process of his personal history. Then, under the cover of a relatively conscious ego ideal, it becomes rooted in representations of a profoundly unconscious nature. The ego ideal always implies a certain idea of perfection, but there is nothing necessarily neurotic in this process of self-reflexiveness. It is a constitutive aspect of the human dynamic, inasmuch as an individual becomes human only by means of his entry into a cultural order that opens up possibilities for him to actualize. Through the ego ideal man becomes a being with a project. His existence is not simply a matter of being-there; he becomes himself, *makes* himself, through this process by which he anticipates himself. But from the moment that his ego ideal becomes fixed in an ideal of perfection used to suppress the libido, he obliterates the projective pole that propels the process of his becoming. As he pursues this ideal, the individual wishes to be only what he imagines he must become.

A comparison may clarify the absurdity of such an ideal: it is similar to the fanciful desire of the author who wants to say everything in one single transparent phrase, leaving out nothing, as if the articulation of meaning could ever be fully achieved in a blast of Truth. This desire for complete mastery, for victory over all doubt and anxiety, for attaining invulnerability against every stirring of the affects, for an unmitigated purity—this desire is the desire for a plenitude in which one would establish an absolute correspondence with oneself alone, eradicating every vestige of internal distance within oneself, as if one's own identity could be completely and incestuously sufficient unto itself. The suffering caused by this perfectionism, which is manifested in the complaints and troubles the subject faces every day, conceals a profound and unconscious desire to obliterate all desire: or a desire for nondesire, which has its source in the fact that all desire arises from a lack. Moreover, it is precisely the instincts that are responsible for constantly reawakening this sense of lack in the subject insofar as they are the inextinguishable source of all desire and insofar as they are, paradoxically, forces both alien to and internally active within the individual's will. The ideal of perfection conceals an imaginary representation of a man completely free of this internal feeling that he is foreign to himself, a feeling that inhabits him as a result of the fact that he is an instinctual and affective being. The neurotic nature and effects of the kind of religious discourse that brands the instincts with guilt and prompts renunciation, self-perfection, and self-mastery as its dominant themes become evident here.

The snares of this religious discourse are all the more effective in that they mobilize and flatter an imaginary narcissism that man has never given up as lost. As Jacques Lacan has shown, the formation of an archaic ego ideal takes place at the "mirror stage," the moment when the child assumes his own body as a totality by rapturously capturing his image in a mirror or in his mother's admiring gaze.[17] In one way or another, in the very depths of man's being, the jubilation he experienced standing before this first mirror never abandons him; he never quite ceases to stand before it. The temptation to return to it is all the greater inasmuch as language deprives man of the completely circumscribable identity visibly available to him through the mirror image. The "I" that posits itself as subject in the act of language cannot be contained within the play of representations in which man perceives himself as he is.[18] The subject remains a question for himself: who and what am I? This non-representability of his identity leads him to aspire to give himself an image to present to others, an image he takes from the values, discourses, and models available to him; in this way he learns to love himself as he loves his ideal ego.

These components make up narcissism. The subject constitutes himself as a being born of himself in a never-accomplished process of becoming himself. But if the ideal of perfection becomes grafted onto narcissism the subject will find himself imprisoned in an imaginary and morbid form of narcissism—imaginary because it inevitably destines him to self-deception, morbid because he becomes encircled by a paradoxical double bind of self-infatuation.

The religious perfectionist discovers that in spite of himself he is a pharisee and the unwitting falsifier of the true meaning of self-abnegation and self-sacrificing love. It is not so much that we must give these terms a moral meaning, because in fact this narcissistic turning in on himself is a profoundly unconscious action; moreover, he greatly redeems himself by a real solicitude for others. Actually, it is through the suffering that accompanies his neurosis that he betrays himself: his incessant self-doubts, his uneasy withdrawal into himself, his exaggerated sensitivity to any remark, all these aggravate the wound of his imperfection.

Clinical experience has shown to what extent the representation of the angel still remains a profound and secret emblem of perfection, even though it is often well protected by defensive humor. We should not let ourselves be deceived by the humorous comments made by some people concerning angelical images. The angel is a representation of the fantastic image of ideal perfection because angels are not the blend of instinctual body and spirit that men and women are. And more importantly, the angel gives us the figure of a being neither man nor woman, a figure completely sufficient unto itself, devoid of the sex that marks division in the body; it is, in fact, the indivisibility of a figure more radically identical to itself than the androgynous figures in mythology. Moreover, because of the illogical associations of the unconscious, it may also represent the ideal of a savage sexuality, as free as the wind and as powerful as a torrent—a figure of absolute disengagement from any place or bond. These contradictory significations of the symbol of the angel are not so surprising, especially if we consider the ambiguous value that religious celibacy can take, particularly in the context of collective neurosis, where man may seem to have achieved a mastery over his bodily servitude—almost a freedom from the body—as well as a superhuman integrity that seems to endow him with a disquieting power. On the other hand, by his refusal of the body he also seems to be deprived of his own obscure power; in other words, he also appears to be castrated.

So powerful is the representation of asexual perfection that it has inspired theological speculation on the state of man before sin. On the basis of Neoplatonic tradition, various church fathers, such as Gregory of Nyssa, proposed the notion that prior to the fall man was neither male nor female but a "perfect" being, indivisible and unencumbered by an instinctual body.[19] It is a strange and imaginary theology that seems deliberately to ignore the biblical passages stating that God created man as male and female, a sexual being like the animals but at the same time in his own image and likeness.[20]

Legalism, or Renunciation for the Sake of a Guaranteed Love

The wish to be perfect in the eyes of others corresponds to the narcissistic desire for perfection. The system of communication we will now examine is correlative to what we discovered in our preceding examination of the psychic system. Legalism is the main characteristic of this system of communication. It should be understood as the search for a love that is guaranteed, a search that subverts faith. We will then see that this form of religious relationship implies a representation of God that contradicts the idea of God to which religion testifies.

Legalism is the practice of an absolute respect for religious laws taken strictly to the letter. It can be a sincere manner of situating oneself with respect to God, though it is often accompanied by intolerance, authoritarianism, and presumption—all of which are responsible for the negative connotations of the term *legalism*. In any case, legalism characterizes a faith governed by guilt, and an analysis of the relations involved will clarify the psychological motives involved.

At first glance it may seem that a morbid sense of guilt is produced by those legalistic religious communities that place unnecessarily heavy burdens on their adherents. How then can we explain the system of communal legalism? Is it simply the result of the appetite for power to which all authority eventually falls prey? In my opinion this is only a secondary factor, for in order for legalism to establish itself the community of believers must support the established power. As a matter of fact, legalism is often prevalent in those who follow the law scrupulously and give it a rigorous legalistic interpretation. In the chapter on obsessional neurosis in religion we pointed out these patients' demand for absolute clarity and rigor from the law, as well as their anxiety about and rebellion against the margins of uncertainty and freedom the law leaves open. Whether legalism is communal or individualized, it is surely more apt to be the result than the cause of a morbid sense of guilt, used to restore something that must be lost through the recognition of one's faults. And yet, like all symptoms, it is also ambivalent: it lets through what has been repressed and defeats the very thing it aims for; in this case it winds up in the subversion of faith itself. Legalism is a defensive system belonging to the category psychoanalysis calls secondary processes—that is, belonging to the order of language.[21]

Let us examine the intrinsic links between morbid guilt and legalism. Guilt is the suffering caused by the loss of the other's love and esteem. It is parallel to the narcissistic suffering caused by the loss of self-love. Guilt normally occurs within the context of an affective bond; it belongs under the rubric of love, which is the desire for communication and union. Because it is also desire, love involves a demand as well as a gift, and implicit in desire is also the need to become a desirable object of love for the other. Therefore love implies a certain adjustment to the desire of the other, which confirms the subject's value in his existence. Insofar as it involves the subject's perception of his unworthiness because of his imperfections and faults, it always entails the fear of being unworthy of the esteem and desire of the other. Of course, the desire that gives rise to guilt need not necessarily be love in the sense of an intense bond. In any situation where man seeks the other's esteem the link is strong enough to make his existence depend on the other.

Fear of the loss of love or esteem is only a diffuse or vague form of guilt, an uneasy feeling of unworthiness, sometimes simply a general fear of not being loved, without the idea of unworthiness actually becoming fully conscious. The subject, painfully anxious to be worthy of love and not to displease the other, can even go so far as to anticipate the very loss of love he fears. In this way men and women often discover just how neurotic the bond between them really is, built as it is on the unsettling preoccupation over whether or not they deserve the love of the other. This is an endless preoccupation because it is never resolved by the other's gift of love. Moreover, the effort involved destroys love itself by creating a mistrust that is never quieted but finally turns into a constant demand. Such comments of course only summarize, after the fact, a whole gamut of motives and relations that take shape throughout a long history of interactions between two people: at the time of their unhappy love they are not so explicitly acknowledged or recognized.

Religious guilt reverts to legalism so that the individual can assure himself that his behavior and actions receive God's sanction. He compensates for impurity and imperfection by multiplying the prescriptions accompanying his actions; every action that is allowed becomes a duty and hence a formal religious act. The aim of this transformation of all activity into legalistic practice is to assure God's good will. The fear of losing God's love is never explicitly recognized, but the subject is always aware that he depends on God for the final outcome of his life as well as his present daily existence. By legalistic behavior he seeks God's confirmation. Fear of God's negative judgment is, of course, a desire to be acceptable to God and consequently a sign of the desire to be loved; but love as the desire for union and communication appears only in its negative form, the fear of being rejected.

The reader may note the paradoxical inversion that legalism brings about. Its aim is to bring as many correctives as possible to imperfection. The individual places himself in an ideal and completely dependent position with regard to the one who ministers his life and his death. He defers all pleasures because if they are not directly warranted by God he fears he may fail to acknowledge the master provider of all life's gifts and that God may consequently withdraw his benevolent providence. The wish to become—as far as possible—a pure receptacle having no other thought or will than what is thought or willed by God (and thereby canonized by his laws) becomes paramount. In short, the subject surrenders all his desires to the Other in order to remain the object of divine benevolence; he seeks to make certain of this outcome by bartering for it with his own merits. In the last analysis the subject behaves as if by his own actions he could force the Other to give of himself. At bottom, then, he really does not have any belief or confidence in the Other. Faith is falsified and becomes instead the search for a guaranteed benevolence; the harsh facade of the legalist turns out to conceal the weakness of incredulity.

Legalism is more the cult of law than of God. The truly neurotic individual will feel the benefits of this cult only intermittently, inasmuch as the entire span of experience can never be completely covered by any network of laws. Consequently the effort to master or banish disorder increases rather than decreases the subject's anxiety in light of the incoherence of his own thought and desires. Moreover, the ambivalence toward God that the obsessional tries to repress by his legalism becomes displaced onto the imperatives of the law. In the context of a collective neurotic guilt, however, the psychological benefits to be reaped from religious legalism are undeniable. Guilt anxiety is reduced, even prevented, by the sacrifices and renunciations consented to by the community, and the ambivalent polarization in their relationship to the law deflects them from any direct confrontation with a God whose sanctity they might find troubling. It is also generally assumed that faith supplies the specific references needed to integrate and suppress the inconsistencies inherent in the world. Legalism interposes an institution between God and man that codifies what one must think and do. These mechanisms insure the subject's acceptability and raise his certainty of being loved.

If we wish to understand something about the dramatic nature of faith that mystics and others, such as those who truly suffer from guilt, pay witness to, both believers and disbelievers should learn to step beyond the facile confusions between law and legalism, between ritual and ritualism, between the affirmation of faith and a dogmatic attitude, between hope and compensatory certainty. The treatment and cure of the morbid sense of guilt manifested in legalism requires a process of working through to renunciation just as surely as does the therapy of patients who have a neurotic relation to love. This renunciation is the price one must pay in order to attain both love and a faith lived in freedom.

Like any other form of love, faith is a hope, a confidence in the promise of the other, not a guarantee, for the love of the other is always a free gift. One can never earn love, even if one can indeed cease to deserve it. Legalism gives the appearance of desiring everything from the other; that is why it constantly postpones for the future the happiness it awaits. But in fact it actually attempts to win what has been promised. Instead of grounding itself on hope, it subverts it. Faith, on the other hand, welcomes with joy and pleasure the gift it has already received, celebrating it as a sign of something more to come. The temporal arena of desirative faith is primarily the present, and it is in the present that it recognizes the sign of a future promise.

Legalism is the most insidious perversion of religion, especially of that form of religion that reveals the free and personal nature of one's relation to God and that also gives evil a religious dimension as sinfulness. Attempting to forestall his every fault and seeking always to be intact and unblemished, the legalist sets himself up in such religious wealth that there is no longer any lack left in him to open him to desire. A great part of Jesus' message was his forceful confrontation with legalism; hence the shocking and subversive effect of his paradoxical symbolic narrative through the parables.[22]

God as in a Mirror

Narcissistic perfectionism as an organized psychic system has as its correlative a particular legalistic mode of communication that, in its underlying logic, implies a particular representation of God, one that causes morbid guilt. The inverse, however, is just as true: the psychological mechanisms just discussed give rise to an idea of God that sustains the psychological disposition of one who has imprisoned himself in his own guilt.

Closely examined, this idea is indeed a strange contradiction of sublime savagery. This most perfect being, this model of the highest purity, this grand, powerful creativity devoid of desire, this God is nevertheless also represented as terrifyingly demanding, an absolute master perpetually concerned with being recognized as such. He casts the shadow of death on every thought and every desire that is not offered up to him. The love of this God—a perfect being and hence demanding of perfection—is strangely akin to the possessive love with which totalitarian regimes govern their subjects. This unacknowledged theology reflects and sustains the psychological incoherences that were pointed out in the foregoing comments on the paradox of the double bind: God and the psyche look at each other as if they were mirror reflections of each other.

This game of seductive imitation, in which the subject makes himself as perfect as his master by offering up his will to the divine will, this game is often played out in the scenarios of masochistic fantasies. Religious iconography has produced an imaginative and rich variety of works in which the subject's consent to the extermination of his own will, his gift of his personal desires, is apparent in the contortions of his body and easily visible on his face. There are the frequent scenes depicting martyrdom: St. Sebastian's beautiful body penetrated by arrows; saints whose breasts, symbols of pleasure, are torn off by burning tongs; those who allow themselves to be devoured by beasts in the arena, just as Christ gives himself to be consumed in the sacrificial meal; Christ on the cross, transfigured by the helplessness to which he is reduced by the nails embedded in his flesh. The important thing here is the idea that is figured by the martyr's body; delight is taken in the imaginary dispossession of the strength and desires of the body. The martyr makes himself small, helpless, annihilated because God loves the weak, the suffering, those who have become diminished human beings.

The contrast between this idea and the baroque exaltation of the martyr is an eloquent one. Consider first the immense paintings that covered the walls of churches during the Counter-Reformation. They exalt the triumph of divine glory over the executioners who knew only how to destroy the mortal body. The broken bodies of the martyrs already radiate that glory because, in spite of the suffering inflicted upon them, faith remains the most powerful conqueror of all. What is striking about the masochistic images is in fact that God is only a distant referee, the absent master of this spectacle in which the executioners are but instruments of his will. In the triumphant forms of the baroque, however, the martyr, whose prototype is St. Stephen, sees the heavens open wide to receive Christ in divine glory. The martyr is indifferent to his suffering; he submits to it in divine sovereignty, triumphing over his apparent destruction.

Morbid guilt engenders a specific form of masochism; it is not the perverse pursuit of pain for the sake of gratifying one's pleasure. Pain and suffering are rather the price one must pay to win the master's love. The underlying idea of God is the same one we found prevailing in neurosis, when unconscious representations are uncovered by the process of free association: it is the idea of a jealous God who does not allow his subjects any desires of their own.

In cases of neurosis where affective ambivalence has been repressed, fantasies often depict a God who takes the role of an executioner bent on victimizing the subject. This unconscious hate corresponds to the representation of a hateful God, who in turn provokes hatred. The infernal mechanism of neurosis produces an endless cycle of aggressivity and counteraggressivity. Thus one obsessional had imagined since his childhood that a black man, hidden in his garden, was waiting for him at night in order to smash his skull with a club. One day he discovered that the unknown sadist was God himself. The fantasy was based on an advertisement for a medicine to cure migraines, which pictured a man's head being beaten by a wedge. After having worked out his masochistic fantasies and his ferocious hatred through analysis, this individual, who had regularly suffered from migraines, found he no longer had them.

We may ask whether the sense of guilt that accompanies legalism conceals a profound unconscious ambivalence. Its similarity to obsessional neurosis leads us to suspect that this may be the case. It is difficult to imagine how the instincts could allow themselves to be so ill-used just for the sake of gratifying narcissism. A strong ambivalence, the residue of precocious conflicts, must have sought a protective shield in the system of repression; for man experiences hate as so threatening an emotion that he needs to develop some mechanism of defense against it. Because of his intense narcissism, the obsessional patient is often led—through a process of self-reflective correspondence with his mirror image—not only to his love of perfection but also to idealization of the other. We have seen how the representation of divine perfection can lead the subject to paint an image of a God whose purity and power the subject desires for himself and to take a divine model of a renunciation and mastery so great that the instincts can no longer prevail. But this God is also a substitute for the idealized father, and the outrageous demands he makes in fact simply reproduce the specter of the superego-father. However, idealization invariably turns into disillusion. Where then does God exercise his power? The world looks more like a junkyard in shambles than a masterpiece, and the erring masses gladly avoid the force of

God's hand. And why, moreover, was the earth so poorly made that even believers have called it a "vale of tears"? These are just some of the enigmas that become obstacles for any believer. And these same uncertainties prevent man from elaborating a totalizing and exhaustively comprehensive discourse out of his faith. This compels him in turn to purify it from his demand that he find a guarantee for it on earth. But the individual who overidealizes God's power will find the test too difficult, and, rather than suffer a rupture of his narcissism or incur the risk involved in sacrilegious questions, he represses his feeling of scandal and revolt. Thus, at the heart of every idealization lies a profound ambivalence that is pushed into the unconscious by a reinforced system of order and organization.

The price paid for this system of repressions organized around a mystified concept of God is high in renunciations. The profound sense of deception experienced when God's power is perceived to be lacking contributes to the return of repressed material. So it happens that believers too soon and too zealously devoted to accomplishing the world's salvation abruptly discover, when they reach adulthood, that they have just been dreaming of a heavenly Jerusalem. Some are astonished to find that they can live without the myth of an almighty God. But others, feeling that they gave themselves wholeheartedly to God, cannot shrug off the bitter feeling of having been tricked into a chimerical adventure. The desire for sublimity, however, is a tenacious one; the absence of God becomes a void characterized as the loss of an absolute object, and love, now bitterly disappointed, turns into hate. These people never cease their quarrel with heaven.

Culpability, Real or Imaginary

The profiles of the shadow of guilt are numerous. Is it possible to determine the characteristics that would allow us to specify its shape in normalcy? It would be helpful to trace a sure boundary between the kind of guilt that contributes to mystification and that which brings clarity and truth to one's life. A simple opposition offers itself: a guilt that separates imaginary transgressions from real faults. One would not question that the guilt felt as a result of committing an odious crime is justified. Nor would we hesitate to call imaginary the guilt of a melancholic individual who holds himself responsible for an ecological disaster because thistledown from his garden has spread over the entire world. Equally imaginary is the purported transgression of the obsessional psychotic who confesses in panic and anguish that his sperm, ejaculated through masturbation, has evaporated into the clouds and will poison the whole of Europe.

But what meaning can such terms as *real* and *imaginary* have when used to describe feeling or desire? Is, for example, a feeling of guilt that does not seem (from the observer's point of view) to correspond to any incriminating act to be considered an imaginary one? The claim could be supported only if it were possible to determine the seriousness of a guilty act according to an objective measure, independent of any subjective evaluation. The norms established by society are already objective in the sense that a common form of consent among its members withdraws judgment from the arbitrary opinion of individuals. But the difficulties are insurmountable when it is a question of deciding not on the attribution of an action but on the responsibility for it. Not even a psychiatrist called upon to present expert testimony can decide with certainty. And this is understandable, for the will of the individual accused of an incriminating action remains an impregnable secret. How much more impregnable it must be to the subject himself who is caught in the turbulence of his feelings and fantasies. The feeling of remorse that follows a wicked act is in itself no guarantee that the subject's perception of its malice is in any way commensurate to the act. There are too many obscure memories and contradictory desires involved. We may even ask whether the feeling of guilt is not in itself morbid insofar as the subject uses it to build an interior refuge where he keeps to himself instead of becoming engaged in the task of building the world.

This is the point developed by A. Hesnard in *L'Univers morbide de la faute*.[23] Hesnard was so struck by the vagaries of guilt that he concluded that it spoils existence by the useless suffering it causes. To Hesnard feeling is an unreal form of interiority; the only real thing is action turned toward the exterior world. He also condemns the idea of sin for its "interiorized and private concern with immorality."[24] "Sin is more a subjective spectacle, a troubling one perhaps but a sterile one, than a reaction to the drama of interior life. In short, it is little more than a thought marked with the sign of Evil. This is in fact the essence of sin."[25] In this definition of sin the issue is not just a semantic misunderstanding, as theologians have supposed. Hesnard characterizes sin as a morbid form of guilt because to him there is no moral or religious sense of guilt that is not a form of psychic illness. Only an ethic of constructive activity that suspends all forms of interiority can avoid being called pathological.

This is a radical position, fit only for angels, we might say, since it belittles any psychic reality that cannot be simplisticly reduced to a form of pragmatic action. The debate around Hesnard's thesis belongs not in the field of theology or moral philosophy but psychology. We may begin by noting that by virtue of his phenomenological reinterpretation of psychoanalysis Hesnard does not acknowledge the reality of the unconscious. He treats any pathological form of guilt as if it were simply a feeling of guilt. But it so happens that in cases of obsession (if it is not religious obsession) and of phobia, the representation of guilt never reaches consciousness; the particular operative logic of these pathologies maintains the repression of guilt.

Hesnard's objection to a morality established on the affective perception of guilt is certainly legitimate; he might even have used the *Critique of Practical Reason*—where Kant demonstrates with incomparable lucidity that sentiment cannot decide the moral value of an act—to support his argument. But does it follow that all sentiment is nothing more than the brief stir of superfluous moods? If guilt is placed under the rubric of morbid disturbances, is it not then necessary to do the same with all forms of affective experience: indignation, love, joy, pleasure? Even if these other sentiments are not unhappy ones they must nevertheless also be considered magical and imaginary, if this objective and pragmatic concept of behavior is taken as the measure.[26]

Freud's attitude, on the other hand, is completely different. No one has taken as much care as he to show the illusory nature of feeling. Feelings leave their messages inscribed on the immediate surface of consciousness in a scrambled and distorted fashion. Thus the feeling of guilt can be displaced, concealed, and even annulled by the disguises and reversals that take place in dreams and various forms of discourse. In spite of this Freud did not belittle the importance of the feeling of guilt. On the contrary, he considered this a universal and fundamental form of knowledge available to man, but also so conflictual that one could accept it only in the process of denying it. Thus, Freud contended, the Jewish people wrote their epic history basically in order to repress the memory of their having murdered Moses.[27] Groups of people and individuals alike behave like King Boabdil, whose story Freud recalls in "A Disturbance of Memory on the Acropolis": after learning that his city, Alhama, has fallen " 'he will not let it be true,' he determines to treat the news as 'non arrivée' " and he kills the messenger.[28] The silence or noise made by guilt will not directly inform us about the moral quality of our conduct. And because of the strange peculiarity of moral consciousness, even the feeling of guilt is not, apparently, a sane guide. Moral conscience "exhibits a peculiarity ... for the more virtuous a man is, the more severe and distrustful is its behaviour, so that ultimately it is precisely those people who have carried saintliness furthest who reproach themselves with the worst sinfulness. This means that virtue forfeits some part of its promised reward; the docile and continent ego does not enjoy the trust of its mentor and strives in vain, it would seem, to acquire it."[29]

We will have to bring an important nuance to bear upon this comment. Nevertheless, Freud's explanation warrants our attention. The more exacting and vigilant moral conscience is, the more this renunciation arouses the instincts and raises temptation. This is common sense, and yet it is contrary to simplistic psychologies of adaptation that suppose guilt can be eliminated by satisfying the instincts, for Freud held that "cultural renunciation" is the very condition of ethics as well as of civilization. We might also note that according to this passage guilt can emerge from temptations themselves, not just acts. Consequently guilt cannot be determined in reference to observable acts: it arises from the conflict between instincts and ethical norms. Of themselves the instincts encourage ideas of theft, lying, incest, and murder, and it is precisely the "most saintly" people who become most aware of these temptations because they remain so vigilant in their effort not to be deceived by their exorbitant or hostile desires.

Moral conscience retains the diachrony of its genesis with the synchrony of present conflicts. We can illustrate this by an analysis of sympathy, which, though not equivalent to ethical conduct itself, is nevertheless the spur and support of such conduct. As the word itself implies, sympathy is not the natural product (as some might suppose) of an *élan vital* but a specifically human relationship based on a form of identification with others. To feel for someone means to put oneself in the other's place, as if one were the other, suffering his misfortunes, rejoicing in his pleasures, and experiencing his conflicts and revolts. This feeling, however, is neither as simple nor as innocent as it may appear. First, it is the result of a reversal in the instinct for domination, an instinct that would willingly inflict suffering; so this benevolent sympathy is already a form of victory over the tendency to have others experience pain. Second, this sympathetic form of identification arouses jealousy: by putting oneself in the other's place one tends to want to usurp his place.[30] Both clinical experience and child psychology have abundantly illustrated the snares involved in sympathy.[31] It is also known that if a respect for the autonomy of the other is not transmitted as a corrective, sympathy and empathy—whether clinical or charitable—can easily become a form of manipulating others. The analysis of any ethically inclined feeling will show from what transformation of instinct and affect it derives. Ethical conduct is the result of a laborious process working with and on the instincts, a process whose memory is well perserved in the negative formulas of the Decalogue, reminding us of the permanent necessity of this labor. Once the mutation is accomplished, the subsequent formation of "virtues"—as they used to be called—eases instinctual conflicts by inscribing on them patterns of ethical conduct that still retain the memory of a primordial pleasure, which is then transferred over to a larger, more inclusive order of loving. But unlike biological mutations, ethical transformations are never definitive. In the psyche, information deposited long ago subsists side by side with more recent acquisitions. The emergence of moral conscience from transgressive desires is continually reproduced in present temptations, which are not just externally transposed over one's good intentions but actually interfere with them. Dramatic literature probably produces cathartic effects by making us experience, mentally and affectively, the trajectory traversed by the tragic hero; thus we purify ourselves, as he does, of the hubris whose traces we obliterated.

But if the individual does not actually commit an act of transgression, isn't his guilt as imaginary as the imaginary crimes that inhabit our spontaneous instinctive representations? We insist that the passions, however antisocial they are in their brute state, are not in themselves evil. But neither are they simply pure biological forces completely extrinsic to desire. They are intrinsically bound up in desire, and the subject clings to them even if only by an inchoate assent that he immediately retracts by reversing its original aim. A man is not absent from the "temptations" that confront him, as if he were nothing more than a screen on which some machine projects immoral spectacles; but neither is he the cynical producer of desires he would disavow. If the movement and thrust of his passions were completely foreign to him, he would not be capable of transforming them from within, either by reversal or sublimation; and if they were simply a perverse fruit of his own deliberate machinations, he would not have to fight against them or repress them or transform them into ethical aims. The immoral acts committed in the imagination are already active desires that a vigilant conscience judges to be immoral. In order to explain the universal phenomenon of guilt, Freud did not need the theoretical fiction of a first crime that leaves its disturbing impact on the entire history of mankind. In the conclusion of *Totem and Taboo*, Freud brings out the full psychological dimension of the issue when he asserts that for the primitive psyche there is no difference between the imagined act and the accomplished action.[32] We might add that in this respect every psyche is primitive. The gospel is psychologically accurate in saying that the angry man is already a murderer in his heart and that to look at another with desire is to commit adultery in one's heart.[33] When these intentions that are acted out in man's imagination become conscious, they are translated—because of their complicity with the spontaneity of the instincts—into a feeling of painful discord within ourselves and with God. But the message of guilt tells us precisely that nothing is definitively fated and that when we surprise the assassin in ourselves, we are called to exert ourselves in the name of peace and life. Nothing can be more convincing of the catharsis brought about by the authentic assumption of one's guilt than its contrary: the obviously harmful effects of its repression. When the guilt that follows the repression of aggressiveness is itself repressed, the result is depression; it follows with certain and enigmatic fatality, but therapy allows us to uncover the logic of the passions that underlie it.

Guilt, then, is an essential part of the consciousness that wills itself as a specifically moral conscience. The imaginary interiority that Hesnard denounces characterizes the density of a psyche that is the locus of the conflict between the desires that lead to the affirmation of life or carry one to destruction.

From the Voice of Conscience to Confession

We have interpreted the feeling of guilt as a signal that warns the conscience of an ethical conflict, past or present, which has been either disguised or recognized on its own terms. We have also detected in this signal an appeal to a transformation of those instincts in conflict with the ego ideal and with God. Now we must examine the difference between the self-accusation characteristic of religious obsessions and the confession of one's sins.

First we must recapitulate a number of points. In the self-accusations of the obsessional patient an unconscious ambivalence of the affects repeats itself indefinitely, without, however, the patient's managing to articulate something he does not, consciously, even know himself. The narcissistic idealism of his ego prevents him from accepting his impure desires as constitutive of his personal history: so, not being able, like St. George, to kill the dragon, he destroys himself morally.

What about those who, as Freud described them in *Civilization and Its Discontents*, are the most advanced on the path of sanctity but who are precisely the ones who accuse themselves of being the greatest sinners? This extreme example can serve as a paradigm for religious self-accusation. If it is true that "virtue forfeits some part of its promised reward," then, indeed, their guilt is a morbid one, even when it is inevitable, and even if it plays a useful role in their lives. That they accuse themselves is merely half of the process of the avowal of sin—precisely the part that predominates in obsession. This reflexive language betrays the specular circle in which a wounded and exacerbated narcissism encloses itself.

The comment from Freud quoted above accentuates the clenched attitude typical of narcissism: "The docile and continent ego does not enjoy the trust of its mentor and strives in vain, it would seem, to acquire it." And yet Freud leaves out the most essential point. The confession of sin is, in fact, only an indirect form of auto-accusation; it is primarily an avowal made before another. It is curious that Freud should have misunderstood the guilt expressed in an act of faith by reducing it to a dualistic rapport with oneself and misunderstanding the structure and the power of the word in the interlocutive use of language.

To clarify the function of language in the act of confession I will apply the categories elaborated by J. L. Austin and D. D. Evans in their analyses of language.[34] There are two components in the act of confession, the one assertive and the other performative. The first is a proposition that states a fact and can therefore be true or false. If we take the example of the "internal sin," we see that the individual who accuses himself of sinning in his heart makes a statement about his transgressive desires. But in this context, this assertion of fact takes on the character of performative language: it carries out an operation. It means, first of all, that the subject is taking responsibility for the movement of his desires, that he is committed to keeping a guard over his malevolent tendencies and working to transform them into a benevolent form of conduct. If he has committed a harmful act, confessing it implies that he is committing himself to pay for the damages. The difference between an assertive and a performative act becomes apparent in the fact that an individual will resist confessing his faults, whereas he will find it easy enough to talk about them in another form of discourse that does not require him to take future responsibility for them before his interlocutor.

The obsessive's confession of sin certainly tries to be a performative act; it is not for us to doubt the sincerity of his intention. But his excessive concern with professing a rigorous accountability betrays a fixed preoccupation with his past more than a commitment to the future. We have already mentioned the unconscious reasons for this: his real past, which ought to be assumed through confession and opened up to the future, remains unspeakable for him because of his neurosis. In contrast, the cathartic effects of a religious confession signal that the construction of a future outweighs regret for the past. Narcissistic perfectionism can also interfere in the performative act and annul it at the very moment of its enunciation. Austin's analysis will help to illustrate this mechanism. The promise or the commitment implied in the performative act can be sabotaged in two ways, which Austin calls "misfires" and "abuses."[35] A misfire occurs when the subject does not have the competence to carry out what his enunciation implies; for example, the confession of someone in a delirium is inoperative. The commitment implied in confession can also be vitiated by abuse, as when the speaker's intention does not correspond to the intention expressed in his enunciation, or when he does not hold to his promise.

Now, one always knows that his confession engages him in a promise that he is, to some extent, incapable of fulfilling: because of the density and weight of his instincts, an individual never has complete control over his performative promises. This is something the obsessive cannot tolerate. He would like his commitment to be immediately and absolutely accomplished, whereas in fact his human instincts will never completely give way to pure good will. As a result he turns himself into a sort of reflexive cramp, unconsciously more bent on attending to himself than concerned about actualizing his only partly good intentions through effective projects. He idealizes what he would like to be and consequently devotes all his love to an ego ideal he desperately exalts. The very moment he commits himself, he knows that he does not have the competence he imagines to be necessary; then he feels he must take back his promise so that he will not be adding new lies to his past one. Therapists have often noted this movement of retraction in patients who obstinately hanker after a therapy that will definitely resolve all their failings. Initially they give themselves over to a true word addressed to the other, only to destroy it subsequently by their complaint that the future will be the same old eternal repetition of the past.

In religious faith the fact of fallibility does not present an obstacle to commitment: man sees himself as he really is, and in contrast to the narcissistic obsessional he does not despise himself for what he is, nor does he resent the Creator for having made such poor work of him.

The recognition that one is sinful is equivalent to destroying one's image of oneself as the idealized infant.[36] By putting away this image of omnipotence and purity the subject becomes reconciled to the development of a faith and an innocence that is never fully attained. At the risk of diminishing the element of dynamic conflict such a process involves, one could say that men and women must learn to accept themselves. To affirm that we are incapable of fulfilling our commitments in one purely transparent act is not to minimize the value of life; it is rather to recognize that the subject is essentially decentered within himself, that he is enveloped by obscure forces that bear the mark of sinfulness. For St. Paul no less than for Freud, man is not entirely master in his own house. The "power of sin," this indefinable reality that one can adequately designate only by the mythical term *force*, penetrates into the conscience and causes the very evil man would avoid. That Freud called the idea of sin a devaluation of life is surprising, considering that he was so intent on convincing others of the power of Thanatos and that he said repeatedly that man is at once worse and better than he believes.

Religious confession is also governed by a different representation of God than is neurosis. Let us recall some of our previous observations. In guilt anxiety God becomes the figure of a fierce judge at once grand and repulsive, an object of respect as well as hate. We found this figure to be an avatar of the idealized father transposed onto an infinite scale. This aggrandized father figure, who is represented as flawless, both ennobles and crushes the child by the fantastic heritage he leaves him, thereby condemning the child never to realize an imaginary ideal of himself. Although the father challenges the child to be equal, he will not tolerate any encroachment on his exclusive rights. The qualities religion attributes to God tend to evoke the image of an idealized father: the almighty Father, who alone is holy and immortal. If man represents himself as the chosen heir of such a father he will inevitably feel obliged to meet his godly standards and demand God's own perfection for himself, or he will feel impelled to imitate God's omnipotence by acquiring self-mastery, or he will try to gain immortality by the abnegation of his instinctual body. But then he denies precisely the structural difference between man and God that religion bears witness to.

There is no doubt that, outside of religious delirium, no one proclaims or even conceives of God in such terms, but this idea governs the logic of religious neurosis. Faith, on the other hand, bears the message of another sort of divine paternity, one that liberates men and women from anxiety and invites them to call him "father" with confidence. Faith recognizes, along the lines of belief, that God's desire for man is more powerful than man's hesitations and infidelities, just as parents—usually stronger than their children's aggressions—do not usually respond according to the law of retaliation. Faith both precedes and solicits the avowal of sinfulness. And confession, in turn, dissipates the vague representation of an almighty divinity that would refuse man the right to his weakness and would betray him by not warding off his faults. As an act of the performative word, confession articulates and accomplishes the very faith from which it receives its authority.

This whole process is contained in the structural relations defined by the symbolic laws of language. Once the conflict between one's rebellious desires and one's image of divine omnipotence is overcome, there is no further need to conceal one's passions and defects, and instead of fabricating myths to cover one's failures it becomes possible to discover the stuff that men are made of. At the same moment one also discovers that others are equally involved in a drama whose scope and finality no man can completely encompass. Isn't this the significance of the commandment that stood as an obstacle to Freud's understanding—to love one's enemies? When men and women truly come to terms with themselves through an authentic recognition of their defects, such love will cease to be based on illusions and fairy tales, but will be as indulgent toward others as it is toward oneself. By reconciling man with himself, the confession of sins (an act elicited by a divine movement) reconciles man to the human condition. The word as a performative act is altogether singular because it engages the speaker in the very depths of his being, and for this reason it has a universal value.

One need not dissociate himself from human realities in order to participate in a divine destiny. When he is touched in the core of his being by something higher than himself and carried by the movement of the divine, man can be delivered from the obsession to overcome all his human limitations. But a certain renunciation in the life of faith, comparable to the cultural renunciation, remains the condition for this liberation. In order to believe that the divine circulates through the world's fabric, man must renounce the quest for signs of the narcissistic dream of omnipotence, both his own and God's. Life is only the promise, a promise without any tangible guarantee that there will be new life.

The aim of this analysis was to clarify certain characteristics of morbid guilt by illustrating how it is overcome. The "normal" is very close to the pathological. Wherever illness gives way to the conflicts, the substitutions, and the self-mutilations that are repeated through an individual's life, man should attempt to overcome them by the psychological means available to him; he must undergo a psychological labor. In the context of a religious rapport, this psychological labor that restructures one's relation to oneself and to the Other is intrinsically linked to a labor of faith. Far from being a happy state of health occasionally threatened by disequilibrium, the "normal" lies at the end of a long trajectory that one must traverse, constantly giving birth to oneself and to the other. The act of life does not reveal its complex pattern, but a scientific analysis can expose a few of life's vague traces, like the film of a jump shown in slow motion.

4 • Ritual Impurity and Debt

Religion is a symbolic practice through which believers commemorate and reenact the emergence of a divine force in their lives. As a religious and symbolic act, the ritual embodies a faith in God not only as a meaning to which the believer adheres but also as a divine power that operates in the human act. A sociological approach to ritual may abstract certain characteristics from the specifically religious significance of the rite in order to isolate various lateral functions, such as that of contesting or affirming a certain type of culture or establishing a cohesive religious group. Psychology, however, should not fail to recognize the inherent intention articulated in the ritual action. Therefore we will take the practicing believer's frame of reference, the believer for whom ritual is neither a religious film nor a social action but an effective communication with the supernatural. Nevertheless, we will concentrate on one specific facet here: the manifest transformation and meanings that the pathological experience of evil injects into ritual.

The Ritualization of Rite and Magical Action

Rite: A Symbolic Operation

In order to trace the difference between ritual and ritualism we must first shed some light on the process through which the ritual is articulated. I impute to the term *ritual* the significance it has in religious faith, using the more pejorative term *ritualism* to refer to the definition often given for *ritual* in recent usage, that of stereotypical behavior or obsolete ceremonialism.¹ This is not simply a matter of verbal substitution; the definition of ritual according to its negative connotations derives from the a priori notion that the meaning of the act has withdrawn, leaving nothing but an empty form.

By the phrase "religious ritual" we mean, then, a symbolic action whose aim is to establish or to restore a bond with the divine. Two properties characterize the ritual: it is an action having its own finality, and this action is a symbolic one. The two elements are intricately bound to each other.

The ritual is a human action. It combines several elements that correspond to various forms of discourse. The ritual expresses feeling; it is a reasoned and deliberate expression, in contrast to a spontaneous manifestation, like a shout. The ritual is also a form of conduct. By its very actions it establishes a rapport between man and God. The gesture of raising one's arms, for example, signifies what is being expressed through a ritual pronouncement such as "I praise you, Lord," just as bowing down corresponds to the phrase "I confess my faults" or "You alone are holy." The posture and the attitude presupposed by the ritual language must really exist for the ritual to be true. The ritual is, in addition, a commitment; its gestures and actions contain a promise that its words may actually express: the promise of fidelity in faith, the promise to amend one's conduct. Finally, ritual is an operation: it intentionally aims at an effect and it accomplishes itself by carrying this aim into effect. In this respect, we may say that it is the nature of all ritual to operate by itself, on its own terms, as it were. The thing it carries into effect is the sacred, as is indicated by the word *sacrifice*, whose etymology exemplifies the religious ritual par excellence. For it is characteristic in religion that God becomes linked to human actions and accomplishes these, when man takes the requisite steps to create in himself the necessary disposition. Moreover, these steps and this disposition are accomplished through the various components of ritual, such as the expression of one's feelings, a form of conduct, and a commitment of faith.

Ritual is a symbolic action. The aim of ritual is to transform existence by establishing a bond with God that will activate a divine force in one's life. Insofar as it is a human action it consists of acts that bear upon things in the world, but these things and acts have been adapted to the ritual with the aim of representing and effectuating a dynamic bond between man and God.

The basic characteristic of the symbolic ritual is that it conjointly symbolizes the religious man and the God he addresses. God manifests himself in the ritual as a God who acts with and upon man, and he does this in accordance with specifically human meanings. It is because of this correspondence in the way man and God are symbolized that the representation of God will affect both the form of the ritual and its experience and, inversely, that man's representation of himself and his world will determine his representation of God.

Ritual can degenerate into ritualism when it becomes desymbolized. In this case the symbol becomes a symptom, a sign that expresses and fulfills some private meaning. Ritual is paradoxical in that it can maintain its symbolic valence only if it incorporates meanings that have been established. This means that a ritual is symbolic only if it draws man into a divine movement and if this movement is incarnated in some expressive form or human activity. The body's spontaneity and the transformation it works in nature must be joined to a living language and to established forms of meaning in order for ritual to be effective.

The established character of a ritual does not, however, imply that the meanings animating it are either uniform or rigidly fixed. Precisely because the meaning of a ritual exceeds its conceptual representation, the subject can always attribute a private sense to it. Nevertheless, this meaning is not fortuitous; it is still oriented by the ritual forms and objects and still elicited by the whole system of religious meanings. Moreover, an excessively rigorous codification of the ritual will destroy it in two ways: on the one hand it will inhibit its expressive function, for codes that are genuinely symbolic only provide the models according to which cultural groups modulate their own expressive styles; on the other hand, an excessively fixed codification is equivalent to imposing an abstract and anonymous dogma, whereas religious truths are too comprehensive to be exhaustively formulated. This excessive codification is characteristic of pathological ritualism.

Magical Action

The term *magic* here has only a differential meaning. It designates a type of action represented as efficacious, but one whose efficacity is not explained as the intervention of a force identified within any specific system of references. It follows then that a religious ritual is not magical in this sense of the term because the efficacity of the ritual is justified by its religious frame of reference. Cultural anthropologists, however, often use the term to refer to rituals whose efficacity is explained by a larger system of beliefs. Here *magic* simply refers to the unfamiliarity of a ritual system to which the observer does not adhere.[2] But anthropologists are nevertheless careful to distinguish ritual magic from individual magic in the cultures they study.

Applied to ritual, our definition of magic designates a form of practice that deviates from its given system of references. It is not a real magic we are dealing with here but rather a form of practice that tends toward the magical, a quasi-magic resulting from the split between an individual's subjective experience of the ritual and the symbolic meaning attributed to it and established by the community's intentions. Such a dysfunction of the ritual may occur for several reasons. We will limit our focus here to the effect guilt has on the quasi-magical use of ritual.

Guilt leads the subject to raise a quasi-magical defense against punishment. The belief in punishment is an important element of the guilty conscience. Piaget's study of this issue, which has been verified by additional research, is useful here.[3] Considered a form of primitive behavior, magic is defined as "the use an individual believes he can make of his participative relations in order to modify reality."[4] Magic forms a part of the "ego-centric attitude, proper to the child, in which the incorporation of objects into his activity prevails over adaptation, so that he only has to situate himself in the objective world by degrees." The child transforms the links of resemblance and contiguity he observes into links of causality. Assimilating "primitives" to children, Freud attributes the same magical behavior to the former.[5] What is significant is that as a result of guilt this magical mentality is prolonged in the child. The child interprets any misfortune incurred after a transgression as a sanction. Piaget calls this interpretation a "reaction of immanent justice" because of its automatic quality. I would stress, however, the fact that it is a matter of immanent punitive justice. Thus the child perceives nature as animated by immanent and intentional forces that reestablish whatever harmony his actions have perturbed.

Piaget does not explain how or why guilt can elicit this magical reaction when this attitude has already been relinquished. This question is correlative to another: is it possible to explain this reaction of immanent punitive justice by a general theory of magic, a theory that appeals to a desire which the egocentric attitude imagines as being automatically satisfied (through magic)? Since this relation is an inverse one to that of desire, we must conclude that the magical process desire resorts to is not the same as that used by guilt, even if they have in common that transitivism by which internal representations are externally projected. Guilt characteristically attributes knowledge of its transgression to the external world, and it is in this sense projective. It travels the same road as the development of moral conscience, but in the inverse direction. The authority internalized by conscience becomes spontaneously endowed with the same power of observation that conscience, by virtue of its internalization, has in the subject itself. Consequently aggression, which also constitutes the essence of the transgression, returns to the subject as a form of retaliation.

In guilt neurosis, ritualized acts become forms of defense against the subject's aggressive representations, as well as against the retaliation he fears because of the law of retaliation. Although apparently insignificant, the obsessional's ritual acts are elucidated in the course of analysis as being unconsciously charged in this way, which explains his anxiety if they are not accomplished. Obsessional subjects recognize the absurdity of their ritualism, but something inside them compels them to carry it out. Because that something remains unidentified, unnamed, the ritual takes on the character of an automatism. The ritualized action could be reconstructed as follows: if I don't do it, I'll be overcome by anxiety; I must do it; if I don't, something terrible will happen to me; that something is a punishment; somewhere there is a force that knows my evil thoughts. These ritualized acts, then, contain a belief, one without any apparent context, but one that analysis will show bears on a dangerously punitive power.

If the subject believes in God a recognizable identity is conferred on the anonymous power in which the subject unconsciously believes. I do not claim that religious faith derives from this belief; on the contrary, insofar as faith is founded in religious discourse, it cannot be understood strictly in terms of a psychology of guilt. And yet the unconscious belief, searching for some identifiable reality for the punitive agency, then becomes transferred onto "God." Still, religious ritual can easily become an area in which ritualism will seek the means to defend itself against a punitive supernatural power. These changes, however, do not affect the formal character of the ritual as much as the way in which it is subjectively experienced. In this way, a cult of guilt encourages a quasi-magical form of ritual, thereby stripping the ritual of its expressive symbolism and imposing on it a fear of divine judgment. In such a context, a ritual can easily assume the character of a quasi-obsessional protective action whose omission is accompanied by anxiety. In fact, I tend to believe that the formalism of certain religious practices is primarily due to this sort of psychological processes rather than to causes of a social order. We can clearly understand, in this context, how it happens that the practice of religious ritual diminishes when the climate of guilt disappears.

Up to this point we have seen how a cult of guilt can cause ritual to degenerate by desymbolizing it. Now we must examine how this form of ritualism affects the subject's faith in the efficacity of the ritual. It is a complex problem because the ritual always remains integrated within a community's frame of reference. Consequently the deviation critiqued here is a variable one, one that an objective observer may not even be capable of measuring. Only the individuals involved in this phenomenon can give an account of it, as they explain why they abandoned a specific ritual practice when they realized it had become magical for them and they could no longer distinguish magical belief from religious faith.

To understand this drifting of ritual toward magic it is necessary to isolate and trace the internal logic of ritualism. This logic contains an implicit theory of faith; it is a practical logic elaborated under the guise of official religious discourse.

If we reconstitute this logic we find that in terms of human activity it pushes toward the elimination of expressive forms and then becomes incapable of recognizing God as being latent in the contours of the world. Responding to the void in man, the divine act, abruptly transcendental and radically exterior, plunges into a world from which God is absent. God is not a being whose presence could be announced and promised by the existing signs of the world. He is not inherently present or even implied in the wishes and imaginings of the kind of desire that inhabits the world. As a result, God's otherness is vaguely and abstractly depicted as an almost purely anonymous force. If men and women cannot pray to him in their own voices, if they cannot address their feelings, experiences, and desires to him with those signs that constitute the poetry of their lives, then God loses the quality of a presence established through dialogue; he becomes the purely other, a stranger, a cosmic center and cause of activity.

By a paradoxical reversal of the type well known to psychopathology, ritual, which remains nonetheless a human act, becomes an instrumental manipulation. The desymbolization of ritual and the representation of God that corresponds to it thus concur. Once the ritual is desymbolized it becomes an instrument whose force of action is perceived as an instrumental causality that produces a supernatural power. Then, since God is perceived as a virtually anonymous force, he becomes himself the object of man's manipulation. Here we see the paradoxical reversal of ritual into a form of quasi-magic: by depriving ritual of its human density and attributing all its efficacy in practice to an absolutely divine power, man acts as if he could instrumentally control that power. Of course, ritual practice does not explicitly articulate all this in the form of a theory, but it follows this logic in practice, until one achieves a certain distance from this form of ritualism and discovers to his own astonishment the belief that governed his behavior.

The psychoanalysis of obsession shows that, in cases of neurotic guilt, an unconscious motive is added to the logic of ritualism, which is itself organized at the manifest level of preconscious representations. We can start with the analysis of the typical obsessive ritual of repetitive counting, counting, for example, the books on a shelf or the number of steps in a stairwell; this is an absurd act because it is of utterly no interest and because the answer, once the exercise has been completed, is known in advance. As is the case with every symptom, several themes are combined here: it fixes the subject's attention on an object, a well-known defensive strategy against temptation; the subject complies with an internal command by displacing his obedience onto a harmless neutral object; and he extends his attitude of mastery and control to even the minor details of his life. But what is most important and most essential here is that the ritual provides the individual a means of taking possession and seizing the object ("object" in the psychoanalytic sense of the term). To my knowledge, Freud never uncovered this feature of obsession. V. von Gebsattel described it very well but did not explain its function in the logic of guilt.[6] The obsessional ritual forms a part of the general structure of perception. To perceive—whether by counting with one's eyes, measuring with one's feet, or feeling an object with one's hands— is to seize an object by penetrating it with one's own mind and sensation. But what marks the obsessive ritual is that it is the compulsory, yet involuntary, exercise of an urgent need to appropriate the object mentally; it systematically clings to it, whereas in normal perception the object perceived is received and then restored to its appropriate place as one presence and one sign among others in the world. We may wonder if this obstinate seizure of the object in the obsessional world does not correspond to a form of anal retention familiar to psychoanalysis. This bodily schema undoubtedly predisposes a subject to this form of ritualization of perception and ritualized unification. But clinical experience has shown that it is a matter of attachment rather than retention, *attachment* being a term that better describes the movement of active seizure visible in the ritual. This active attachment is more easily understood if we situate it within the experience of guilt as we analyzed it in the chapter on obsessional neurosis. Because of his transgression—unconscious, of course—the subject feels that he has broken his bond with the object (mother, father, loved one) whose love is indispensable to his self-assurance and sense of vitality. The subject takes possession of a substitute object by means of the ritual and thereby reassures himself with a guaranteed presence. However unlikely this motive may seem to those who have not observed the logic of the unconscious, they may understand that it is well founded if they reflect on the ritual activity those in mourning will perform: classifying their things, counting linen, noting expenses. The emptiness left when a bond has been severed is then somewhat filled by some form of substitute object or activity.

In religious ritualism the same function can be ascertained and the same meaning inferred from it. The subject literally clings to the prescribed words and established forms in the same way that the obsessive appropriates the exact number of objects by counting them or the legalist clings to the law as if it were the divine substance itself. The ritualist takes possession of the divine substance incorporated in the letter and the object-signs of the ritual. An unconscious anxiety, produced by his fear of being rejected, leads him to cling desperately to the Other.

Once caught in the web of pathology, the ritual becomes overdetermined in meaning, charged with contradictions and paradoxes. Psychologists sometimes suppose that pathological formations are more simple than those of normal existence, that the normal is composed of an organized system of elementary forms that in pathology become isolated into distinct elements. In fact, however, pathology is much more complex than this, precisely because the same elements that form the basis of normalcy become transformed in pathology, mixing both positive and negative components. The obsessive ritual will take a symbolic form that has already been established by culture, partially desymbolize it, and then introduce its own more or less unconscious intentions, disguised as signifiers of faith.

The Dualism *Purity/Impurity*

The opposition between the sacred (or the holy) and the impure—an opposition basic to all religion—grounds the religious laws that constitute the basic requirements of purity for cultic practice. It also determines the rituals of purification so essential to the structures of religion. But although it recurs frequently in poetic and religious metaphors its significance remains obscure. A memory of the opposition is preserved in religious rituals, but in a culture such as ours, which has lost the vital significance it once held, these rituals can be easily misunderstood, often becoming the vehicle of morbid motivations.

The Sacred and the Impure

Let us first recall the original meaning attributed to this category, which is significant only if it is taken as a polarity. My position counters those studies, rather old ones admittedly, that interpret the sacred as an ambivalent category produced by the primitives' confusion between two opposed forms of experience, the sacred and the impure, the divine and the demonological, the beneficial and the malevolent. In other words, the sacred becomes assimilated to a dangerous defilement and vice versa. The concept of "taboo," so fascinating to anthropology in the past, is the prototype for this notion, which was largely propounded under Frazer's authority and influence. Freud uses it in *Totem and Taboo*, where he tries to give it a psychoanalytic foundation. Even Mircea Eliade bases his work upon it: "This ambivalence of the sacred is not only in the psychological order, but also in the order of values; the sacred is at once 'sacred' and 'defiled.' Commenting on Virgil's phrase *auri sacra fames*, Servius remarks quite rightly that *sacer* can mean at the same time accursed and holy. Eustathius notes that same double meaning in *hagios*, which can express at once the notion of 'pure' and that of 'polluted.' "[7] These semantic inversions of the word prove nothing in favor of the ambivalence of the sacred; they are simply due to the rhetorical play of language in tropes such as the litotes or the hyperbole. As for the real substance of the sacred/impure, more recent anthropological studies have shown that the dichotomy is little more than a phantasmagorical construction elaborated by ethnologists attempting to suit all religious phenomena to the evolutionary scheme prevalent in anthropology and psychology at that moment in history, a scheme according to which all culture and all religious experience purportedly followed a line of development from the confusion of affect to the clarity of reason.

We might take the following text from Isaiah 6 as an example. "I saw the Lord Yahweh seated on a high throne. . . . Seraphs cried out to one another in this way, 'Holy, holy, holy is Yahweh Sabaoth. His glory fills the whole earth.' . . . I said, 'What a wretched state I am in, I am lost, for I am a man of unclean lips and I live among a people of unclean lips, and my eyes have looked at the king, Yahweh Sabaoth.' " A seraph then comes to purify his lips with a live coal taken from the altar. Isaiah is not proclaiming a psychological terror for his people's widespread defilement; his fear of impurity is not the primary experience here. If Yahweh's holiness is dangerous, it is not because it radiates a dangerous ambivalent substance. Nor is the impurity that terrifies Isaiah the uneasy conscience of a sinner. The impure consists here in the transgression of the difference in essence separating man from God. When Yahweh approaches, when he traverses the abyss that veils and separates his radical otherness from man, he comes too close to man and causes Isaiah to become suddenly aware of man's impurity in light of God's holiness.

We might note that the original meaning of the word *holy* was that which was separated insofar as it was entirely other to man. The nearness of the two cannot be maintained unless man is first purified. Purification is the symbolic act that allows men and women to present themselves before God yet at the same time maintain his otherness. The ritual has two aspects. On the one hand, man expresses and confirms his human status before God, who is in turn recognized for what he is. On the other hand, through symbolic forms of fire and water man can temporarily participate in the divine quality and approach God without transgressively denying the difference between himself and God. The same structure can be found in the sacrifice.

Purification rites consist of two movements, retreat and contact, separation and binding, disinvestment and reinvestment. The two movements are interconnected. When a Muslim washes his face and hands and takes off his shoes before going into the mosque, he already belongs to the circle of the divine even before he actually enters the mosque. In the Christian rite of baptism the two meanings of purification and being born into a new life are also inseparable. But the rite's actions and discursive pronouncements are temporally developed and diachronically distinguished. The same is true in the Eucharist, where the succession from the offertory to the communion develops temporally the dialectical movements of dispossession and assimilation. The dialectic of these two movements in the purification ritual is fundamental to the human order: it specifies human beings; it characterizes their desire and demarcates their customs and social behavior. It is a fundamental property of language insofar as language both supposes and creates the necessary dialectic of distance and appropriation through the intermediary of signs, which allow the subject to posit himself as a subject and to relate to things as what they are. Consequently, by these two movements—signified by their appropriate symbols—the two most basic rituals of purification and sacrifice both institute the relationship between God and man and identify the structural difference between them.

Ritual implicates the whole of man's life and then inscribes this religious dialectic into his very body: through his spirit, which structures difference; through his sensations and his instinctual life, which give rise to the metaphor of impurity. This is not a psychological sensation projected onto the sacred in the manner of some confused and archaic notion; on the contrary, it is the perception of a structural difference that is then given a symbolic shape, one charged with the whole range of affective corporal meanings present in man's life.[8] If there is any confusion it derives from an a posteriori condensation of two different perceptions of fear: one awakened by the manifestation of the divine other, and one aroused by the threat of being polluted.

Language uses this resemblance and bridges the two phenomena by rhetorical mechanisms. In this way the sacred comes to signify something that exerts a dangerous and mysterious attraction for man. Then the notion of impurity or defilement, which is itself perceived as dangerous when it is confronted with the sacred (thus itself taking on significance as a religious category), also becomes interchangeably used with the term *sacred*. But the sacred itself becomes dangerous only when it is not respected. Religious defilement is on the order of profanation, the kind of human act that profanes the sacred. It is present for example, in the act of sacrilege, that paradoxical action that recognizes the status of the sacred only to subsequently disregard or subvert it. Sacrilege is the religious perversion par excellence, and like all perversions, it presupposes the very law it then takes pleasure in transgressing.

Strictly speaking, the category of the impure is not opposed to the pure but to the sacred, or the holy. The reason is that this relationship is not primarily moral but religious. The polarity of these categories so profoundly defines the religious rapport that I would call it an ontological-religious category, one that defines man and God with regard to their difference in being. But the impure should not be given an independent and substantive value, because it has meaning only within the religious process that binds man and God. Since the impure is only one moment in the whole movement that establishes this bond, the subject transcends the experience of the impure once the rapport between God and himself has been achieved through the ritual.

To recognize and pinpoint the pathological use of the category of the sacred and the defiled, we must look more deeply into both its metaphorical significance and the way it is transferred onto the symbols of ritual.

Contrary to the psychological concept that derives the metaphor of defilement from the feeling of disgust for filth, more precisely excrement, I will argue that it derives from a specific category of thought. One of the functions of language is to differentiate; what is primary to the working of mind is the pure, perceived as simple and unmixed, and—on the order of the mind's perceiving—the perception of the pure form, perfectly and distinctively identifiable through the language that differentiates it. At this level the pure takes precedence over an impure, whose identity is confused and deformed. Himself formed by language, man is the being that creates things by giving a form to the formless. And for him the deformed is a monstrous thing, filling him with horror. Thus Hieronymus Bosch used an imaginary world swarming with human monsters to represent the radical evil that brings about destructive deformation: evil first disfigures its author. In his painting of Jesus carrying the cross Bosch shows how the executioners, with bulging eyes, crooked teeth, and twisted mouths, are packed like flies around the Holy One of God. When confronted with the holy, evil manifests itself as the monstrous destruction of creation.

Our familiarity with works like these in our culture allows us to understand the impure as a religious category in other cultures. We might take as an example the strange taboos described in Scripture, taboos which orthopraxic Jews still follow and respect.[9] These taboos are a function of classification, the means by which a culture distinguishes different categories of being according to specific and identifiable forms; those forms of being whose category is unclear or mixed (such as the pig) are subsequently perceived as impure. None of these biblical texts explicitly states the principle of impurity. When I once asked a celebrated orthodox Jewish thinker for an explanation of the impure he replied that it was "that which swarms," a definition that supports the foregoing interpretation of taboos because it calls to mind the disagreeable sensation that a confused, formless, or deformed object evokes. It does not, however, associate the impurity with bodily filth, as psychological interpretations frequently do. But it is still interesting to note that only a structural analysis of texts can adequately specify the principle of impurity operative in the Bible. This shows how the function of classification inherent in the cultural unconscious organizes the world according to a signifying order that separates the formed from the formless. Moreover, it is because this division represents a system existing in the world that it has a religious meaning.

By refusing contact with anything monstrous, a group of believers chooses its adherence to the Creator and refuses to align itself with the opposed forces of chaos and evil. In this way, they pay homage to God in their daily life. We might point out another image that eloquently demonstrates this idea: the representation of the devil in traditional iconography often combines in one figure the differences between male and female or between man and the lower animals by depicting the devil—God's antagonist, hence the symbol of impurity par excellence— in a variety of monstrous forms, having, for example, both a penis and breasts, and brandishing a tail while preserving a human posture. Consequently I would argue that physical impurity, dirt, and excrement first take on the symbolic meaning of impurity and then come to signify religious impurity in the same way that deformation can symbolize religious impurity because it depicts formlessness or decomposition.

Man in the presence of God experiences himself as a mixture of good and evil, a being made of dust and of a principle that likens him to God. It is by contrast to the holy that man discovers his impurity, just as deformity appears as such only in comparison with a form endowed with unity of meaning. Insofar as it performs this differential function, there is nothing in the category of impurity that necessarily evokes the ethical terror caused by the pervasive sense of evil that may envelop men, such as we find in some neuroses, and such as the moralization of religious impurity has helped to diffuse.

Rituals of purification express man's consciousness of his impurity as he stands before the Holy; they permit him to cross over to a state in which he resembles the pure. The symbols of physical purification are used for this purpose: water, for example, is used to wash away dirt, and fire to destroy decomposing matter. So, by virtue of metaphorical transference physical impurity becomes the symbol of religious impurity.

It is the entire dialectic of ritual, however, not just this specific aspect of it, that is given shape and concrete expression through the symbols of purification. Water, for example, is also the element from which life originally emerged, as various cosmogonic myths asserted long before science did. Fire too has a twofold symbolic value: it consumes corpses and waste material but it is also a divine element. By means of these two symbolic operations the purifying elements place man on a level with God. In its very principles Christian baptism exemplifies the two dialectical movements that make it the fundamental rite of passage.

Psychological interpretation adds an important element to this hermeneutic polarity of the sacred/impure; it also exemplifies the meaning of the purification ritual both as the experience and the production of religious meanings. Because of the ambivalence inherent in and necessary to instinctual life, the religious act is in fact an ambiguous one: it risks turning into its opposite, the sacrilege.

The transformation of aggressivity finds expression in the various symbolic gestures and acts where psychoanalysis distinguishes and uncovers the twofold dialectical movement we mentioned above: the negation of aggressive negation and the positive signs of recognition. When man extends his bare hand to another he lays down his weapons; this already constitutes one step toward establishing the pact of friendship. Both movements are apparent in the various symbolic and almost ritualized gestures involved in the act of love, gestures whose aim is to evoke the experience of love as well as to prepare one to receive it. In the same way religious experience becomes concretely accomplished and exemplified when it is given symbolic form through ritual.

The Pathological Drift of Religious Impurity

Under the impact of monotheism, biblical religion progressively developed a notion of sin as a "religious dimension and not a moral one."[10] Taken in this sense sin is a form of religious impurity revealed within the context of the prophetic message, and not the product of a subjective moral conscience. Nevertheless, as the subject stands before the God who speaks in and to the prophets in the first person, the "I am," the meaning of sin becomes interiorized as subjective guilt over the wrong for which the subject must take responsibility. And correlatively, the ideal of the just man, in the biblical sense of the term, transforms religious purification into a necessity for becoming holy; this in turn adds a distinctly ethical character to the religious attitude. This evolution undoubtedly marks a type of progress that we could call, along with Freud, a form of "spiritualization."[11] At this point, however, the category of the impure, taken in its limited usage and as a metaphor for sin, can easily take on the significance of a religious sense of unworthiness due to one's personal faults. We might recall briefly that Christianity took the term *impurity* and used it as a metaphor for sin, sin being the tainting of the soul, a stain (*macula*) that defiles it. It is no longer a question of man's ontological impurity as a consequence of his being essentially different from the God before whom he stands. Here the category of the impure has lost its differential and relational meaning. In its ritual context, physical impurity is taken as a symbol opposed to the symbolic purifying element. But when impurity is taken as a metaphor for sin, the impure can become a substance that adheres to man. What we have here is a process of progressive materialization that winds up desymbolizing the category of the impure.

In addition, the derogation of sexuality and an excessive emphasis on sexual purity then leads theology to associate all bodily pleasure with impurity, thus reinforcing a further degradation of the metaphor. At the extreme, all desire and sexual pleasure become completely identified with the physico-religious concept of impurity. The category of impurity originally lent itself to this progressive materialization because it is an irrational concept, irrational in the sense that it is not reflected upon but rather proceeds directly from the classificatory and differentiating function of the collective imagination. The category belongs to that kind of mythical discourse that men do not think out rationally but that "thinks itself" in men. In this cultural universe men perceive all creatures as bound to one another in a bond of solidarity; consequently, the transgression of a taboo by one individual can infect his family and even the entire group with impurity. And if the transgressor happens to be a king, as in the case of Oedipus, who made himself impure by patricide and incest, his impurity will be transmitted to the entire community, poisoning, as well, earth and water itself. Once the mythical discourse that bound together man and cosmos is lost, the power of communicability once attributed to the impure as well as the divine becomes progressively rationalized and eventually articulated in terms of a physical causality.

The subjective moralization of sin and the quasi-materialization of the impure—now having become a metaphor for sin—have both greatly influenced the Christian notion of guilt and significantly impoverished the religious significance of the purification ritual in Christianity. Accordingly, research on the subject has shown how baptism can be perceived as a virtually automatic, instrumental form of purification.[12] This representation of sin-impurity as a substance that affects the soul of man reinforces both the concept of and the practice of ritualism. The same realism in the concept of sin is also implicit in representations of the Christian redemption by means of Jesus' death on the cross, according to which man transfers all his evil onto Christ; thus the lamb of God, seen as a scapegoat, becomes responsible for assuming unto himself all the world's iniquities. Consider the inversion implicit in this reasoning. The scapegoat ritual was originally a form of collective purification in which the collective unit symbolically transferred its impurity onto an impure animal, thus affirming its adherence to a divine order, just as it does when it respects communal prohibitions against impure animals. In the sacrificial act, however, a pure animal representing both God's holiness and man's resemblance to him is chosen, then sacrificed in order to establish a bond with God. To interpret Christ's sacrifice according to a model of the ritual scapegoat is in fact to pervert the religious meaning of the sacrifice and to corrupt the category of the impure.

We may recall that in obsessional neurosis the instinctual body, especially the sexual instincts, is condemned by a largely unconscious judgment proceeding from the superego. Infantile representations associate the sexual act and the act of giving birth with excremental acts and products, and this association gives the unconscious prohibition the added quality of being based on a shameful physical fact. Under the influence of cultural rules that the infant assimilates when he enters the network of differentiated human relations, the excremental becomes the figure of everything dirty and repugnant. Thus two distinct realities become associated and eventually confused: on the one hand, the impure as a category on the order of the illicit transgression, the destruction of laws regulating the order of men and creatures; on the other hand, the impure as a physical quality. The nature of the regression consists therefore in the fact that the quality of physical impurity overtakes and absorbs the impure as a cultural, moral, or religious category. The effects of repression are apparent in this regressive process. The representation of physical impurity becomes associated with the idea of sin, then the impure as a religious category becomes identified with the body that committed the forbidden act, and thus the body itself becomes a sinful object.

In the phobia of touch, an external, often unidentified object becomes the locus of an impure substance, which circulates around it like an anonymous fluid and which receives the full affective charge of an evil that evokes horror in the subject. In this manner, the subject appeases his anxiety by projecting it onto the exterior world; he frees himself from it internally by situating it in an object outside himself and protects himself by various mechanisms of avoidance. Because, however, he feels constantly besieged by a form of impurity that cannot be easily fixed upon a specific symbolic object, he often finds himself compelled to seek purification by means of symptomatic rituals that frequently develop into cleansing or washing manias as compulsive as obsessional rituals. It is clear how representations of phobic impurity can easily become associated with religious representations and how a phobic ritualism can assimilate religious ritual, endowing it with an unconscious meaning and a compulsive force equivalent to the anxiety against which the ego must defend itself.

In psychosis, the impure has a more fundamental status. In a preceding analysis we saw that it is linked to the unconscious representation of monstrous forms of violence that rend and dismember the body. In these representations, blood-lust and sex commingle in representations of a body torn apart and devoured. Among some primitive peoples it is the sorcerer who represents the figure of radical impurity in that he is believed to practice cannibalism, vampirism, and incest. Similarly, the act of murder rendered a Jew ritually impure—in other words, barred from all participation in communal worship. The impure in psychosis more clearly resembles the impure in religion than neurotic impurity, and it is in the works of someone like Hieronymus Bosch that we find the monstrous imaginary realm that best figures the radical evil haunting the worlds of both psychosis and sorcery.

In conclusion, then, the pathology of impurity exists on three distinct levels in analogical relation to the three forms of meaning that constitute the category of the religious. In obsessional neurosis the desire for pleasure is represented as an impure transgression; it corresponds to the subjective moment of sin as an evil internalized by the act of transgression. In the phobia, which is the pathological precipitation of hysterical anxiety, the impure is transformed into objective form as a substance in the outside world; we see here the materialization of a religious impurity that, by virtue of the laws of interdependence, affects the subject's whole environment. In psychosis, finally, the impure coincides with a corporeal entity that is both the agent and the victim of torture and dismemberment. This is the radical moment of the impure; it corresponds to the essential principle of religious impurity, which consists in the negation of all differential and signifying forms of relation.

Whenever pathological impurity is found it contaminates religious impurity by condensing evil into a quasi-physical substance and freezing the dialectical process that effectively relates religious impurity to a concept of the sacred. In their ponderings over the impure, neurotics often come to recognize that there is a link between the idea of sinfulness and the pathological representation of the impure. Once this link is recognized the idea of sinfulness may take on a different significance for them, but only if they can move beyond the duality of purity/impurity to the recognition that the authentically religious opposition is in fact a relation of the impure to God. Then can the rites of confession and purification free them from their obsession with purity.

Sacrificial Debt: Self-Mutilation or Symbolic Exchange

The logic that governs neurotic guilt leads to the problem of the debt. "All pleasure is stolen from God." In his torment, the obsessional relives the torture the gods visited upon Prometheus, who was fed upon by an eagle sent from the heavens into which Prometheus had ascended in order to steal fire for man. In the fantasy recounted earlier, the black man waiting in the dark to crush the patient's skull is in fact the specter of God come back to avenge himself. Caught in the anxiety of his guilt, the patient incessantly repeats a phrase similar to those in a dream recounted by Freud: "It serves you right if you had to make room for me. Why did you try to push me out of the way? . . . Ote-toi de là que je m'y mette."[3]

According to the logic of the obsessional, there is only one place. Father and son, God and man cannot occupy it together; it belongs by all rights to the Father. To affirm oneself, to succeed, to enjoy oneself, even to exist is to dispossess the Father, to kill him in one's imagination—which, according to the psyche's laws, is equivalent to killing him in reality. It is impossible, then, to avoid incurring an insolvent and incessantly renewable debt toward him, unless one surrenders everything to him.

We have outlined the "psycho-logic" that governs the obsessive: it is a reflexive, specular logic that sets off the *perpetuum mobile* of attack and counterattack, of submission and revolt, simulated death and murder, self-mutilation and parricide. The idealized father is the only one with right on his side. He is also singular, unique, and therefore he is the only available model. Thus he incites the son to take his place, which is also the only desirable place. In this logic love and hate are inseparable, two facets of the same polarization. An idealizing and thus necessarily ambivalent love projects a fantastically exaggerated image of the father, and, in turn, the image of a father who sets himself up and apart in his solitary heights provokes a love disposed to rivalry in the son. In this perpetual play of specular reflection the one engenders the other: their reciprocal justification prevents us from isolating any one cause that might have initiated this perpetual movement between the two. In order to release the subject from this repetitive movement, a different logic must be put into effect, in the same way that the idea of immobility resulting from Zeno's paradox can be dissolved by introducing a logic of movement. Freud's reconstruction of the origins and the history of religion is based entirely on the obsessional logic that perpetually knots and unknots the same conflict, even though it invariably arises in different forms and disguises. According to Freud the conflict began with the murder of the first, primal father, who alone held the power that his sons wished to claim for themselves. This parricide did nothing to modify the basic coordinates of the conflict, because the father later reemerges in the form of guilt and other substitutive figures on whom the original parricide is repeatedly reenacted. This psychoanalytic reconstruction, offered as a fantastic saga of the history of religion, dramatizes for the larger theater of the world the logic underlying the psychology of the obsessive. Is this the unconscious truth of religion, one that is exhumed from under the surface of the textual evidence whose lacunae, displacements, distortions, and incompletely erased traces only the psychoanalyst can correctly interpret? First of all, the psychoanalyst must read those texts, study those memorials, and interpret the gestures of religion with the same vigilant attention he lends to the discourse of his patients.

Some of the practices and some interpretations of the sacrificial ritual can be understood in terms of a conflictual dualism. The story of Abraham's sacrifice, for example, illustrates the obsessive sacrifice as well as the first step toward its resolution through a first moment of dialectical reversal. Yahweh demands the immolation of the only son promised to Abraham, the son who was to ensure Abraham's paternity over a great nation, the only project and aim that gave some direction and meaning to Abraham's adventurous, nomadic life. On the basis of several rabbinic commentaries, we can see that this God who lays a bloody hand on man is a projection of the father's homicidal tendencies onto Yahweh.[14] We might add, however, that insofar as he is a paternal figure, Yahweh invites this projection. And if Abraham attributes these intentions to Yahweh, may we not suppose that Abraham harbors a secret rivalry between Yahweh and himself? Much as Jacob will later struggle with the angel of Yahweh on the banks of the Jabbok, the father of the future nation experiences his paternity as a stake in a duel with God.[15] In sacrificing his son, Abraham would make reparation for what he experiences as a usurpation. Abraham no doubt took as his model the Canaanite custom of sacrificing children by fire. But the context here is no longer that of a fertility cult. According to the mythical notion that life flows through all creatures at once, the sacrifice of one life fertilizes the whole and thus, by virtue of the homostatic law that distributes vital energies equally, the flow of life is intensified by removing it from one member and injecting it into the general system. However, when confronted with the concept of a personal God, this equilibrium is transformed into rivalry over the only position of paternity. Here, though, Yahweh himself takes the initiative and stops the sacrificial suicide by instructing Abraham to offer him a male animal instead. Henceforth the "law of the first-born" will require a substitutive offering for their redemption. This resolution of the debt constitutes a dialectical reversal, since the initiative coming from Yahweh himself confirms Abraham's paternity, giving him the right to assume his paternity even as he recognizes his debt toward God. Now Isaac truly becomes the son of Abraham insofar as he becomes a son of the covenant. By recognizing the assymetrical relationship between Yahweh and himself, Abraham overcomes a fatal rivalry on the imaginary level and is able to occupy a position comparable to Yahweh's.

The story of Abraham outlines a passage through the perilous conflict that faces the obsessive. By means of this mortal confrontation where both the temptations of pride and a perverted notion of God's power find their resolution, religious faith is affirmed as a sort of reversal that fundamentally changes the subject's perspective. This resolution of faith neither disguises nor displaces the conflict: it moves beyond it. The difference between this resolution and obsession is crucial. Obsession is the constant repetition of the same, whereas Abraham's sacrifice is a sequence measured by three different stages: the sacrificial suicide that Abraham imagines is demanded by Yahweh as vengeance for a usurpation; Yahweh's intention confirming Abraham's paternity; the sacrifice through which Abraham recognizes his debt and assumes his allotted paternity.

This analysis also sheds light on the significance of the circumcision of Moses' son. The Bible recounts how the cruel hand of Yahweh threatened Moses with death and how Moses saved his life by the circumcision of his son. As a form of symbolic wounding, circumcision is a type of sacrifice: through metonymy Moses symbolically offers up his sex. In a culture where procreation is a sign of man's life and its extension through his lineage, castration is the equivalent of death, just as it is in the unconscious representations of our day. Thus on the one hand Moses accepts symbolic castration as a sign of his debt toward Yahweh, and Yahweh, on the other hand, accepts this symbolic inscription on the body as a recognition of the debt by making it the emblem of his pact with Moses and his people. The contrast between symbolic castration and the neurotic castration complex is striking. In neurosis, it is the fantasy of the castration threat that haunts the subject. When the analytic process stirs up repressed ideas, it will invariably uncover representations of castration, either as something that the subject undergoes or as something he performs upon himself in order to prevent "the other" from inflicting it on him. These imaginary scenes are experienced as real, arousing internal anxiety as if they were actually going to happen. But Moses does not remain caught in an imaginary confrontation with a bloodthirsty god, for when he renounces his will to omnipotence by a symbolic gesture the savage deity becomes the God of the covenant for present and future.

The least one can say is that these amazing stories disguise nothing. Rather than warranting all sorts of suspect interpretation, the language in which they are couched elucidates with considerable insight the tortuous evasions of the obsessive imagination. These texts bluntly state the obsessive idea underlying a neurotic guilt: the dark violence of God hunts man down. One can infer from these texts that man's unconscious affective ambivalence is universal. But these biblical heroes do not pursue the unconscious folly of denying their affiliation, an ambition that to Freud's mind remains the fatal vocation of the great man—the hero who always "rebels against his father and in the end victoriously overcomes him."[16]

Moreover, it is remarkable that the history of both Moses' and Abraham's relation to their God opens with the word of Yahweh, who declares himself to them, entrusts them with a mission, and promises them the paternity of a whole nation. This confirms the law that according to Lacan contradicts the Hegelian dialectic of master and slave: "The pact is everywhere anterior to the violence before perpetuating it, and what I call the symbolic dominates the imaginary."[17] It is precisely because the pact precedes and consciously dominates the subject's imaginary confrontation with God here that he can resolve the subsequent violence by a renewed pact instead of being carried into revolt against a filiation that he experiences as fatal.

Nevertheless, the Christian idea of the death of the Son as a substitutive reparation for sin—this "primitive theology of bloodshed," as Bultmann calls it—ushers in again the representation of a bloodthirsty God.[18] Can one imagine a more obsessive fantasy than that of a God who demands the torturous death of his own son in order to assuage his anger? The assertion that God delivers his son to the inevitable sacrifice out of love for mankind is only an attempt to mask this idea, a form of denial meant to obfuscate the monstrous fatality of the notion. But these primitive concepts of debt and justice have their basis in a profound insight. The experience of a radical evil led one obsessional patient, who was not herself a believer, to think that only a radical sacrifice, that of life itself, could possibly redeem man from crimes such as those repeated since time immemorial. André Malraux had an analogous idea when, to his horror, he was faced with the gratuitous torture of a child: "The sacrifice alone can look into the eyes of torture, and the God of Christ is not God without the crucifixion."[19]

As a witness to horrible crimes man senses that this evil affects humanity as a whole and he perceives that only the sacrifice can redeem him by virtue of the mysterious links of solidarity between human beings. Thus one can grasp by an immediate sort of intuition that the death of Christ on the cross is "the death of sin" and that it gives man back his integrity. But when one explains the effectiveness of the sacrifice by affirming that it is meant to satisfy God's wrath and wounded honor, the primitive notion of a mortal conflict between man and God is introduced once again, and this, in turn, simply confirms the logic of the obsessive in theological discourse. While this theology has alleviated some people's sense of the insolvable debt that burdens them by displacing it onto Christ, others have seen it as a sign of their condemnation to imminent death.

By way of conclusion, I will give a brief sketch of the dialectic governing religious sacrifice. The sacrifice reproduces the twofold movement of disinvestment and reinvestment that marks the rite of purification, as well as Abraham's sacrifice and the rite of circumcision. But in contrast to these rituals, the religious sacrifice from the start posits a third factor between man and God: the symbol that the debt has been recognized. A number of elements taken from and representing the earth are set aside by man, and in the offering he then acknowledges that earth belongs to God but has been given to man as the domain of his autonomy, for his joy and pleasure. By symbolic means he expresses the fact that he simultaneously invests and disinvests himself of the earth and the life that have been given to him as a gift. He does not cling to them with the lack of moderation of one who would seek to be his own father, nor with the uneasy conscience of the usurper. In this way, those elements that have been set aside become the sign in the world of a divine presence that heightens existence without suppressing it. The sacrifice expresses a discontinuity between man and God, which is symbolized by the topographical separation between the earth as the place of human habitation and the heavens as God's dwelling place. The sacrifice affirms that the earth is man's by right, but by divine right. Nevertheless, the sacrifice is an act, a procedure; in answer to man's symbolic recognition of his indebtedness to him, God establishes continuity in this discontinuity. Insofar as it is a process that enacts and establishes a link within a recognized difference, the sacrifice goes beyond the specular relation implied in the imaginary struggle to occupy one and the same position. The sacrifice is a symbolic gift, not a self-mutilation carried out in despair of man's utter insolvency. It does not seek to pay a debt, but affirms that the debt need not be repaid.

PART THREE

Failings and Troubles of Desire

5 • Desire: Psychological Sources and Criteria

Desire and Love in Religion

I do not conceive religion along the same lines as Henri Bergson, who once defined it as "the crystallization—brought about by the chill of wisdom—of the burning element that mysticism has lodged in the soul of men."[1] Religions teem with diverse forms and interests. As a language about the world and man's existence, religion offers a first and all-encompassing discourse whose ultimate aim is to render the meaning and truth of this existence; it does so, however, without taking recourse in speculative or explanatory forms of language. Religion offers principles and models for an ethical praxis. It gives man various ways of situating himself with regard to death—that enigma and suffering essential to his existence. Different types of religion respond to specific human needs, and, because they are inscribed in a particular historical, sociological, and psychological context, they appear to be intelligible within a problematic studied and verified by the human sciences. Thus, there are certain sects that are specifically characterized by the privileged position given to the adherents' subjective relation with regard to evil, to illness, and to their society.[2] In the hope of understanding religion, some psychologists and sociologists have based all their studies on these marginal sociological and psychological phenomena, as if this very marginality did not indeed place the sects in question inside a closed field very specifically determined by their partial motivations. Nevertheless, although religions overlap any or all *particular* interests, they are not for that reason reducible to some sort of philosophical world view, nor do they completely coincide with their ethical dimension—however essential that dimension may be.

In religion a fundamental dimension—one that can, in fact, become the dominating force of religion—is often overlooked and misunderstood by both the human sciences and theoretical reason. It is precisely that dimension which participates in the order of love and desire—insofar as these are experienced in relation to a being which, according to religion, is both within and outside of ourselves, a being designated and named as a divinity. In any case, this sense of being linked to a God who is the source of that deep mystery present in the world and who is a personal presence before whom the individual recognizes his responsibility—a presence, moreover, which also guarantees that man's efforts to construct the world are not in vain—this sense of God is an essential dimension of the Christian faith.[3] Even if it is inconceivable that man can be religious without deriving some interest from it, the interest involved in his experience of this relationship with religion cannot be conceived in terms of partial motivations. What we have here is a relationship that concerns all of existence as it is aligned with man's center of being. This "ego-totality" is where Freud situates the source of love, which, in turn, he distinguishes from the instincts that are themselves partial. It is often asked, however, what possible interest love and desire of God can afford man if we disregard the particular interests that arise from his circumstantial needs. It is the whole question of the significance of love and desire that is at stake here. Moreover, if on the human order this question concerns an area of experience that the human sciences have enough trouble outlining as it is, how much more enigmatic it must become if the issue is raised at the religious level. It will be necessary then to proceed with circumspection as we evaluate the phenomena pertinent to this register of experience.

Mysticism is undoubtedly the most paradigmatic form of this religious dimension. For this reason I consider it the phenomenon that most clearly manifests both the significance and the likely pathologies of desire in religion. It is not my ambition to propose a psychology of mysticism but rather to examine a number of salient examples of it, in order to clarify how religious desire and pathology can become intertwined.

It may seem rather offhand to speak of mysticism as a whole since there are so many varied forms of it. What are the common features of Pythagorean, Neoplatonic, Buddhist, naturo-cosmic, Christian, cabalistic, Islamic, shamanistic, and drug-induced mysticism? Historians and phenomenologists who study the variations, links, and cultural conditions of mysticism are attentive to the plurality of its forms, but they do refer to the same center of interest throughout that allows them to identify the phenomenon.[4] This interest seems incontestably to be situated in a common movement reaching for the experience of union with some element that is conceived as the secret center and permanent source of life, the object of man's desire: the sacred, a divinity, God, the One. Because it is possible to designate a unity of interest among the different forms of mysticism, as well as to note a diversity of themes, formulations, and approaches, we may deduce that different mysticisms are the result of a conjunction between certain psychic dynamics and the signifiers and symbols of specific cultural and religious environments. Consequently, the two sets of given data, subjective and objective, are not disassociated in this approach, for in this case as in all other human contexts, cultural and religious messages are woven into the psyche and thus awaken aspirations of a qualitatively different order. But to link mysticism to psychic dynamics does not mean that one simply reduces it to some elementary tendency or experience,[5] nor does it mean that mysticism is treated as a superstructure without differentiation of meaning or internal truth of its own.

As in preceding chapters I will concentrate on an examination of the Christian religion. To keep in mind the circumscribed themes and references of this study, I will aim this inquiry at those universally psychic elements, and this will in turn allow us to pinpoint and understand the corresponding forms of disorder and illness. Any incursion into Christian mysticism will therefore suspend theological considerations. In any case, as mysticism represents for me the most articulated and developed form of a dimension I consider essential to religious experience, I will call that vector which deploys man's love and desire as a specifically religious love and desire, the mystical vector of religion. I will not, then, concentrate primarily on the extraordinary or bizarre features of mysticism, such as ecstasies, visions, or hearing voices. These phenomena, which have so often sparked the curiosity of psychologists and psychiatrists, will be considered only insofar as they enter into the context of mysticism.

A number of recurring phrases, such as those that express the pain of separation, suffering, the desire for union, love, and enjoyment, all attest to the fact that the comparison of highly diversified manifestations and their unification under the rubric of mysticism is not an arbitrary procedure. The evident analogy between the mystical vector and the register of human love even has a paradoxical effect. On the one hand it seems to correspond perfectly to the supreme command of biblical religion: "Love your God with all your heart, with all your soul, and with all your might"; on the other hand, to many it appears so strange to love God in such extreme fashion that one immediately suspects this love of drawing upon rather opaque and somewhat preternatural fantasies. The Renaissance, influenced by Platonic thought, was not quite so fearful or reticent about religious desire when, for example, it represented divine love in the unveiled theophanous nudity of Botticelli's Venus.[6]

It is a question, therefore, of appreciating and evaluating the erotic in religion. Religious desire is born in those for whom certain words and signs carry more meaning than they do for others, even other believers. "Near is the God and difficult to seize. . . . " These words, opening Hölderlin's evocatively titled poem "Patmos," attest to the pain of separation and mark a religious desire. The obscure appeal of a divine reality can lead through any number of paths. Some individuals, those particularly sensitive to the hidden mystery of their lives or those who wish to link their being with the divine source of being itself—some even avid to feel its active force flowing through them—obstinately pursue the way of union with the sacred or with a God who is both manifest and hidden to them. Why should these people rather than others find themselves so affected by an insistent sense of a vertical reality, at once sublime and profound, permeating the web of scattered phenomena. Why do they draw a very particular form of enjoyment from this experience? Insofar as it touches upon the Christian faith the question is even more intriguing in that this religion explicitly organizes existence according to the perspective of a personally present God, disclosing himself specifically, even though this presence does not necessarily address each believer in the same way. From my own point of view, the mystical quest is not an especially privileged one. Nothing authorizes us to consider as religiously inferior the sustained consciousness of a discretely divine presence who accompanies, simplifies, and illuminates the Sundays of life as well as its dramatic moments. No less authentic is the hope that confidently accepts one's allotted span of life in a bleak world, leaving for later the "face to face" encounter pledged by faith. But inversely, neither have we cause to judge as abnormal the impatient desire to penetrate the fund of silence in which God is held by the very words and signs that mediate his presence. One may wonder whether these differences in attitude do not stem from deep psychological structures. The believer may, like St. Paul, attribute this diversity to various supernatural gifts (charismata); the psychologist, however, has the right to suppose that these "gifts" are not arbitrarily appended onto an inert mass of human material but rather are written into psychic processes that predetermine their direction. We should try to see what these structures and processes are and thereby lay groundwork for the identification and articulation of a pathology of desire in this domain.

Psychological Sources and Corresponding Dangers

It is my working hypothesis that religious desire derives from human desire and that this derivation results from religious signifiers acting upon desire. The pathology of this vector is consequently dependent upon a pathology of desire, in which case religious signifiers lend themselves to a displacement—in the twofold sense that they bring about a partial resolution of a conflict but also furnish it with material and contain it within the unconscious. The guiding interpretive principle here is the same as that developed with regard to the neurotic sense of guilt. Taken in its absolute sense, desire is the aspiration to replenish a void; it is a force that pushes toward the conquest of an object the subject believes will abolish this lack and quell his desire. Thus all human activity is impelled by desire. Desire is not, however, a simple separable force whose action is, in itself, oriented toward some good automatically accomplished for, or by, man.[7] It is the cruel law to which mankind is subject that our desire takes its form, is transformed and deformed by the historical inscriptions that constitute the remembrances and record of our pleasures (pleasures lost in the past never to be recovered as such) and of our disappointments and frustrations of desire. The permutations of desire cannot be traced here, but the following interpretation will stake out some of the guideposts. I rely freely on the work of Freud, Lacan, and Szondi.

Lack and desire are correlative. By the nature of our corporal being the first recurring experiences of lack are hunger and thirst. The mother's breast, or its substitute, is the first appeasing object of pleasure. This primordial experience of lack and the contact with the object of satisfaction imprints upon the psychic apparatus the whole matrix of desires and strengths that support a subject's ideals of happiness and his sexual fantasies, as well as the pathological forms of avidity, which the German language designates by the untranslatable term *Süchtigkeit*. It also forms the supportive base for the symbolic discourse of mystical desire. In psychoanalysis this enduring primordial form of desire is called orality. The expression "oral stage" might lead one to suppose that this first form of desire is one the subject must leave behind, lest he condemn himself to an infantile regression. In order to avoid this misunderstanding, it should be emphasized that insofar as it is a foundation of experience, the oral stage marks the desire for (and is proper to) the oral position, or state, mainly because desire is constituted in and by the individual's experience of want, of relation and contact, as these have been organized by the body's organs. The act of drinking and eating, centering on the mouth as an active and receptive opening, prints upon the psyche the existential schema through which the subject experiences and represents to himself his manner of being in the world and with others. In an analogous manner the eye organizes man's existence and world according to patterns of light and dark, perspective, color, panorama; then the desire that is formed through this visual organization of the world will in turn make colors speak and light sing.

Is it surprising, then, that according to Freud every object of love is in some sense the first object—the mother's breast—which was lost, then recovered in a different form?[8] The poetics of desire, modulating as it does various metaphors of drinking and eating, is one of the languages frequently used in the discourse of religious desire, and it receives concrete form through symbolic gestures and action used in worship. The Flemish mystic J. Van Ruysbroek exhorts his disciples "to cling with mouth and lips to the celestial pipe," and one can say about mysticism the same thing that Freud said about love: "The infant at his mother's breast and the lover returning to home and nourishment at the same breast after twenty years of separation, these are the prototypes and princes of mysticism."[9] These symbolic figures are inscribed in the archival memory of man and mark him as a creature of lack, an active hollow. The aspiration for an imaginary plenitude can predispose the individual to something which, in the language of a still indefinite and imaginary desire, one may call an "absolute" and which can, after having effectuated a demanding transformation, eventually be identified with God.

The oral position in desire comprises both possibilities and dangers. Even though it arouses active impulses, the lack that it gives rise to is marked by a passivity that can also take the form of receptive capacities. Without the oral position, the instincts of mastery, domination, and organization of the world dominate the subject, who in turn becomes driven by the urge to possess. And this in turn abolishes all the potential derived from the capacity of enjoyment and play, capacity whose proper place is the field of culture itself.[10] Without this receptive capacity the subject cannot learn to love, even though his archaic memories and the bidding of language may cause him to wish for it as a sort of utopian felicity; for the other cannot be caught or taken, whereas he can give himself. Likewise, the religious bond, if it is the result of a journey, is reserved for those who are poor enough in their desires to remain open to an offer of union. The oral state of desire exhibits its own pitfalls in specific forms of pathology. The term *avidity* designates a kind of insatiability that devalues anything that offers itself as an object of desire and empties out every promise of pleasure or joy.

We should not seek a causal explanation for this state; it would be impossible to pinpoint one. We must be satisfied with understanding these pathological forms according to the features that emerge through psychotherapy: certain unconscious representations disclosed through dreams and fantasies compulsively and repetitively drive the subject to seek a satiation whose phantasmagoric memory haunts him, but which no object or occasion can fulfill. God is as susceptible as any drugs can be of becoming a substitute object for an orality that seeks desperately to quench itself by means of such substitutions.

The oral position of desire when it is newly born predestines the child's attachment to the first object that presents itself: the mother. Through this first bond the child experiences the qualities that will continue to exemplify what he will want of all other bonds, the expectation of which will actually constitute the form of his tendency to establish other relationships. Because he becomes attached to his mother on the basis of what she offers him, the child develops the capacity of attachment. The desire is born in him to find again the life and the pleasure he once experienced: security, warmth, affection, the narcissistic confirmation he received through the other's acceptance of him, the desire to live that is transmitted to the child through the mother's desiring the life of her child, the stability that results from being able to adhere to another. This initial attachment,[11] insofar as it is the first direction of desire, develops in man the capacity to form bonds as well as the positive presumption that such bonds will provide the satisfaction and pleasure that are sought. But this attachment also entails the risk of a certain inability to tolerate the experience of a reality that opposes the values desired by the infant, values we can call maternal values. Because it seeks security and refuge above all, this form of desire as predominating attachment tends to misapprehend and flee from conflictual relations. It readily abstains from launching into the conquest of an uncertain future and does what it can to avoid facing any threatening loss of love, even at the expense of making painful concessions. I will use the term *clinging* to designate this defensive turning inward of desire onto things that recapture and prolong maternal values.

As one etymology of the word suggests, the one that derives *religion* from *re-ligare*, to establish a link, God represents (among other things) all the desired values entailed in attachment; unless, that is, a neurotic sense of guilt superimposes the figure of a ferocious persecutor upon God. Everything leads us to suppose that interest in religion develops predominantly as a prolongation of attachment, and that God first addresses the subject's desire insofar as he represents the same qualities evoked and proffered by the mother. The predominance of maternal values determines each person's vector of attachment, and consequently also determines religious forms of attachment. Religious desire, like all forms of desire, emerges from this attachment, which actually also constitutes the libido as something deriving from need. Religious desire can also be directed laterally toward a human community peacefully unified under the sign of a divine reality. The properly mystical desire of insistently wanting union with God is driven on the one hand by the call of the religious message and on the other by the pain of separation and the radical lack that characterizes the oral position.

Before we trace the processes that constitute religious desire on the basis of its mediations, it is important—in the psychopathological context—to underline the seeds of danger implicit in desire according to the mode of attachment. The wish to promote understanding and to conciliate the opposition among men feeds a longing for the celestial Jerusalem on earth. This leads to a misapprehension of the conflicting dynamisms that act as the motor of history. The culpabilization of all aggressivity described earlier is probably promoted by this misapprehension. Much of the religious discourse on charity or on absolutely disinterested love betrays an affective intolerance for the intractability inherent in conflicts that make inevitable the opposition between fundamentally different options and interests. When it confronts historical necessity and successive frustrations, the desire for attachment can too easily take on the demanding and suspicious attitudes of depression. Because it concentrates excessively on religion as the appeasement of desire, this form of faith—even as it adheres to the Christian message—voids it of the prophetic inspiration gathered from the paternal wish that God has for men: the construction of a world ruled in truth and justice. Unless the desire that issues from attachment first transforms itself, it can never be suited to the task of recognizing and standing up to the conflict that arises from the confrontation between the message of religion and the reality of the human condition. This danger of the human and religious spirit's becoming narrow does not yet constitute a clear case of pathology; nevertheless, we see the germ here of a growing tendency toward a depressive state or a paranoid position.

Insofar as it is both a radical opening and a bond established on the basis of attachment, desire is shaped and deployed within the context of language into which men are born and which they inhabit.

We should begin by pointing out the link between religious discourse and one of the basic characteristics of language. Language is actually the milieu of a spiritual universality in which man participates by the very fact that he enters into language. As a matter of fact, of itself language establishes the universal reign of the spirit. To speak is, in principle, the power to communicate with all men on the significance of all things. It is quickly apparent how, on the subject of language, desire becomes permeated by the universal virtuality of communication and attachment. To be more precise, man would not be a creature of desire if foundational experiences of his life, those of orality and attachment, did not take place within the opening and the promise that constitute his entry into language. Now, one of the characteristics of religion is that it is a discourse about the world and about man's existence, articulated along a universal and an ultimate dimension. Symbolic rituals as well as various pronouncements on origins, on good and evil, on destiny—all organize existence with reference to the whole of being, by linking everything to the divine being. In this way, religious discourse enables man to tap a power of being that transcends his contingent interests.

Belief is a second characteristic of this mode of language that finds its achievement in religion. The exercise of language as such always implies an adherence to a meaning that goes beyond perception itself. As the space where the meaning hidden by the perceived world can become manifest, language contains within itself the promise of meaning and thus solicits faith in an ultimate revelation. Let us recall Freud's comments on the tie between language and paternity. The recognition of the paternal function entails the act of going beyond sensation, hence entailing a belief; paternity is correlative to one's accession to the reign of language.[12] Moreover, according to Freud, the spiritualization of culture takes place through the biblical promotion of a divine father and, correlatively, through an adherence to the revelation of the divine name, after the abolition of all representative figures.[13] Religion is the domain where the act of language displays and accomplishes to the highest degree its function of belief. Both myths and religious signs render present that dimension of the real that remains most radically withdrawn from immediate experience but that nevertheless asserts itself as more real than anything that appears to the senses. In the biblical religion the attitutde of faith explicitly affirms itself as constitutive of a religious rapport with a paternal God who affirms his radical otherness even as he reveals himself in his declarative word. The two etymological meanings proposed for the word *religion* thus meet and fulfill each other through faith: man is bound to God (*re-ligere*) as he carefully gathers (*re-legere*) the messages through which God communicates.

Language contributes to the formation of desire by instituting man as a subject. The subject is a being who, through his assumption of language, posits himself as the "I" in an act of speech.[14] Everything psychology has stipulated as progressively constitutive of the ego also subtends the self-positing subject who speaks in the first person. However, without this speech act there would be no way of speaking about, or as, an ego who is the subject of desire. As a being centered within himself in singular subjectivity and decentered from himself because he is open to the other, existing simultaneously for himself and propelled toward others as a result of the subjectivity that separates him from them, man is basically a creature of desire, the desire to communicate and desire for union. The religious message addresses this most essential sense of self, this intimate consciousness of self where man recognizes at one and the same time his existence for himself and his participation in a humanity held in common with other subjects whose "I" is both within and beyond any specific function or role imposed upon him or her by sexual difference or social orders. But the "I" addressed in biblical religion, the ego in the first person, affirms itself as a specifically personal interlocutor, for there God declares himself as a subject of enunciation and thereby manifests his paternal acknowledgment of every particular human being as well as of a universal humanity.[15]

We should keep in mind, against the dualism of psyche and reason (an offshoot of the dualism between body and mind), that the psychic apparatus enveloped and inhabited by the power of language is a two-sided phenomenon: instinct oriented by the signifiers of language. The oral position of desire, permeated by the archaic experience of attachment, receives from language the power of symbolization and the power to move and evolve beyond itself. Now on a new and personal level, desire can orient itself toward a bond that meets the subject's aspiring for free recognition, a bond that confirms him in his power to be and has a universal dimension as well. Desire, triggered by the message of religious discourse, can become a religious desire, a desire that hollows out and fills the oracular promise of an infinite transcendence, desire for a union that accomplishes the subject's primary experiences. As one of the mystical poems of Hadewych of Antwerp attests: "For me all things are too narrow; while I have stretched my grasp toward the uncreated." And Plato, the first actually to think out the meaning of desire (*eros*), represents it in the *Symposium* as the product of a god's making love to a mendicant woman; in other words, eros is a median being, a virtually divine being.

Although desire may experience the presence of the divine being in many diverse ways, it always seeks to recapture the quality of infinite being held out by the divine being. The specific danger that threatens the diastolic ego is, according to Szondi's use of Jung's term, that of inflation: an imaginary self-aggrandizement that abolishes all sense of limit and, losing all anchorage in contingent reality, believes everything is possible. In extreme cases, through a narcissistic concentration that rejects all the suffering caused by time and separation, inflation can engender a religious delirium culminating in the act of self-divinization.

Once transformed and broadened by language, oral attachment can also lead to the desire to comprehend the whole of being within a conceptual network, thereby grasping the intimate essence of things.

Thus various means are tried to abolish the lack left by the first lost object. Passion for intellectual dominance can sometimes take the place of a religious attachment which is rather more oriented toward participation as a personal bond with a singular being. The passion for intellectual mastery can also become installed in the very heart of religion, transforming it into a sort of philosophical faith whose main endeavor is to exclude all contingency and reduce all misgivings.

The forms and vicissitudes of the sexual instinct also contribute to the formation and the content of religious desire. How could it be otherwise when the strength of desire and the capacity to love develop inside the family constellation? Love and desire are grafts implanted in the child by his parents as they address their desire to him and as they manifest the desire circulating between and uniting them. And that desire is evidently sexual. Consequently it arouses fantasies that give imaginary shape and sexual identification to pleasure born on the margins of the child's bodily functions and the mode of his attachment. As a witness to the affection and desire that flow between the parents, desire in which he is included as well as excluded, the child progressively becomes a being of a desire transformed by the complex processes of identification and oedipal attachment.

We can only mention a few of these issues, with the aim of better understanding the normal and pathological vicissitudes of religious desire. If sexuality were only an instinct whose form, aim, and object were part of a predetermined biological scenario, it would be absurd to relate it to religious desire. But human sexuality is libidinal; it is marked by the pleasure arising from the bodily functions through the exchange between the subject's demands and the gratifying responses he receives. Thus it contains within itself a premonition of that intersubjective rapport called love. The desire between a man and a woman and that between parent and child are the prototypical forms of love. If man can become capable of loving God, it is because he is a sexual being and has had the experience of sexual love, as a witness to it and as an object and a subject of it. On the basis of this first capacity to desire and to love sexually, desire and love can then develop according to a mode of sublimation. Sublimated libido detaches itself from the sexual function, meanwhile remaining libidinal to the extent that it preserves the essential qualities of sexuality: desire and pleasure in union. As a mode of sublimation love can appear to be a gratuitous gift, an absolutely disinterested love. It appears to me, however, that the opposition between love and desire arises from a false spirituality, one that fails to recognize, because of its own sense of guilt, the ever-presence of desire. There is no love that does not also entail the desire to be loved and the wish to confirm and broaden—through an exchange of gifts—the self as well as the other. I reject the dualistic opposition between eros and agape, between love as desire and love as pure disinterestedness.[16]

Faith in a God who reveals himself to man, in the first person and as the presence of love, must necessarily address and evoke man's desire and love. Desire and love emerge, at their source, as the subject's response to the invocation of the other. In Christianity, too, religious love and desire are implanted in man like a graft. This occurs through the declarative word that comes to man, soliciting him to enter into a new intersubjective relation. Here again, psychology should take the religious message into account if it is to understand the actual human being, who is a psychic being, and one transformed by the signifiers that become inscribed in his psyche. By addressing the actual nature of man's desire and love—in other words, its libidinal nature—religion mobilizes the same representations that the human libido uses and then transforms them. The human figures to which the libido has attached itself and those with which the subject has identified will remain as the symbolic supports of his religious desire. These influence the modalities of the subject's religious desire. They orient its aim and determine its representation of the object. Moreover, because the human figure of Jesus is so central to the Christian faith, it is only natural that religious desire should be all the more permeated with the human figures that have presided at the formation of the libido. There is not only an analogy between religious love and desire and human love and desire; it is the expressive effectuation of human desire that becomes transferred and amplified with relation to God. As St. Teresa of Avila says, there is only one love. The question of eroticization of religious desire is inherent to its constitution. But if there is only one love constantly at work, the term *eroticization* is too ambiguous at this point to mark the moment when pathology begins.

By considering all the elements that constitute religious desire one can understand that its forms are very diverse, even if they are unified by a common tendency to annul a fundamental lack by attaching oneself to a divine being and to find in this bond a confirmation and expansion of one's own being. Love, understood as a relation of the "total-ego," derives from all the psychic vectors that make up the human being and from the work through which the subject maintains an active equilibrium. Consequently love and desire are plurals. Any diagnostic judgment that fails to recognize their peculiarities winds up imposing a psychiatric violence that would have them normalized according to some judgmental code. In order to discern what is or is not pathological one can only rely on one general principle: a religious transfer of desire is to be considered morbid if it cannot support desire or guide it toward a bond that appeases it through the fulfillment of love. It is only natural, then, that in the religious vector the borderline between the normal and the pathological is particularly mobile.

Criteria

By what traits can one recognize that the religious orientation of desire is a free stance, one that liberates, and not the *mise-en-scène* of an unconscious scenario? The task that puts psychology to the test more than any other is that of distinguishing the type of desire that is freely constituted psychologically from that which is held captive by the scenes hidden behind consciousness. If one remains strictly at the level of "subjective impressions," one is struck by the similarity of traits and impressions testified to by those individuals whom religious tradition considers authentically "spiritual," those who induce extraordinary "mystical" experiences by techniques such as trance, and those whom psychiatry considers patently ill, seriously hysterical, or delirious. J. H. Leuba, one of the first to study the phenomenon scientifically, has noted that a group of "impressions" is commonly observed in all these cases: problems of spatial and temporal perception; "photism," or the perception of luminous phenomena; powers of levitation; increased moral and intellectual energy; the sense of an ineffable revelation; and so forth. For Leuba, these impressions, emotions, and sensations proceed from common psychic needs: for example, the need for self-esteem and self-affirmation, the need for moral support and tenderness, or needs that arise from sexual drives. These are "the sources of Christian mysticism," as of all mysticism.[17]

The mystical plunge into the unconscious intensifies to the extreme the impression of "exaltation and the perfection of vitality," which is the end sought by all religions.[18] The difference between mysticism and the erotico-hysterical trance or the drug-induced trance lies in the "interpretation, which transfigures the basic experience of trance and turns it into a religious ecstasy."[19] Leuba concludes that religion "is paralleled in the realm of reason by the development of science. Both lead, if in different ways, to the physical and spiritual realization of man."[20] A strange conclusion indeed. If mystical ecstasy is psychologically void, an unconscious phenomenon in every way comparable to a drug-induced trance or to "neurasthenic and hysterical symptoms,"[21] how can the mere subjective interpretation of such a state—in other words, an external and artificial personification of a strange impression—in accordance with a given set of beliefs constitute a great spiritual realization of man? P. Janet is more consistent in this matter, as I will demonstrate in my later discussion of St. Teresa of Avila.[22] When he compared the subjective drives of patently mystical deliriums to those of venerated mystics he boldly concluded that they share common pathological roots. It is difficult to understand how a doctrinal explanation provided externally and after the fact could possibly authenticate and spiritualize a hysterical loss of consciousness, neurasthenic void, an enthusiastic trance, or a hallucinogenic experience.

The Catholic church has also, in obstinate and frequent opposition to infatuation with marvels, proved to be mistrustful of subjective impressions by refusing to grant special significance to extraordinary phenomena, whether of a physical or a psychological order. In its determination of sanctity it considers only those attestations of "heroic or exemplary virtue" that testify to a life distinguished by its accord with the faith professed. Pope Benedict XIV, who consecrated a vast critical study to the canonization of saints, stated that "those who while in ecstasy speak in the person of Christ or the saints, as if Christ or the saints would avail themselves of their organs, either deceive or are themselves deceived."[23] Because the logic of faith itself remains the actual locus of truth for the church, it bypasses psychological questions and considers only the way in which its followers effectively fashion their lives according to meanings grounded in faith.

Clinical psychology cannot base itself either on the subjective impressions of a subject or on objective criteria completely external to the subject. It does not have to determine the issue of sanctity—unlike the Church, which must do so but hence remains sovereignly independent of any psychological theories of "normality." Nor does psychology have to regulate its clinical judgements according to the variable and precarious philosophical convictions concerning the real or the imaginary, as classical psychiatry from Kraepelin to Janet was apt to do by refashioning the academic schemas of the faculty psychology of the soul and its innate psychological needs. It makes no sense to observe that the mentally ill or the so-called mystics share the impression of being guided by God and that in both cases the psychological faculties of perception and memory have been modified at a certain point, and then conclude from this that it is either the irruption of some obscure and beneficial force (the wild unconscious or a romantic nostalgia) or a morbid alteration of "reason." All these phenomena attest to the fact that the limits of ordinary signification have been exceeded. One may ask, however, whether it is existence itself that is expanded by an expressive act through a refashioning of meanings already available in the field of cultural signifiers, or whether the experience appropriates them only in order to blindly fulfill the wish to recapture a previous satisfaction. It is clear that the only basis for a clinical appraisal is the subject's discourse itself, not as an impressionistic or momentary discourse, but insofar as it testifies to the presence or absence of a labor that elaborates (*durch-arbeitet* in Freud's terminology) those messages proceeding from the unconscious by confronting them with the promises and demands of the signifying referents. Hence, the sources and transmutations of desire surveyed above have important consequences.

The important thing here is not the ecstatic sense of well-being or the sense of awareness suspended in trance, whether it comes from the use of hallucinogens, from a momentary hysterical effervescence, or from orgasm. In themselves, representations of oral plenitude and the subjective experience of attachment do not denote either a morbid regression or any special means of attaining the summit of existence. When listening to a subject's discourse one must take it as the text of his love and desire speaking on its own behalf, to hear both what is and what is not said, to hear the lapses, contradictions, evasions, and erasures. One must also attend to all the signs of the subject's vigilance—whether it is fleeting or sustained—toward whatever romantic illusions or complacent satisfaction he finds in the spectacle he presents to himself and others; attend, too, to whatever presumptions he holds that he is exempt from the universal laws that govern the psychic body, the world, and language. Any discerning grasp of these phenomena must be based on a reading of the dynamic and topological structure of desire insofar as it extends between, on one side, archaic formations, which are anticipations of the future and the origins of adulterated messages, and, on the other, the external signs of that presence with which the subject wants to be united, the signs which prescribe the intrinsic conditions necessary for the advent of the desired presence. In this way it is possible to distinguish if the voices that relate their experiences betray too many discordances or if they change at the same center of enunciation; if they are ventriloquistic voices or the expression of a self that has moved beyond itself to the Other by whom the subject believes himself called forth.

Because of its multiple vectors and vicissitudes, and because of the labor that it implies, the course of desire does not usually allow for any simple opposition between black and white or between glorious success and lamentable failure. More frequently we will attend at an initial or repetitive oscillation, where unconscious messages, struggling between repression and attempts at sublimation, support and overlap each other.[24] From this point of view I will interpret phenomena such as visions, auditory hallucinations, stigmata, and other sorts of altered states, which I believe are always of a psychological nature (but not necessarily pathological). I do not accord them any supernatural honor, but neither should they necessarily be taken as pathological symptoms.

6 • Hysteria: The Moments That Structure Desire and the Repetition of Their Failures

Desire strives to accomplish itself in joy or pleasure, but it is not obliterated by doing so. Religious discourse fundamentally reminds us that joy is an essential part of religious experience, so that worship, for example, becomes a celebration. The feast days that seasonally punctuate a faith recall its mysteries, so-called because these are the events through which the divine dimension of life erupts into the human dimension in order to heighten and expand it. Moreover, Christianity paradoxically declares that the beatitudes are its most fundamental law. Consequently any displacement of the essence of this religion onto any of its other possible features—its ancestral tradition, world-vision, or utopian symbol of a better world—is tantamount to revoking its essential feature.

Unlike love, the enjoyment of pleasure does not necessarily tend to reciprocity. Desire can even become mere pursuit of enjoyment to the complete exclusion of reciprocity. When a subject's aim becomes explicitly fastened on enjoyment, the other is reduced to a useful means of pursuing this interest. Any persistent search of pleasure for its own sake eventually corrupts its own intention. I mentioned earlier that this avid quest for pleasure can be dictated by an ideological superego that holds man to the obligation of achieving happiness *hic et nunc*. In this thirst for enjoyment a prevailing oral position only repeats the archaic fantasies of a pleasure once derived from an immediate sensorial contact.

The idea of a pure enjoyment of pleasure is consequently an abstraction, just as the idea of desire is an abstraction: its specific quality depends on the actual structure given to desire. In saying that desire tends toward the achievement of pleasure and enjoyment I merely state a psychological law; I do not describe an explicit intention on the part of the subject. Any desire that finally becomes transformed into love necessarily has passed through the moments that constituted its structure. Desire mobilizes pleasurable representations and delights in the signs that the other has fashioned. But there is also a moment of reversal in which the other's presence dispossesses desire itself. At this point a certain relation is attained in which the existence and desire of the other give a joy and a fulfillment that are not avidly sought but nevertheless are gathered and received. Thus did Pascal discover one night the hidden meaning of religious enunciations: the divine "I" in the act of enunciating itself. By means of a discourse he had often heard and reflected upon before, a certain presence broke in upon him; then, caught in the grip of an existential relation that dispossessed him of his ability to master through language this gift granted to his desire, he found only one word to express his rejoicing, a cry articulated, "joy."[1]

As an act of desire opaque to itself, the fulfillment of pleasure becomes manifest in joy, and, somewhat more discretely, in the attainment of peace as well. Although the absence of these feelings may augur a deficiency or a perturbation of desire, their presence does not necessarily verify a form of desire that has become capable of divesting itself of its past in order to allow for the gift of presence. Like Freud, we are certain that every feeling is in itself quite real. Nevertheless, feelings can be displaced onto persons that are neither their true cause nor the object of desire. In the preceding chapter on the sense of guilt we took note of this characteristically illusory nature of feelings, but now it is necessary to analyze it specifically with regard to desire. Moreover, because hysteria, the disorder most specific to affect and desire, is often placed in perspective to religious love, it seems appropriate to study the links, confusions, and differences between them. I will develop the idea that hysteria may well be a receptive structure for religious desire precisely because, to the extent that it remains a neurosis, it represents a repeated effort to master the more difficult passages of desire, as well as the residue of its failed attempts.

Hysterical neurosis is the failure and imbalance of the two processes that structure relations between two subjects: idealization and identification. We might, with F. Perrier, call desire that is sustained in a love relationship a "successful hysteria."[2] The ill-repute with which hysteria has been saddled outside psychological milieus testifies to a gross misunderstanding of the vicissitudes of desire. This misunderstanding can be explained by the effect hysteria has on those it implicates in its demands: husbands hurt by the sexual and affective dissatisfaction of their partners; doctors blamed for not being able to heal a body suffering from unsatisfied desires that are speaking through the body; clergy harried by demands to help appease affective suffering or assailed by excessively ostentatious and indiscreet expressions of devotion.

The many and diverse wiles with which hysterics complicate their relationships often provoke a reaction of voluntaristic authoritarianism that imputes hysterical disorders to a sort of moral perversion. Any individual who is constantly importuned by the hysterical demand for love or help, who is wearied by its refusals, displays, and continuously displaced torments, may well be tempted to accuse the hysteric of imposture. But psychoanalysis has shown us that although hysterical behavior may seem to be a fraud (and sometimes actually is), it is the hysteric himself who is caught in the wheels of his ever-recurring desires. These desires, moreover, reappear in remarkably acrobatic forms throughout his troubled and confused history.

The hysterical pathology of desire is more difficult to identify and analyze than is obsessional neurosis. Because it is primarily a defensive strategy, obsession has a more rigid structure, whereas hysteria is less circumscribed and more mobile insofar as it borrows from all the various processes that structure desire while still maintaining a check on its development. One should not expect a complete analysis of these processes here; we must content ourselves with a description of them and their repercussions on religious desire.

Idealization, Repression, and Desire's Refusal to Be Satisfied

Freud defines idealization as "a process that concerns the object; by it, that object, without any alteration in its nature, is aggrandized and exalted in the subject's mind."[3] This last element distinguishes idealization from sublimation. The latter has its source in sexual drives that are transformed and diverted toward a nonsexual and socially valorized aim.

All forms of love exalt the qualities of its object, but the hysteric's deadlock consists of the impossibility of dismantling his dominating need to idealize. The subject suffers with his passion because he aspires to a person, an idea, or a cause in which he must be able to place his absolute belief, one that must be worth his complete commitment and adherence. The strength of belief and commitment that animates hysterical desire might not be recognized if one looked only to the passions that become so embroiled by disappointments and deceptions in hysterical behavior. Although the following discussion necessarily concentrates on demystification I would also like to call attention to the hysteric's search for the signs and tokens to which he can attach himself.

The hysterical woman, for example, dreams of a man without lack or defects, but men always seem to be two-faced, hiding their weakness beneath a mask of arrogance; their humility is no more than a defensive weapon. In any case nothing in the world is so whole or absolute that it can be turned inside out like a glove whose inside lining is identical to its outside. There are many descriptions of the hysteric's seductive attachment to a man who represents power and who is in principle inaccessible to the desire she has for him; the doctor, priest, therapist. This form of attachment partly derives from idealization and thus exhibits its basic nature. Because this type of man holds a position that prevents him from responding to the desire addressed to him, he is outside the hysteric's reach; this conceals any lack that would destroy his ideal status as a man without shortcomings. Here is the paradox implicit in hysterical idealization: it seeks to arouse the other's desire, and yet the will to mastery feeds on the secret hope that the other is devoid of weakness, hence devoid of desire. In other words, the hysteric wants to be desired by someone who cannot manifest desire; hence her frequent curiosity about the possible love-life of someone whose personal life is unknown to her. She wonders constantly about the intimate life of someone on whom she can make no claim, looking out for his private feelings, hoping someday to become the one chosen by him, but fearing from the start that she will be disillusioned if he does yield. The hysteric needs to worship an ideal object whose adoration, in turn would exhalt her but would also disappoint and deceive her, finally becoming unbearable to her. According to Lacan's formulation, the object of a hysterical desire can be qualified as the idealized phallus, *phallus* signifying here a symbolic entity whose obvious sign and actual organ would be the penis. The idealized phallus is the imaginary representation of a being that could confer a complete fulfillment of joy and pleasure, if it were not for the fact that by the act of conferment it would be deprived of the very power the hysteric longs for.

It is clear that for a woman the ideal object would be figured in the father. His very position would enable him to assume this status for a twofold reason: the prestige he holds for the little girl and the interdict that separates them. Circumstantial factors can accentuate Oedipal idealization. For example, when a father is humiliated by his wife, the daughter may, in order to protect her nascent desire, spontaneously love him with a sort of devotion that will, in fantasy, heighten his prestige. On the other hand, the impression that she is being seduced by him can promote a phobic retreat from sexuality and lead to a reactional idealization. But whether or not circumstances reinforce it, the idealization of the object is inscribed in the very formation of desire, and all desire must pass through it in order to achieve any effective relationships and have access to the enjoyment of pleasure. In any case, hysterical idealization does not manage to dismantle itself because it is defensive. Having contributed to the repression of an incestuous desire, hysterical idealization preserves the ambiguous nature of neurotic symptoms whose function is to maintain the first attachment—and its prohibition—but to maintain them suppressed through repression. The expulsion of sexuality becomes understandable. Aside from the horror evoked by the vaginal wound, an unconscious memory of incestuous representations also orients the subject toward a platonic tenderness, which in turn feeds the process of idealization.

We should also mention the narcissistic process of turning in upon itself that corresponds to idealization. The exaltation of the other for whom the subject uselessly longs also heightens his own self-esteem as a desirous being and as an object of a privileged election. This imaginary self-aggrandizement shares something in common with delusions of grandeur that, in the case of neurotics, stay in the background and are staged in fantasies scarcely perceptible to the subject himself. They are disclosed by the touch of fabulist mythomania or the subject's desire to set himself apart, by the compulsive refusal to submit oneself to everyday tasks, by defensive lying—all forms of behavior that are not explicitly conscious to the subject.

This analysis, though based on feminine hysteria that is by its very nature clearer, is mutatis mutandis equally valid for male hysteria. The idealization of the desired woman leads to an exaltation of the virgin or noble woman, who becomes the object of a platonic love or an impossible passion like that echoed in the cult of courtly love.

This hysterical idealization condemns desire to perpetual dissatisfaction. Desire can be experienced only as the desire of desire, desire as a yawning lack. Hysterical desire is of the same order as an amorous passion, except that it is a passion that destroys its own real future.

The process of idealization consists of a passion for the absolute, which predestines hysterical desire toward religious love whenever the given cultural context invites it. Various historians have noted that in the Middle Ages several poets of courtly love turned to monastic life,[4] transforming their cult of desire into a mysticism of desirous love.[5]

As we have seen, a passion for the absolute is a sign of the oral position, whose important link to hysteria has always been stressed by clinical observations. The oral position can become translated into symptoms of bulimia alternating with anorexia; basically, it is the avid search for the mythical object of attachment that would abolish any interior sense of emptiness. Hysterical ambivalence, however, is not between love and hate as in obsession; it is rather an oscillation between an avid attachment and a disillusioned, indifferent detachment, between absorption and rejection, between hot and cold, fullness and emptiness.

On considering the elements at work in hysteria one may recall the poem by Hadewych quoted earlier: "All things are too narrow for me; toward an uncreated have I extended my reach...." But the choice of a religious life taken by such a desire cannot confer peace unless it undertakes to work through the narcissistic idealization from which it originates and which it enlarges. The main obstacle in working through one's idealization is the insistent demand of unconscious incestuous representations kept active but out of the range of consciousness by repression. As we have seen, idealization both derives from and acts as a defense against these desires. Idealizing the object of desire distances it infinitely from sexuality and hence eliminates any recollection of a forbidden incestuous relationship.

My development of these ideas may seem rash or arbitrary. The links established here between desire, orality and clinging attachment, hysteria, incestuous representations, and religious desire may seem all the more uncertain in that we are used to separating religious aims from their obscure germination in the psyche's substratum. An unbiased and clinical attention, however, dictates "theories" that may seem fantastic to those who have not tested them in their own experience. I can offer one example that, although it may not settle the issue for those who find it too marginal, may at least give content to theoretical concepts that are difficult to think through without concrete terms.

This case concerns a gifted young woman who became quite successful professionally after having completed her studies brilliantly. In the course of an analysis that she undertook because of intermittent depressions and spells of anxiety, she slowly discovered, in bits and pieces and each time to her surprise and initial incredulity, that during puberty and adolescence she had fantasized having erotic relations with God and Christ. First she remembered that as a child, in bed, she used to imagine Christ invisible at her side, placing his hand on her breast, an image that gave her a feeling of intense warmth. Young children frequently have such "visions" at an age when the child cannot understand how or why real living people can absent themselves and not answer him when he calls; hence the child may "hallucinate" in his own fashion that he sees and hears them when they are absent. In this particular case, the patient's impression of physical contact already implies a religious and idealized transposition of her father's caresses. In the shadows of her fleeting adolescent imaginings, Christ appears to her in the flesh and runs his hand through her hair. A number of memories that she recalled with considerable difficulty and reconstituted against her will and with great reticence subsequently revealed their explicit erotico-religious content: she imagined herself sucking on Christ's penis. She also had fantasies about being lovingly chosen by God, being impregnated by him, and becoming the destined mother of Christ. At this point she remembered feeling hostility toward the Virgin Mary, a feeling she had never understood and had since forgotten, but she had the clear impression that it was a feeling of jealousy. This affective memory, whose content now became clear, then made her feel the weight of a real memory linked to this reevocation of fantasies concerning her sexual intercourse with God and Christ (it may be noted that we have here one of the laws of therapy: remembrance is effective only if the experience that reemerges in the course of treatment brings to the fore feelings that are linked to repressed representation). A multiplicity of associations intervened and revived the memory of her adolescent fantasies. Subsequently she worked through her sense of a vaginal wound, her distaste for sex, and her displacement of this aversion onto substances that became objects of a phobia that triggered in her a mania for washing. During this time, and with increasing evidence, memories of incestuous representation concerning her father forced themselves upon her. These, however, were not as straightforwardly figured as her erotico-religious imaginings, and even these were figured only while she was in a dreamlike state so fascinating to her conscious mind that she was rather more absent than present to herself.

It is undeniable that in this case the patient's religious representations were to a significant degree nourished on incestuous representations and that these provided the terrain for displacement and for a defensive and narcissistically gratifying idealization. At the time this person undertook therapy, there were no longer any conscious traces of her previous religious eroticism. In her relations, however, as well as in her experience of faith she often suffered doubts that paralyzed her and that were the obvious reverse of her exasperated demand for signs of love and appreciation. These in turn revealed a problematic that was continuously being replayed in another scene, that of the unconscious. Nothing here authorizes our supposing that a durable religious love is simply the transposition of an Oedipal complex that has not been worked through, no more than this could account for a professional interest or human love. All the registers of this woman's life indicated nonetheless the existence of a desire too close to repressed representations, one that consequently kept all representations of sexual desire at too great a distance for them to be openly accepted or to serve as a symbolic support for a sublimation that might bring her peace.

In masculine hysteria, one finds the same set of associations between religious desire and the idealization of woman in an unconscious attempt to overcome a repressed incestuous bond. Take, for example, the case of a man who saw a beautiful girl by a lake—an apparition of a pure and perfect beauty in contrast to which he could only represent sexuality as something gross and brutish, like the image of his father, whom he perceived as a heavy and opaque man. His aversion for his father contrasted with his admiration for his mother, with his rather exalted feeling for the beauties of nature, and with a religious faith that motivated a real devotion on his part. Here the work of sublimation was clearly in progress; this generated a personal investment in cultural values that found their support in a religious desire that in turn was reciprocally nourished by the sublimation. But the difficulty of his relations with women—relations the consultant deemed truly neurotic—demonstrated the defensive function of a sublimation marked by an exaggerated sense of the sublime and the pure, too obviously opposed to the density of the flesh. The opposition between his openly expressed scorn for sexuality and a luminous world of the purest love had the following result: once he consented to a sexuality experienced as virile but brutally transgressive, he also abandoned all religious practice. Does this consent to his own sexuality constitute a lifting of the repression? Was his previous religiosity a false one, then? Neither one nor the other. Abettors to their opposition—the opposition between idealization and the imaginary world of autoeroticism—his faith and his sexuality were still caught up in something that enmeshed them from beneath, as it were.

I mentioned above the importance of idealization for obsessional neurosis, but its function is different in the two forms of illness. In the case of obsession it enhances, on an imaginary level, the ego ideal to which the subject wishes to conform; it thereby invests the personage whose authority he has interiorized with a powerful and frightening exigency. Obsessional idealization thus contributes to the setting-up of a fiercely exigent and judgmental superego. In the hysterical type of neurosis it is the object of the libido that is transformed by idealization. The opacity of sexuality arouses aversion, and only one emotion becomes possible: the lyricism of a transfigured body. Every object of desire is deficient. Therefore one must posit a transcendent object in order to authenticate and confer the desiring self with a unique dignity.

The fact that idealization can be inscribed in the psychic apparatus in these two different ways does not preclude the existence of obsessional defensive mechanisms in hysteria. Nothing human is foreign to any individual. All these neurotic processes are at work in everyone. One should not be surprised to find defenses of an obsessional character in hysterical neurosis, or vice versa, for to do so would be to suppose that a particular diagnosis can encompass the whole meaning of the subject's existence, whereas a diagnosis actually comprises a limited number of specific prevailing forms of activity that repeat the same impasses and contradictions.

Affectivity and Autoaffection

Certain forms of behavior whose features classically have been considered hysterical suggest that there is an intimate link between affectivity and identification. It is said, for example, that hysterics are markedly theatrical. They give the impression of playing a part, and their emotive expressions often seem exaggerated. Any especially volatile affectivity will oscillate between extremes: anything that happens takes on such excessive proportions that those around suspect that the hysteric's personality lacks interiority, that he lives life on the surface and can truly experience it only if everything is dramatized. The hysteric's suggestibility also shows a certain plasticity in the way he will quickly adopt and change models whose gestures, bearing, expressions, and intonations he will copy and whose affective inclinations and passions he will appropriate. It is this sort of symptomatic behavior that frequently causes the hysteric to be rejected by his environment, and all the more so when such behavior is accompanied, as it frequently is, by an imperious aggressivity and a tendency constantly to denounce other people's shortcomings.

Here again, we must move beyond what is immediately visible in order to gain access to something that both disguises itself and reveals itself in this type of behavior, something that, according to those characteristics already mentioned, lies at the very juncture of affectivity and identification. Because these two elements comprise man's basic center of gravity and the path of his desire, it is on this basis that we must try to understand hysteria as the partial failure of something universally human.

Let us consider affectivity. In itself it consists of a whole register of elements that different forms of language will render somewhat differently: feelings, emotions, passions, affects. The links and distinctions that have been elaborated regarding this issue do not much matter for our purposes. It is essential, though, to recognize that affectivity is an attribute of consciousness, that it always connotes pleasure or pain, that it anticipates an action, and that its relationship to representations varies.

Affectivity, whether it is a feeling or a more intense emotion, is a form of sensitivity, the capacity to experience subjectively something that affects one—danger, beauty, erogenous forms, an unsolicited gift, rejection, or esteem. The messages that thus affect man from the external world awaken both conscious and unconscious affective memories that have been deeply inscribed into the psyche. In this way affectivity is also a form of knowing. But affective consciousness always exceeds the power it has to represent to itself the meanings that have been sensibly apprehended, especially if the messages received affect one intensely. For this reason, the real world on which man exercises his assured hold becomes to some degree de-realized through affective experience.[6] Consequently, some measure of disorder is always produced[7] whenever a disconcerting anticipation disturbs the mastery or insensibility that are sought. But we should remember our Euripides: man learns by what he suffers, by what affects him.

However wide the range of feelings, they all have the generic characteristic of pleasure or pain, which can become paradoxically mixed up—without thereby necessarily signaling masochism. This generic character tells us that affectivity has its source in the drives whose aim is to achieve pleasure by modifying the tension created by the drives themselves. Therefore affectivity is also inextricable from the passions, for it is through the passions that the drives are deployed. Being more than instincts, these drives flow into psychic formations shaped and dismantled by events and encounters.

From this sketch of a psychology of affect we see that it is essential to a life of desire. A secret presence that the dominion of thought cannot encompass makes itself felt in affect. Whether in joy or terror, love or hate, guilt or peace, affectivity opens up a trajectory to something other, another locus, a future in which the subject will find himself, as it were, outside of himself, but which radically addresses his singularity. Feeling has the twofold quality of being subjective and, because it affects man, of also causing the other to appear. Because it proceeds from elsewhere, affect always catches us off guard. But this "elsewhere" is also twofold: it is in the messages sent by the outside world and in those rising up from the depths of instincts and our archival memory. These two messages converge, and in that convergence lies the ambiguity intrinsic to affectivity, the possibility of its affectation and its latent illusions.

As a pathology of affect, hysteria is characterized by the predominance of affective memories over the advent of the other into the subject's life, and it is in this context that the phrase "religious illusion" takes on its full meaning. Freud turned psychiatry upside down when, without quite knowing where his discoveries might lead him, he understood that the hysteric's affective expressions are linked to an unknown personage—one originating in his personal history but buried in his unconscious memories. "Attacks of giddiness and fits of weeping—all these are aimed at another person—but mostly at the prehistoric, unforgettable other person who is never equalled by any later one."[8] Although lost in the shadows of time, this first other who presides at the birth of feelings still reigns over and precipitates them, relegating the one to whom his present feelings are eventually destined to the role of provisional support. Thus it can happen that the God to whom these feelings are addressed becomes a representative figure for this prehistoric other. Inasmuch as they are always experienced, feelings can always be said to be true; nevertheless, they can be illusory as to their cause and their object. However, to suspect them as a matter of principle on the basis of their latent and inherent ambiguity is to destroy the cultural space they open up and, consequently, to reduce man strictly to the dimensions of having and knowing. Finally, the problem of sublimation is raised by the question of the veracity of feelings. How is it that man, through his prehistoric experiences and the archaic figures of his desire, becomes part of something that lies beyond him? And what signs can tell us that a real transformation and exchange have taken place?

If we wish to answer this question while maintaining a psychological point of view, we must consider the presence or absence of neurotic symptoms as the decisive factor, for these are the evident signs of what the neurotic has paid for a failed attempt. I have said that affectivity catches us off guard because it is an excess of meaning, but what particularly marks hysteria is the fact that this excess cannot spend itself through the expressive power of the signs available to it. Affectivity then turns, knotted, into itself, precipitating itself upon the body in a sort of reflexive autoaffection of its own sentient, instinctual being. Once its access to a presence generally mediated by perceptible signs is cut off, affect, not finding a means of expression that might respond to the signs addressed to it, then becomes muted, using the body as the vehicle for its speech,[9] such as the trembling, convulsions, and spasms of uncontrollable weeping or laughter. This body language expresses, unbeknownst to the subject, something he himself cannot express. Although it seeks representations that will orient the subject to move outside of himself, his affectivity cannot become invested in them because these representations evoke forbidden desires and painful memories. "In hysteria, the incompatible idea is rendered innocuous by its sum of excitation being transformed into something somatic. For this I should like to propose the name of conversion."[10] In the domain of religion we can interpret the celebrated phenomenon of religious stigmata (whose hysterical character has frequently been noted) as an example of affect speaking through the body. Although I will come back to this issue later, I would note here that there is nevertheless a problematic difference between hysteria and stigmatization: far from seeing their condition as the muted incarnation of an occult memory living symptomatically in their bodies, those who have received stigmata have consciously assumed the affective significance of wounds they experience as symbolic wounds.

The autoaffection of affectivity is analogous to the precipitation of affect speaking through the body. The volatility and avidity of the hysteric's affectivity have always struck clinicians as being characteristic of hysteria. It is a subtle property to appreciate correctly, and only by placing it within the context of the individual's subjective life is it possible to decide whether affect, self-inflated, has closed in upon itself. We might take the following observation by André Green and apply it to hysteria: "Affect is an object of hypnotic fascination for the ego. In psychoanalysis the spell cast by affect maintains the ego in a position of dependence with regard to its narcissism. Any act of conscious recognition is barred by a conscious affect that cannot be questioned as such."[11] The dramatization of the smallest adversity and the exaltation of pleasures and joys are signs of this turning of affect in upon a sentient ego so captivated by its own sentiment that it dissipates and dissolves into its fleeting variations. Thus one will observe those exalted religious conversions whose sudden fevers metamorphosize the subject, buoyantly lifting him above all the weight of his past. But the tricks life plays soon reveal that affectivity was so strong it could allow for only a magical leap over the obstacles encountered. An affectivity that feeds largely upon itself deepens its own void. The presence of the other for which it strives is plunged into indifference. The signs the other produces do not open out onto what they signify: instead of leading to an Other that is yet to be discovered, they are taken as incitations to an emotion closed into itself by self-fascination. Religious fervor slips into depression, thus fulfilling a hyperbolic figure pursued by any number of the diurnal or nocturnal dreams and fantasies that the subject, raised by some secret magical power, flies off with, only to fall back into a void of anguish.

This captivation of affect by its own presence to itself makes one think of narcissism. It is, as a matter of fact, an indefinite idea one has of oneself that gives affectivity the particular representation of itself that it wants to appropriate. Here again, one must keep in mind the idea, so necessary to psychology, of reciprocal causality. On the one hand, the obscure existence of an aggrandized image of the ego, an image situated at the limits of consciousness and unapprehended by the subject himself, moreover an ego that finds its own source of pleasure in itself, attracts sentiment to itself, pushing the subject toward increasing autoaffectivity. On the other hand, feeling, because of its instinctual origin, always has the power to amplify its sense of pleasure, and this also augments its narcissistic quality. In the final analysis, it is the narcissistic fixation that maintains emotion as a captive of itself. Further observation will show that the exaltations of affect, even those of a mystical cast, conceal a hidden world where are deployed the memories and fantasies in which the subject has become absorbed, paradoxically, without being much aware of being so. The content of such fantasies consists precisely of representations of distinguished actions or brilliant missions or privileged election. Psychoanalysis recognizes in these fantasies the offshoots of an archaic experience in which the child, *his majesty the baby*,[12] on finding himself the center of loving admiration, responds by taking the imaginary posture of sole desirable object, the all-powerful idol dazzling his round of worshipers.

But this account must be further developed if we are to understand hysteria in its religious configurations. Affectivity, although not reducible to sexuality, has its source in the libido. However, precisely because of the repression of certain representations and sexual desire—a repression that simultaneously holds these too near to actual feelings and too far from consciousness—affectivity then folds narcissistically upon itself, thereby serving as a fortification against sexual excitations and providing them with a substitute. This accounts for the oblique impression of the eroticization of feeling given by the dramatization of affect in hysteria. This perspective allows us to understand the disturbing and evanescent character of certain types of mysticism in adolescents—not that we should judge these forms as pathological or even as devoid of meaning.[13] It is simply that these mystical phases receive their charge from an ambiguous experience in which a defensive function has been linked to an anticipation for a possible transformation of the subject. Only those states hovering indecisively between two functions should be considered pathological, and this becomes evident in the demands of the affective dissatisfaction that may dominate a religious life chosen in a moment of ambiguous fervor. Adolescent mysticism feeds on both the awakening of sexual interest and the narcissism it produces; religious meaning then endows it with a cosmic dimension, the promise of a beatific expansion of existence on a scale as large as the universe, thereby helping the subject to overcome the incestuous bonds revived in the unconscious. A tone of voluptuous satiety indicates that this mysticism is at the edge of eroticism; the subject's captivation with himself becomes clearly apparent in this oneiric flux.

As the preceding analysis has shown, idealization adds an element of fascination to these experiences. If they then evolve toward hysteria, a fantastic eroticism remains active behind the mystical stance, and this prevents words and representations from becoming progressively filled by the very presence they actually anticipate.[14] Once it is stimulated by the erogenous power it imparts to the domain of religion onto which it has been displaced, the subject's sexuality remains unavowed and marginal to his existence, condemning him to a refusal of all pleasure. The sense of existence as a sterile lack can thus deepen in three ways: by distancing God far from the subject; by regressively clinging to a lost past; and by the tacit appeal that his sexual desire addresses to an other the subject mistakes for someone else. The hasty denunciation of the joys and pleasures of mysticism as hysterical manifestations does not testify to a very deep understanding of psychology. In light of this analysis we may even presume that this form of enjoyment and fulfillment is a victory over hysteria, or at least that it is, like all truly affective love, a "successful hysteria."

The Hazards of Identification

Affect is also shaped and transformed by the process of identification. In the reflexive sense of the word, to identify oneself with, identification is the process through which the subject assimilates the traits and properties of another: a gesture, an intonation of voice, an affective reaction, a somatic ailment, or, on a more fundamental level, a way of relating to others. Although it is analogous to imitation, identification is a more complex involuntary, even unconscious process, and it also contributes an essential element to the constitution of the personality, whether neurotic or not. It is exactly because identification is such an essential process in the formation of the differentiated personality that it becomes both a deficient formation and a defensive mechanism in the structure of neurosis, especially of hysterical neurosis. Identification is always the installation, in the ego, of a specific relationship of desire between two subjects, as the subject himself perceives it. Thus the Oedipus complex is the assimilation into the psyche of the sexually differentiated position that the child perceives in the desire that binds his parents. As a witness to the scene of their desire, in passing through the positive form of the Oedipal complex, the child assumes his differentiated sexual identity by appropriating into himself the specific rapport of love or being loved that the parent of the same sex represents to him. Identification, then, is a transformation that initially shapes the personality, thus defined by its way of relating to the world and to others.

It is important to understand how, from a structural perspective, hysteria can become a pathological form of desire as a consequence of some failure in the process of identification. It can be seen from clinical observation that this failure—a partial failure, of course—can be pinpointed to three general moments that overlap with and mutually reinforce one another. In therapy hysterics frequently say that they are always conscious of playing a role and cannot prevent themselves from taking on the gestures or intonations they presume others expect of them. They suffer from the feeling that they are always on stage, but they cannot do otherwise. Often they feel as if they were inhabited by a variety of latent psychic individuals, which actors are summoned at the will and pleasure of other spectators; yet the hysteric himself does not know who is really at the bottom of this impressionistic explosion. Other people are in any case convoked by the hysteric, so that he or she can detect in their gaze the very thing the hysteric then displays before them. For the hysteric others perform the service of a mirror, as if the mirror had been pierced through by the eyes of the other. This specular rapport through which the hysteric finds an instant personality in the doubling effect of the mirror-image he himself has produced reminds us of the intense fixation to "the mirror stage" that Lacan has described.[15] Leaving aside the subject's assumption of his body as a unified Gestalt, which occurs during this stage, I would rather stress the pleasure the child takes in seducing his mother's or father's desires by gestures and mimicry: this is one of the characteristic moments that shape the hysteric's rapport with the world. The pleasure taken by the child here, a normal and necessary pleasure, can become engraved in him as a fascinating, captivating memory if his seduction seizes hold of one parent whose desire for the other parent is shattered.

Because it prolongs and reshapes a specular identification to the image of oneself exhibited before the seduced gaze of the spectator, the Oedipal identification also produces an oscillation—characteristic of hysteria—between the images of man and woman. Whatever the contingent causes, hysteria maintains a twofold identification with both parents; this produces a certain psychological bisexuality. This also serves as a good defense against the basic lack that any assumption of a differentiated sexuality might entail. Moreover, it confirms a somewhat megalomaniacal representation that one is able to be everything. The ensuing gratification will maintain the oscillation between two forms of desire, the masculine and the feminine. Not being deeply identified with either sex, the hysteric may reproduce this unaccomplished identification on an imaginary level. This accounts for the tendency to accentuate feminine seductiveness or else to assume virile attitudes, effacing feminine traits.

The hysteric's life is also shadowed by fantasies of rejection. This fantasy adds its own motivation to the penchant for staging seductive scenes and the tendency to hesitate with regard to what place to occupy in relations of desire. Without always being aware of it, the hysteric feels excluded from love. The insidious fear of not being desirable, of not deserving love, of being incapable of loving, insinuates itself into his relations of desire. The foregoing analysis of the first two moments of identification obviously justifies this fear, but it does not reveal its deeper causes. This fear is a signal to the conscious mind of a real distortion, but the situation of exclusion established by the Oedipus complex seems to be the deeper source of this fantasy. An image that forced itself on one hysteric's imagination clearly translated her sense of exclusion, experienced as a rejection, into geometric figures: she saw two circles that overlapped at points but could not be superimposed on one another. The tension between the two circles aroused discomfort, even anxiety, in her. These figures appeared to encircle an area of affective communion, one with the child and one parent, the other with the child and the other parent, or both parents. Neither of the two circles opened up to make room for the third person, who remained present as an intruder, a pole of attraction that decentered the whole space of desire and prevented it from closing itself off in dualistic harmony. Whatever place the third wished to take in this complex field of three polarities, it never embraced a singular vector that closed in upon itself. The family circle makes the circular desire explode. This is what the hysteric experienced with such particular intensity that she continued to feel rejected, remaining always outside the two circles that structured the phantasmic base of her desire.

The most apparent hysterical symptoms, those of the unconscious speaking through the body, always express these different moments in the process of identification that we have just analyzed. A somatic conversion, therefore, is a sign that condenses a variety of themes inscribed in it. A symbolic symptom can become localized in the painful experience of some part of the body—whenever the traumatized body can form a collusion with psychic wounds. The evicted sexuality that also renders the body painfully erogenous will then find a refuge in such symptoms, expressing themselves by a negative means (one that symbolizes the refusal of sexuality, such as vomiting, coughing, paralysis). Such symptoms can also result from a spontaneous identification with someone else's trauma. The subject takes the other's place in the affective relation he has with a third party, like the well-known cases where groups of children imitate, by a spontaneous autosuggestion, a handicap suffered by one of them, a handicap that seems to confer some special affective privilege.

All these elements that constitute hysterical identification as a more or less deformed formation of affect will undoubtedly shed some light on religious phenomena. The dramatization of affect will find reinforcement in these if the cultural milieu valorizes, by the models it chooses to privilege, the hardships of mystical desire. In the Renaissance, for example, we have the great epoch of affective mysticism, when religious people exhibited their feelings with such ostentation that even St. Teresa of Avila was repelled by it. There is no doubt that an ostentatious religiosity, if it is consciously motivated by the wish to imitate specific models, will unconsciously revive both the subject's archaic specular captivation by an admiring gaze and the game of seduction played out with a mirror image in which even the subject himself is alienated.

The fantasy of rejection will favor certain forms of religious outburst that reproduce that tension equally distributed between the two circles of adherence mentioned above. Let us take the example of a woman who has remained an atheist since puberty. At seven or eight she sought consolation for an indefinable sense of rejection in the assurance of having an affectionate bond with God. Being a child of lively intelligence, she realized at puberty the exclusive nature of this bond and found herself facing the following dilemma: either her affective bond with God was intimate, excluding the presence of others, in which case it seemed illusory, with no guarantee of objectivity; or else it included others, but then it lost its affective value, in which case she is once again excluded from a love relationship that does not include her. Her critical rationalism helped her to settle this insoluble problem. Her first feelings of love, which were particularly intense ones, later constituted an affective circle that deliberately excluded any religious bond as being incompatible. If the religious bond had been pursued with the same exclusive quality, would it have been an illusory religious commitment, and if so, in what way? On the basis of religious messages, this sort of tête-à-tête where desire and egocentrism are confused in one another might be considered as a certain recognition of divine love. It would nevertheless have implied a certain error in her relations to others since the idea of God essentially includes others in his love. The absence of a horizontal rapport to others (as opposed to the exclusive vertical one with the divine) leads us to suppose that God has been summoned up in order to close up some archaic affective rupture caused by the intrusion of a third person into a desire that sought to close itself off. Experience teaches us that sooner or later the fantasy of rejection becomes transferred onto God: then, profiting from the exhaustion of an affective effervescence, it plunges the subject into constant doubts concerning himself and the Other, sometimes even evoking the specter of an almost demonic God of arbitrary malevolence. The dramatic twists of religious desire are in every way similar to those of human love. The two must go through the trials and tests set by man's primordial attachments. The inability to accomplish this labor attests to the fact that because of particularly intense fixations, the hysterical structure can become frozen into a neurosis. What particularly characterizes neurosis is the repetition of failures that consequently revive old trauma, giving them the mythical quality of being a fatalistic destiny.

7 • Illustration by Some Variants

**The Mystical Enjoyment of Teresa of Avila:
Displaced Eroticism or Sublimated Libido?**

It is not my aim to write a psychology of the mystics.
Nevertheless, the often paradoxical nature of their fortunes and misfortunes demands closer attention. Their story seems so
extravagant, they manage so fully to reinvest a sense of joy and pleasure
into the realities of an existence reduced to essentials, and their discourse
makes such an original irruption into the habitual modes of religious
discourse that although they become objects of suspicion for some people, they are exalted by others. Any science given to establishing its
dominion over experience invariably attempts to repress them. For Janet,
for example, there was no doubt that "thought processes during ecstasies
were inferior, regressive ways of thinking, analogous to that of children
and savages."[1] The group of pathological characteristics he studied during his observation of Madeleine Le Bouc, characteristics that he was
convinced could be found "in many disturbances common to mysticism,"
constituted "a syndrome sufficiently characteristic to be given a place in
psychiatric descriptions."[2] The syndrome is that of the "mystical delirium." Dr. Lemesle, who seems particularly skittish on the issue of mystical
pleasures, believes that mystical ecstasy proceeds primarily from an autoerotic inversion of sexuality, close to perversion[3]—a piously camouflaged
masturbatory orgasm, in other words.

153

I will not proceed to an epistemological study of the intuitive forms of knowing operative in mystical states.[4] The central elements in mystical phenomena seem to be that they constitute God as an object of desire and that they mobilize an entire apparatus to liberate this desire, to formulate it in authentic terms, to accomplish its fulfillment in love, and to perfect the quality of joy experienced through this love. One cannot, a priori, raise any doubts regarding such an enterprise, even if one is a nonbeliever or even if one is somewhat Victorian. Why couldn't God penetrate all of existence with his light, like any other desirable being? Not all mystical forms of love or desire, however, are the *amor intellectualis* Spinoza described. Ever since St. Bernard's commentaries on the *Song of Songs*, Western Christendom has developed the affective mysticism that has triggered those strange phenomena apparently related to hysteria, madness, or perversion.

Teresa of Avila (1515–82), for example, proclaims the joys and pleasures of mysticism with unrestrained freedom.

> The soul is suspended in such a way that it seems to be completely outside itself. The will loves; the memory, I think, is almost lost; while the understanding, I believe, though it is not lost, does not reason.... In this state the faculties enjoy without understanding how they enjoy. The soul is more and more inflamed with love without understanding how it loves. It knows that it enjoys the object of its love; but it does not know how it enjoys it.[5]

Like many other texts, this one describes with considerable acuity the experience of intense love, a state of consciousness without self-consciousness, and the experience of a joy that, by self-abandonment, takes pleasure in the other without turning reflexively onto itself. True, the experience itself is articulated only in a moment's reflection, but the clarity and soundness of this condensed analysis at least attest to the fact that the experience is not the product of an "inferior thought process" or a "regressive way of thinking." The "feeling of presence" that Janet describes can certainly be found in clearly pathological cases, but this "feeling of presence" is a rather crude psychological category that tends to erase any significantly distinctive traits. What counts here is the experience of presence as a conscious relation inscribed in the trajectory between desire and love. To judge the experience of a highly articulated love according to the epistemological norms of theoretic knowledge is truly to practice a governmental form of psychiatry.

If we adhere to a clinical point of view we have only to ask ourselves if St. Teresa's experience bears the mark of hysteria—the question of a "mystical delirium" being absurd to anyone who is even slightly acquainted with her writings and with her life, both contemplative and active. After our analysis of hysteria the question would appear, indeed, to be paradoxical. By idealizing the object of desire the hysteric waits for—in fact, tends toward—its presence. However, any effective confrontation would abolish the distance that sustains the desire. For reasons other than those of obsessives, hysterics also postpone the very union that might confer peace upon them and satisfy them with the joy for which they yearn. Hysterics are consequently attentive to the slightest beat of their own desire and constantly tend toward an always imminent but ever suspended union. Instead of telling of the joys of union with the loved object, those hysterics who are conscious of the forces that motivate them might say, with P. Valéry's Eupalinos: "I desire with all my being. . . . Far from receiving those mysterious and abundant favors such as are solely drawn from the great desire, formed, naively, at the extreme point of my soul's longing, oh Phaedrus, I must arrest their movement and let them await my signal."[6]

Is it possible that in relation to God the hysteric maintains an idealizing and open desire that shuts out sexuality but is then addressed to an ideally conceived divine presence and thus surrenders itself to a welcoming love and enjoys the satisfaction of an authentic exchange with the other? In the eyes of anyone who knows and takes seriously the logic of psychological processes, this interpretation of the resolution of hysterical conflicts must seem like a veritable short circuit. One can better gauge the distance between the mystical experience and a hysterical exaltation by listening more carefully to the latter's amorous confessions, whether of human or divine love. In the imagination of hysterics, they deck themselves out in the signs and traits of the overestimated other; always placing themselves in the other's point of view, they try by this narcissistic identification to discover what they themselves are as men or women, thus unconsciously questioning their own identity and trying to find it in the adoration received from the one they adore. Even their choice of a love object serves as a support for the construction of their own myths. It is a myth, however, that they cannot take quite seriously, and so they keep it in the background like a dreamy mystery kept in reserve in order to give special value to their existence. This myth, moreover, can probably be traced back to some lovely role taken from a novel or a movie. Generally, they are careful to protect it from being put to the test in the reality of their everyday life. And if one approaches it, or if it is ever candidly spoken about, one cannot help but be struck by the ill-developed or inane level of its content. For example, one need but compare the texts and drawings of Madeleine, the subject of Janet's study, with Teresa of Avila's spiritual epic to be edified by the difference.

A study of Teresa of Avila's autobiography gives the reader ample occasion to speculate on the snares, twists, and struggles of hysteria, but it also shows the strength of the desire that animates it as well as the labor required for its resolution. Those who mistrust her mysticism will point to the undeniably hysterical manifestations that mark her adolescence: her febrile exaltations, alternating with fits of serious depression, and her moments of loss of consciousness are signs of veritable hysterical crises. A seductive and sensual girl, dreaming of glory and nourished by the courtly literature of the times, burdened by not being a man, too proud to submit to marriage, and yet herself surprised that she could find humiliation a source of intoxication, Teresa had all the requisites for becoming a fine hysteric or a great lover. It is natural, then, insofar as the archaic past anticipates a future, that this mystical passion should emerge from the troubled conditions that first gave birth to it. It is basically a matter of knowing how the future takes up the past and transforms it. Neurosis, of course, cannot occur independently of a desire that seeks to fulfill itself, but the desire that does fulfill itself is different from the formations that define a neurosis.

Now, Teresa of Avila's extraordinary self-analysis makes her work a treatise on demystification such that it could well serve as an inspiration to psychoanalysis. With the constant care she takes to distinguish what is true from what is imaginary she manages to practice a progressive stripping of her own psyche. She pursues this project by moving between two poles that serve as her reference points and clarify each other. Her essential base of reference is her faith, understood as the injunction to believe. She is struck by the religious discourse that surrounds her, and she knows there is an entire universe she longs for and the subject of which she wants to be united with. Hearing and believing are quite different matters, she notes.[7] Illuminations of a diffused affective quality are only premonitory, but belief is an act that implicates her being, not a sort of surprise that robs her of her own self.

Her second base of reference is the anthropological concepts of St. Augustine and St. John of the Cross. These serve as an objective guide for a lucid critique of the mystifications that surround her intentions, attitudes, and emotional experiences. In this way she guards against her tendency to take her raptures and sufferings, either physical or moral, as signs of a divine election. She thus accepts the silence of affect or void of the imagination as effects of the distance that separates her from God—who will not be caught by the web of our sensations. She desires an intimate union because she believes it is announced and inaugurated by the first gesture of faith, but, armed with the knowledge that a higher union with God is not within the reach of human endeavor, she decides then to give herself to a preparation for it by a joint attention to sustaining her faith and the more negative labor of looking out for anything that might deceive or alienate her attention.

In my opinion this trajectory is a good example of sublimation. Here her imperious desire, incubating in dreams of glory, domination, and pleasure, finds its fulfillment and reaches a union with the Other by virtue of a decentering of her own self. To use the signs of a previous hysteria in order to determine the significance of her accomplishment is to deny the very possibility of sublimation as well as the difference between "successful hysteria" and a hysterical neurosis.

In order to maintain such an antithetically crude conception of psychology one would need to be possessed of the positivist spirit of a Janet, or perhaps of a Zola, who considered Cézanne an aborted genius because he suffered from various neurotic difficulties and from a schizoid intrusion-anxiety. But wouldn't it be more accurate to state this inversely and say that his extreme sensitivity to the world made Cézanne especially vulnerable, and that it is his morbid isolation that brought him the very life he saw germinating in landscape? What is important here is the fact that he triumphed over a whole sea of anxieties by dedicating himself with a religious attention to a study of nature, color, and the depths of space.

To discriminate between neurosis and sublimation, I will focus on the mystical experience, studying its content and also the underlying attitudes that inform and organize its significations. Its visible effects in the domain of human realization are certainly an index of the value of the experience that animates it: "by their fruits you shall know them." Consequently, the constructive dynamism Teresa deploys is often cited as proof of the authenticity of her experience. In this balance, found frequently among the mystics, between their description of an exceptional religious experience and the revival (through experience) of previously paralyzed creative forces, Bergson saw the irruption of a God who is the simple concentrated source of creative energy.[8] This evidence then led him to try to disengage God from his terrestrial emissaries, with whom Bergson had often confused God in his previous philosophy.

Freud's few sketchy definitions of sublimation do not add much to our understanding. They are even misleading if one does not think this concept through with reference to the whole context of metapsychology, and they have given rise to simplistic, utilitarian sorts of judgments. Generally, psychology has retained the last element of the most complete definition he gave of sublimation: "a certain kind of modification of the aim and change of the object [of the sexual instinct] in which our social valuation is taken into account."[9] The channeling of the sexual instinct toward intellectual cathexis and artistic production represents for Freud the model for sublimation as "the capacity to exchange the original sexual goal for another goal which is no longer sexual yet which is psychically connected with it."[10] A certain type of utilitarian and rationalistic ideology, by adding a simplistic sense of decorum to the rationalist philosophy of the Enlightenment,"[11] appropriated Freud's few remarks to prop up the concept of sublimation by an idea of what is "socially useful"— science, work, the economy as a means of distributing goods, the comforting illusions of art, and so on. The mystical experience, however, because it is not in itself work that is useful to the world, can never produce anything more than an "autoplastic" change of the same sort operative in the hysterical conversion and defined by Ferenczi as "the realization of a wish, as though by magic, out of the material of the body at its disposal and—even if in primitive fashion—by a plastic representation."[12]

Clinical observation will verify, among other things, the transference of an instinct to intellectual activities. But the notion of channeling instinctual forces onto "higher," socially valorized activities is no more than a facile image. The whole problem of sublimation consists precisely in understanding when and how this "modification of the aim and change of the object" of the sexual instinct comes about. As J. Laplanche writes, "From the very start and to the end [of Freud's work], . . . [sublimation] stands . . . as the sign of a sort of questioning that remains to be carefully worked out . . . an indispensable notion, but one that has never been 'grasped' by a *Begriff* [concept]."[13] Of course we cannot accomplish here the work Freud himself had to renounce,[14] that of resolving the problem of sublimation, but a few pointers on the issue are indispensable.

In order to understand sublimation correctly, we must keep in mind that transforming the sexual instinct nevertheless serves to satisfy it.[15] Otherwise, sublimation would be equivalent to repression, and this is a contradiction in terms. Moreover, the sexual instinct could not lend its energy to an activity with which it did not have some inherent rapport. How then to understand an activity that has been desexualized but remains libidinal in its very source and form of satisfaction? At stake here is the whole concept of sexuality, the very difficulty Jung came up against and one that remains problematic in Freud, as his perplexity in facing the issue of sublimation indicates. In *The Ego and the Id*, however, we find the flash of an idea that illuminates the entire field of this problematic if one elaborates all that remains unstated in it. "It seems a plausible view that this displaceable and neutral energy, which is no doubt active both in the ego and in the id, proceeds from the narcissistic store of the libido—that it is desexualized Eros." Further on: "If this displaceable energy is desexualized libido it may also be described as *sublimated* energy; for it would still retain the main purpose of Eros—that of uniting and binding—insofar as it helps towards establishing the unity or tendency to unity, which is particularly characteristic of the ego."[16]

By constituting the ego as a unity the sexual instinct becomes desexualized while still accomplishing the unifying aims of Eros. It is this narcissistic activity of the psyche that shapes the ego and causes it to move beyond itself toward the beloved object.[17] We might compare these texts to one in which Freud states that love is a relation of the ego as a totality,[18] or to those in which he opposes love to perversion,[19] or to the passage where he defines sublimation as a means of placing at the service of cultural endeavor forces that are "to a great extent obtained through the suppression of what are known as the *perverse elements* of sexual excitation."[20] This desexualization of libido is brought about by the transformation of libido through the ego's mediation. Thus it preserves and transforms the very element that defines the essence of sexuality as an instinct whose basic aim is pleasure. From this emerges also a form of pleasure that is no longer strictly bound to vital activity or the satisfaction of needs.

Sexuality is the genesis of a different domain of experience than that of the strictly vital activities. But this genesis, whose definitive axis lies in the constitution of the ego as a subject of libidinal investment, unfolds in other devices and transformational activities—all of which deploy the constitution of the subject. The characteristics of sublimation are that it emanates from the ego as subject and that it pertains to domains which, because not specifically useful, afford pleasure. Therefore, the phrase "socially valorized activities" should be interpreted with reference to both the ego-subject and the social dimension that constitutes it. As a subject of language, the ego-subject (the "I") is itself caught in an intersubjective rapport; it is also decentered by the universal character of language. These elements then contribute to the evolution of the instincts toward sublimation: narcissism, which is a libidinal formation constitutive of the ego, carrying it toward the other, and the interlocutionary rapport established by the very structure of language.

Any libidinal activity of the ego already constituted as a subject can be considered sublimation, but anything on the order of vital needs where the instincts of mastery exert their pressure or anything pertaining to the sexuality of primary narcissism that "makes its appearance unchanged in the personality in the form of a perversion"[21] is not sublimation. The specific characteristic of sublimation, then, is the quality of enjoyment, and the absence of enjoyment in any libidinally oriented activity marks the failure of sublimation. From the psychoanalytic perspective, however, enjoyment and pleasure do not altogether coincide. Pleasure, which should be distinguished from the economic principle of an automatic regulation of the psyche by the avoidance of unpleasure,[22] is, properly speaking, an autoerotic satisfaction of the partial instincts, whereas enjoyment is an act of the ego-subject.

In human love, then, even sexual love, we find, as Michèle Montrelay has shown, a sublimation of sexuality. The partial pleasure preceding the act of love is taken up and assumed into an I-thou rapport established by the total ego. For love to succeed narcissistic pleasure must forget itself, suppress its own representation of itself in order to discover itself—as if through its own death—in a sexual rhythm similar to the rhythms of language.[23] This passage of the subject to an order beyond the imaginary order (which is the subject's being present to himself through representations of himself)[24] is not accomplished in hysterical neurosis. A fascination with the appearance of one's body image before the other, an excessive preoccupation with the other's defects, a sense of disgust aroused by incestuous representations, the fear of a rupture or an irruption that revives the traumatizing image of an incomplete body not closed self-sufficiently in upon itself—all these factors combine to focus the subject's attention narcissistically on himself, triggering in him a defensive refusal.

This metamorphosis of sexuality in sublimation can be traced through Teresa of Avila's spiritual epic. She reaches the state of the ego's effacement, and through this effacement she wakens to the "I" uttered in the first person, who remains present but forgotten and is made in the image of God, capable of being in him and receiving him in herself. Through this fulfillment of desire in love, she experiences a joy without representation, a state of pure jubilation.

The biblical idea of man made in God's image and the conviction that God is beyond representation combine to erase progressively, in her relation to God, any attachment to any affective experience deriving from the sensations. In order to rediscover herself, her authentic being, and in order to address herself to the Other as he actually is, Teresa seeks to identify herself with God, relating to him as she knows and recognizes him in the faith: as the subject of his word, beyond the order of imaginary representation.

Ascesis is a veritable *mort*-ification, a negation of the ego's sensual pleasures and attachment to representations of itself. Through this death the ego reconquers its forgotten identity as the "I," subject of the word in which the divine "I" declares and presents himself. The solicitation of a suffering Christ serves as her model. But the suffering of ascesis is something other than the mere quest for pain; it is an attempt to triumph over affect from both pleasure and displeasure, both equally signs of the failure of sublimation. We could reproduce any number of texts in which Teresa asserts the insignificance of sensations and ecstasies. She wishes neither to look for them nor to reject them, but she accepts them rather as provisional aids and promises, conscious always of the risk that they can mystify, mislead, or distract her into forgetting her own identity and God's.

This analysis, it may be noted, makes no appeal to any phenomenon of a supernatural order. I only examine here the path Teresa herself followed in the perspective that was her own: the Christian faith. To invoke interventions of a supernatural order to explain her mystical experiences would be to obscure the psychological laws specific to desire and sublimation. Even if theology can legitimately claim that a divine grace is at work in these exceptional phenomena, psychology for its part must elucidate the significance of the work of sublimation operative in these phenomena.

Still, in what light are we to judge the celebrated vision of the "transverberation" recounted in one of Teresa's texts and immortalized by Bernini in a marble that in no way cools or tempers the physical and corporeal ecstasy of the vision?

> I saw beside me, on my left, an angel in bodily form. . . . He was not tall but short, and very beautiful, his face so aflame that he appeared to be one of the highest types of angels who seem to be all afire. They must be those who are called Seraphim. . . . In his hands I saw a long golden spear and at the end of the iron tip I seemed to see a point of fire. With this he seemed to pierce my heart several times so that it penetrated to my entrails. When he drew it out, I thought he was drawing them out with it and he left me completely afire with a great love for God. The pain was so sharp that it made me utter several moans: and so excessive was the sweetness caused by this intense pain that one can never wish to be delivered from it, nor will one's soul be content with anything less than God. It is not bodily pain, but spiritual, though the body has a share in it.[25]

Critics will immediately look to this text when they wish to show that Teresa of Avila is a flagrant case of hysteria or even perversion,[26] for humor is decidedly not the rule in these matters. We will leave for later the hallucinatory character of this vision and concentrate on its erotic nature, which is more to our purpose here. The metaphors she uses lend themselves to a translation of the vision in terms of sexual penetration. But we cannot have it both ways: either we interpret the vision as a dream in which the mechanism of repression disguises in celestial symbols a dream-thought whose content is sexual copulation, or else we interpret it as a text that straightforwardly expresses an actual experience of such intensity that the subject must figure it in the form of hallucinatory symbolization.

The terms of the text exclude the hypothesis of repression inasmuch as the author pointedly recognizes that the body plays an important part in the "excessive sweetness caused by this intense pain." We should therefore read the images that describe this vision as metaphors used in a straightforward text and not as symbols that disguise what Freud calls the dream-thought. In cases where the dream is strictly a return of the repressed, the dreaming subject surrenders to what Groddeck calls the "compulsion to symbolization."[27] What appears in Teresa's vision, on the other hand, is a symbolic sequence with a multiplicity of meanings of which the author is both subject and object. As with all forms of symbolism that are not the captives of a compulsion to repeat, here too the links of meaning that have been condensed into polysemic signs must be brought to light. We might mention just a few of the connotations: that God is a fire passing through man's being in order to purify it and communicate his love to it; that his light enters into man's deepest recesses; and that "the union with Absolute Love . . . takes place in the deepest center of the soul (or rather of one's being)."[28]

Reading the account of this vision one is reminded of Bruno Bettelheim's notion of the "symbolic wound"; he describes this repeated opening and reopening of the body as a ritual form through which a subject assumes his sex.[29] A symbolic ablation, for example, symbolizes the subject's lack of the opposite sex and his acceptance of it; this, in short, is what Lacan called a symbolic castration. The "sweet pain" St. Teresa speaks of evokes the twofold nature of the experience—the suffering of being torn out of her self-sufficient enclosure and the joy of being inhabited, as it were, by the Other. If this assumption of one's sex (through which the subject surmounts his narcissism) is already a form of sublimation, then the experience described by Teresa is even more so, especially when one considers the symbols of the vision and allows the contextual metaphors their full resonance. The spontaneity of the sexual body that has been assumed by the subject contains in germinal form the whole movement of desire; the language of desire then picks it up thematically in order to arouse and articulate this desire. Through this transposition between language of the body (not, as in hysteria, language *through* the body) and the body of language, desire, of whatever order it is, expresses itself through the metaphors of the body, and the body in turn becomes the metaphorical vessel that gives experience, including spiritual experience, a special resonance. Otherwise how would one find joy in spirituality?

This affective resonance can invest the bodily responses with greater or lesser intensity. But St. Teresa in any case is particularly vigilant concerning this and does not allow her own joy and pleasure to become immersed in a bodily experience that, folding in upon its self-affectivity, might go against the transformative aims of God's love. She perceived too clearly the symbolic ambiguity of the "mystical marriage": "I am only making a rough comparison, but I can find no other which will better explain what I am trying to say than the Sacrament of Matrimony."[30]

There is no trace here of pathology, where the absence of pleasure or joy that constitutes the sign of repression would lead us to suppose that a substitutive relation to God maintains a repression of sexuality because it is perceived as incompatible with a transference onto God. Moreover, Teresa feels no shame in simply admitting that she both suffered and enjoyed the experience through her body. Nor does she linger over these ecstasies and visions, which she considers authentic only if they are involuntary and fleeting. As a matter of fact she believed them to be a "weakness of the body," and she was greatly pleased when she finally attained a durable joy in a union with God that no longer enraptured her body but left her free to attend to the many duties of an existence heavily charged with responsibilities.[31]

Once it has been situated in its context and elucidated by a psychology of sublimation, this vision of St. Teresa's transverberation can be taken as a sign of the psychic health and lucid judgment of this woman. She indeed mortified her body, not out of a horror of sexuality but because of her project to grow into a love that might be worthy of him whom she believed herself destined to love in the depths of her identity, an identity she shared universally with all men and women.

Counterpoint: The Erotic Mystics

When a form of spirituality dedicated to the contemplation of the divine humanity of Christ was inaugurated in the Middle Ages, a veritable wave of erotic mysticism, of varying degrees, flooded Catholic tradition. Various authors have studied this phenomenon, some with a discerning solicitude,[32] others in the spirit of psychoanalytic Grand Inquisitors,[33] and others with the aim of liberating women from the humiliating role of "perpetual adoration."[34] It is not necessary here to run through all those mystic pearls of dubious quality, so I will select two cases, which I will examine in terms of their pathological significance.

The "venerable" Agnes Blannbekin,[35] born in Vienna toward the end of the thirteenth century, was particularly preoccupied with the question of what became of Christ's "Holy Foreskin," a question first debated by a number of theologians of the age and one that was first raised—as if by chance—with reference to the problem of the integrity of the resurrected body. God puts an end to Agnes' torment by revealing to her that the Holy Foreskin had risen with him on the day of his resurrection. (Fortunately God did not also reveal to her that he was going to tell St. Bridget that the Holy Foreskin was kept safely hidden in Rome.) Agnes' revelation started a number of sensational ecstasies, reported by her "unworthy confessor," as the Franciscan Ermenic calls himself. Then one year, while she bitterly wept on the feast of the Circumcision—as was her wont—and although she had already been informed by the revelation, Agnes began to wonder once again

> where indeed Christ's foreskin could be. And behold! she felt on her tongue a thin piece of skin, like the skin surrounding an egg, but of greater softness, and she swallowed the skin. After swallowing it, she felt again that soft skin on her tongue, and she swallowed it again. And this must have happened at least one hundred times.... The softness produced in digesting the skin was so great she felt a sweet transformation in all her limbs and joints. During the revelation she was inwardly filled with so much light that she was able to contemplate herself in her entirety.[36]

The Lord then bestowed upon her a number of chaste, tender caresses given by his own hand or by a lamb that had descended from the altar. "During these visitations Agnes felt her breasts filled by such an incandescent glow that it spread and burned through the rest of her body, not painfully, but in a soft sort of way." It is surprising to hear that once when she was being bled the bleeder was shocked to see this girl's blood "boiling from the heat."[37]

Upon sniffing these heady fumes of the mystical wine press we can hear Montaigne mutter, "Just between us, these are two things I have always held as being in singular accord: the views of celestial realms and the mores of the underworld."[38] Is this a "sickness of religious sentiment"? Such is the diagnosis of Dr. Witny, who transcribes a whole anthology of hallucinations of vision, hearing, smell, taste, and touch in support of his thesis that one always finds an erotic quality in these illnesses.[39] If we leave aside for the moment the question of a hallucination in a nonpsychotic individual, then what sort of illness is this? An erotomania? But an infatuation with a man who is divinized by an individual and the experience of erotic feelings toward God or Christ are not symmetrical and merely inverted phenomena. Erotomania is a form of paranoia[40] whose passion, because it is the inversion of a denied homosexuality, does not lead to pleasure.

I must admit to a certain hesitation. Anyone who has any notion of the essential aspects of mysticism might suppose that this erotic mysticism is a sickness of religious sentiment. Is it, however, a form of psychic illness? One could draw a table of correspondences between these erotico-mystical representations and the more distant marginal fantasies that are often detected in incipient hysteria. Only neurosis maintains them as a phantasmic background, finally repressing them along with the incestuous representations for which they serve as substitutes.

The fantasies that broke freely into Agnes' everyday life availed themselves of the mystical themes then current in her milieu, thus allowing the body of her desire to speak. One might suppose that individuals like Agnes use these mystical signifiers as a therapeutic language that allows them to lift a repression by the direct investment of substitute representations. Sexuality no longer runs any risk here because the subject becomes assured of his privileged election by a partner who has been raised to the height of idealization and hence remains beyond all suspicion. And if this credulous or tolerant milieu grants these experiences value as universal signs, it also serves as a means of deliverance from individual alienation.

We are, at any rate, dealing here with a desublimation that illustrates the abyss separating self-affective pleasure from a liberating experience of joy. All of Agnes' attention is concentrated on her own immediate bodily sensations. Hence the erogenous body closes in upon itself in a pleasure that floods and caresses all the variously dispersed libidinal instincts. The experience of joy is limited to the narcissistic pleasure of being singularly chosen as the object of extraordinary favors. This "mysticism" remains in the final analysis little more than a label for an autoerotic mysticism. Even the mystical fellation described does not go beyond this point. It is, without any doubt, an illness of religious sentiment. Is it, however, a psychic illness? I would conclude that we are dealing here with a perversion, of which neurosis would be the negative.[41]

With the aim of isolating principles for discerning between an erotic mysticism and mystical sublimation, I have chosen one case of particular simplicity for discussion. The great majority of mystical ailments are undoubtedly infinitely more complex. The phenomenon of religious hysteria finds a clear example in the case of Marie Alacoque (1647–90), the celebrated apostle of devotion to the Sacred Heart.[42] At the age of eight she was placed in a convent, where "something," she says, seemed to pull her away from the games and activities of children: "This spirit forced me to pray, nearly always kneeling on my bare knees or prostrated on the ground." She becomes ill and cannot walk for four years. Guilt anxieties, ecstasies, visions, and hallucinations follow one another. "With loving violence" her "divine Master" teaches her the most severe and actually self-mutilating forms of corporeal penance. When her family decides she should marry, Jesus informs her that "he is the most handsome, the most rich, the most powerful, the most perfect and accomplished of all lovers."

Under the name of Sister Margaret-Mary, as a nun in the Convent of the Visitation in Paray-Le-Monial, she is visited by Jesus, who loves her "in the fashion of the most ardent of lovers." "His loving caresses . . . were in fact so excessive that they often left me beside myself without the power to act." She sees, feels, and hears her divine lover so near to her that she feels annihilated before his grandeur; and when she is alone with him she wants to remain on her knees or with her face to the ground, "for he would not let me rest, even for a moment, in a less respectful posture." Jesus demands of her a written testament in which she surrenders her freedom to him, and then with a knife she engraves in blood the name "Jesus" over her heart. The passionate relationship that follows leaves her no rest, day or night. Soon after she has the celebrated vision of their exchange of hearts. The conversation with Jesus ends on this medical note, typical of the age: "the ardor [of that flash of living flame in her heart] could not be extinguished and found no relief except only slightly, what an occasional bleeding could afford."

This small detail, with all its picturesque realism, also evokes the symbolism of sacrifice, which in turn betrays how beneath the romantic image of the exchange of hearts, prevalent in her time, Mary Alacoque tends to identify and place herself at the center of a love for the God she wants to love. In this particular we can no longer judge her case to be merely hysterical, since the hysteric recoils from this center from the moment that her desire approaches it. Moreover, Mary never hesitates to pay the price, for the only thing that matters to her is the will of her "Sovereign Master." Through all these torments and demonic or erotic surprises and attacks she always tries to refer—as the objective pole of her judgment and conduct—to a divine will that expresses what God rightfully is. And she is not niggardly in this matter: once, "reproved" by God for her repulsion toward "the least bit of dirt," "when I had to clean up the vomit of a sick patient I couldn't prevent myself from doing it with my tongue."

In order to avoid a hasty imposition of our own ethnocentric categories, we should first consider these phenomena within their proper historical context: an age in which we see a massive irruption of diabolical possessions, which were forms of hysteria largely conditioned by the prevailing religious mentality. The context in part explains both the extreme obsessive manifestations and the reactional movements that perturbed the lives of those like Mary Alacoque. Nevertheless, I would not hesitate to identify the torments she relates as hysterial. Still, in this strange biography we can detect a sustained effort to situate herself in a stable relationship of love.

Phantasms of all kinds haunt many of these seekers of God, provoking bizarre experiences and giving shape to all sorts of horrible or captivating visions—Walpurgis Nights, Dantean hells, or canticles of love. It is as if the great supernatural powers had chosen these visionaries as the secular field for their combat. And these visionaries and their contemporaries perceive in these struggles a mysterious drama that far surpasses them. Religious faith then provides them with the signifiers that permit them to situate these psychological issues within a symbolic universe in which divine good will ultimately prevail over evil and suffering. In this way a subjective solitude can be transcended and the irrational forces can to some degree become liberated by this juncture with a larger, more universal meaning.

The lived experience of these dramas and their healing, however fragile or partial, accomplished in the path of sublimation, thus assume the value of a sign for others, who recognize in them their own obsessions and hidden monsters as well as their own truth and possible destiny. Is it necessary then to denounce the ambiguous prestige bestowed on some of these historical figures? I would not like to see them confined in subterranean asylums, although neither would I raise them to the celestial level of supernatural bodies. Like the heroes of mythical dramas, they have enacted on the public stage the symbolic signs so necessary to the work of catharsis.

8 • Visions and Voices

Religion has always been full of visions and words that have been seen, heard, and stored in the collective memories of their respective adherents. Whether it is of a highly sublimated, mildly troubled, or frankly morbid kind, mysticism also has tales of divine visitations to relate; these tales are especially abundant in popular religion. Most of those who benefit from these visitations do not appear to be mentally ill. Still, this phenomenon does seem to be of a hallucinatory nature. Whether the believer thinks that God or some other supernatural presence reveals itself in these visions or voices does not change matters much: the fact remains that the communication of such revelations does not follow the normal tracks of perception.

These ecstatic phenomena offer such diversity that it seems suspect to call them all by one simple term. Many of the different incidents of God's manifestation in the Bible leave their distinct brand on a particular religious movement, which then becomes defined as an essential part of religious history. These supernatural breakthroughs into the world of man bring about cumulative transformations. The comprehensive expression "the history of revelations" has, then, a meaning even for the historian who has reservations about the ultimate source of revelations. It is not the intention of the Christian mystics, or even for the most part of the visionaries and prophets springing from the general populace, to augment or modify the acquired revelations that their religion considers a closed chapter. Consequently there is already an essential difference between biblical revelations and other forms of divine visitation.

We should also consider that the history of biblical revelation already contains a large variety of literary genres conditioned by the cultural, social, and religious context as well as by that history's interpretative reflection upon itself. Biblical prophecy is therefore a very particular and historically limited form of inspiration in which God breaks forth as the subject of an enunciation in the first person. This form of prophecy has little in common with the ecstatic phenomena found in mysticism, and it would be scientifically ingenuous to reduce all these phenomena to one heading under the pretext that all these forms of inspiration are beyond normal understanding. Given the perspective of this study I will have to limit myself to those ecstatic phenomena found in Western Christianity. I distinguish—for reasons I will later explain—two different categories: mysticism and popular religion.

The interpretation of these phenomena as hallucinatory is by no means an innocent description. It brings to mind something the discipline of psychiatry has identified as contrary to normal forms of perceptive knowledge, something psychiatry tends to view as a psychic impairment. Whereas madness was once interpreted according to religious models, now the category of hallucination places universal religious phenomena under the dominion of the rational, thus forcing them into the realm of unreason.

The problem is commonly envisioned in terms of two alternatives. Either one agrees with the speaker and accepts the supernatural source of his visions or voices, thus disallowing science's pretension in imposing its norms upon these supernatural forms of knowing; or one reclassifies the speaker, placing him within the field of natural phenomena. The latter option offers two possibilities as a means of substituting a human discourse for a so-called supernatural one: a psychiatry of hallucination, or a parapsychology of the enigmatic powers of the soul. It is my conviction that both these alternatives are imaginary. It is first a matter of finding out whether what is involved is a recognition or a misunderstanding of human and religious realities. Whatever the case may be, it must become intelligible to us on the basis of our own human psychic organization.

Hallucination

At the end of his *Traité des hallucinations* Henri Ey defines hallucination as "a pathological phenomenon of the subjective, classically and elliptically defined as a 'perception without object.' More explicitly, it is an unconscious act by which the subject, disorganized in his psychic system, is fooled '*in perceiving*' *perceptions without objects*, either as a consequence of a disorganization of his conscious being or as a consequence of a *disintegration* of his perceptual systems. From this follows: (1) the heterogeneous (*anomic*) character of hallucinations, and (2) the classification of hallucinations into two types: *delirious hallucinations* and *hallucinosic ideations*."[1] For Ey, then, "Hallucination is either pathological or it is not hallucination."[2] It is a psychic impairment that always becomes manifest within the context of a collapsed sense of reality. Ey's negatively formulated definition is thematically linked to Freud's notion of the "loss of reality." Moreover, hallucination is considered to be heterogeneous as contrasted with other imaginary productions, with the illusions typical of magical thought or collective suggestion—all phenomena some authors have called "psychonomic hallucination"[3] in order to stress that although the latter examples are illusions according to the laws of objective perception, they nevertheless follow the normal laws of imagination and affect as they operate in perception.

According to Ey, in order for a hallucination to be real there must be "(1) a sensorial quality to the experience (diagnostically differentiated from an idea, a fiction, or the imaginary); (2) a conviction as to the nonsubjectivity of the experience (diagnostically differentiated from other sensorial anomalies); (3) the absence of a real object (diagnostically differentiated from an illusion, defined simply as an error regarding a real object)."[4] "In the final analysis, the reality of hallucinatory phenomena presupposes an affirmation of the reality of the hallucination (hence the unreality of its perceptum) for others. In other words, hallucination occurs in conditions of an inadequacy between, on the one hand, an experience and a reality affirmed by the subject and, on the other hand, the laws that allow for an accord of communication among those in the group."[5]

Two large classes of hallucination correspond to this definition. In "hallucinosic ideations" the subject perceives an image within his spatiotemporal perceptual field and makes a positive assertion about it, affirming it uncannily present in his perceptual field without thereby necessarily judging it to be real. These "false perceptions" are often imbued with sensorially fascinating qualities. We may note that the same sensory vividness can be found in religious visions and in psychedelic experiences without the perceptions appearing incongruous. Delirious hallucinations form the second largest class of hallucinations. Deliria "are constituted on a mode of knowledge specifically heterogeneous to the forms of thought common to the group and to the laws governing its system of reality."[6] According to Ey not every delirium is necessarily hallucinatory, for it can consist in affects, presumptions, abstract concepts that remain "beyond any reference to perceived or perceivable reality." Still, "within the vast group that constitutes the most important core of *alienation*, hallucination most constantly appears, as it were, '*a media voce*,' as the very voice of delirium par excellence."[7]

What is particularly striking in this treatise is the repeated alternation between an epistemology of perception and knowledge, on the one hand, and, on the other, affirmations of a psychological order concerning the subversion of reality and the destructuring of the subject. Personally I cannot determine whether these affirmations are clinical inferences made from the concept of a "perception with no object to perceive" or are actually based on an analysis of the hallucinatory subject's discourse. Nevertheless, for our purposes here, this point is a capital one. Ey wants to limit hallucination strictly to pathology, and when he gets into straits trying to distinguish it from the aesthetic imagination, he finally has to take recourse in the theoretical conviction that hallucination is a "negative phenomenon," "a hole in the system of reality, a void no figure can represent or reproduce."[8]

But how are we to decide if there is a hole in reality? And who is finally the judge of what is a real and what an unreal perception? Those religious visions that are not seen by anyone else are perceptually unreal; but what piece of reality is missing, leaving the hole they are meant to fill? The prevailing ambiguity becomes clear in considering the phenomenology of hallucinosic ideations. The hallucinating subject perceives a given sensorial datum, but even to him it does not seem to have the same density as reality, since his judgment of it remains strictly an assertive one. What he perceives may be situated within his spatiotemporal field, but he cannot scan, from various perspectives, the profiles of the object appearing to him—and it is the continuity of these profiles that, according to Husserl's phenomenology, sustains and grounds the affirmation of the reality of this object, which remains an unknown that one can only approach without ever seizing it in all its parts.

The hallucinating subject is not oblivious to this difference and consequently feels his perception to be an uncanny one. We are dealing here with a type of perception, described by Sartre,[9] that has all the characteristics of an imagining consciousness but does not present itself as such. Does it suffice, however, to bring it before the court of ordinary perception, in order to decide whether or not it is pathological?

Many of the perceptions Ey describes as magical thinking or aesthetic imagination would, as a matter of fact, have to be considered pathological if one did not know beforehand that they were produced by children and artists. Consequently it becomes necessary to appeal to a theoretical principle that explains the breakdown of reality. But exactly where can such a principle be found? It seems to me we can take as an important sign the subject's consciousness that his perception is strange and compelling. He cannot really believe it, but at the same time he cannot quite disbelieve it.

It may seem, then, that a diagnosis of delirious hallucinations could be more firmly grounded on the universal laws of knowing and reasoning. Frequently the subject's rupture with universal forms of human discourse is offered as an obvious criterion, but in most cases it is difficult to assess with any certainty the significance of this rupture. We mentioned earlier, for example, Janet's summary judgment of Teresa of Avila: believing himself capable of controlling the whole of reality by his unerring logic, he calmly decides that she should have been locked up in an asylum for delirious mystics. As a matter of fact Ey's diagnosis implies two different avenues of approach. His assertion that hallucinatory delirium is discordant with reference to universal principles is warranted finally by his conviction that there is a hole in the system of reality. If, however, one bases the definition of reality on perception, then the very concept of hallucination itself rests on a tautology, with the consequence that the whole issue becomes tainted by that narrow rationalism that underlies certain forms of psychiatry. If, on the other hand, the concept of reality is of another order, it still remains to establish this order. It is clear that an appeal to common sense cannot help us here. Reality, which happens to be a plurality, can only be judged according to transcendental principles of the sort Kant tried to establish when, reflecting on the experiences undergone by Goethe's young Werther, he developed *The Critique of Judgment*. This is obviously not the place to attempt a similar task, moreover such a difficult and unending one. And yet clinical psychology continues to pursue such principles after its own fashion when it goes beyond diagnostic description to analyze the discourses of various subjects and, by its interpretive constructions, attempts to understand whether there is an active and involuntary denial of reality at work in these discourses.

Ey makes the subtle observation that the individual in the grip of a delirious hallucination may not always believe in his delirium.[10] But this negative belief on the subject's part, this compelling impossibility of believing in something he perceives, something presented to him in the form of messages from the world around him, seems to me to be equally important. The various comments Freud makes about negative hallucinations are noteworthy here.[11] I would like to propose that at the "fertile moment" of a delirium there is an oscillation between negative and positive hallucination: ordinary reality loses its thread of believability and other representations impose themselves, offering an alternative belief that is often opposed to the realistic character of what is perceived. Proceeding from somewhere beyond the subject's private world and beyond the world of the commonly shared discourse of those around him, a third world imposes its own rule, a rule over which reasoning and the ordinary prompting of observable reality no longer exercise any control.[12] We have yet to understand the mechanism of hallucination by which the hallucinatory material makes its appearance in perceived reality.

As I analyze different cases in the course of this investigation I will outline a number of points as an answer to this enigma, but it is important first to emphasize that the form of psychical phenomena that I designate by the general term *hallucinatory* is not necessarily pathological. To my knowledge most authors, excepting Freud, have tried to understand hallucination by considering only its pathological examples, thereby neglecting the actual mechanisms of perception insofar as it forms an integral part of the topical structure and dynamics of the psyche. In my use of the term, *hallucinatory* refers to the process by which a hallucination becomes perceived and perceivable—leaving aside for later discussion the issues of the pathological character of its content and of the subject's particular disposition toward this content.

From this rather sparse introduction, intended to orient our perspective on this issue, we can sift out three indications that ought to be kept in mind throughout the following discussion. In hallucination, as well as in neurosis or psychosis, something other—another place, another source, an "elsewhere"—makes itself heard or seen; likewise, the visions and voices perceived in ecstasies also proceed from somewhere else. What is this somewhere else? Who or what speaks and appears there, and from where does it proceed? This is not a theological question but a psychological one, and only an analysis of the content of the vision can give us an answer. Second, how does the subject relate himself to this something else proceeding from another place? What level or degree of believability does he grant his perception? Third, is there a specific portion of reality that he rejects, represses, or denies, and if so, what is it? Since in any coherent theory of hallucination the three questions must necessarily be interrelated, the answers to these questions will also elucidate one another and by this convergence will eventually allow us to make distinctions among the various phenomena that concern us here.

Neurotic Hallucinations in Ecstatic Phenomena

The visions and erotico-mystical sensations experienced by Marie Alacoque commented on earlier are representative of hysterical hallucinations. It is clear that repressed representations have forced themselves upon Marie Alacoque's consciousness by taking a shape in her field of sensations and visual perceptions. It is not, however, this appearance of repressed material in the phenomenal world that allows us to conclude that we are dealing with a delirious psychosis in a personality that does not otherwise manifest any sign of a radical destructuration of the ego. Marie Alacoque certainly believes in her visions and sensations, but she judges them in reference to something she wants to believe and consequently she resists them. Within the records of hysteria, this particular case seems to be an exceptional one, but perhaps we can reconcile it with hysterico-hallucinatory symptoms described by Janet.[13] I might add, though, that the religious context certainly favors the process by which sensations and phantasmic representations take a concrete shape in the phenomenal world.

Repressed representations can easily take the form of hallucinations of sensation, but it is rare for them to speak in audible voices and even rarer for them to be staged in visual spectacles. Here is a simple example: after months of analysis, X, a seriously obsessional individual, finds that suddenly, in the midst of his professional activities, he is gripped by the idea/image/sensation that the whole length of his penis is split into two. He is so overcome by anxiety and panic that he must rush out of his office. Is this a hallucination? He feels, in any case, and with an unbearable pain, that his penis is cleaved. He does not for a moment believe it, for the question of a judgment concerning the reality of the idea does not really pose itself during this intermediary moment of fascination, situated between ordinary reality and his shock at what had just happened to him. This, then, is a hallucination of sensation accompanied by a phantasmic representation, and yet it does not take the form of a visual hallucination. Here, an unconscious representation precedes and causes the hallucinatory sensation and the image—of castration—represented according to his perception of the vagina, which for years had aroused shock and aversion in him.

This anxiety-producing representation of castration, having been repressed, forced its way back by taking concrete shape in a hallucinatory experience. Contrary to the common belief also supported by Ey, hallucination is not simply the projection of a desire. As Freud has shown, hallucination is in some ways comparable to the dream in that both are often an eruption of unconscious wishes into the field of perception. But, like dreams, hallucination can also borrow its material from traumatic representations.

Let us consider a hallucinatory vision related by Ignatius of Loyola in his autobiography, a vision that has a truly hallucinatory quality about it.[14] During his stay at the hospital of Manresa, where he was confined after being wounded at the battle of Pamplona, Loyola, till then "much given over to gambling, women, duels and weapons,"[15] reads a *Life of*

Christ and *The Gilded Legend* and decides to change his life. Wishing to imitate the heroic exploits of the saints, he imposes a rigorous ascesis upon himself and decides to live a life of poverty. After a period of initial gladness a certain doubt begins to obsess him, and he begins to wonder if he can sustain that kind of life. Shortly thereafter he has a hallucinatory vision that lasts for days:

> Often, in full daylight, he happened to see near him, but suspended in the air, something that afforded him great consolation because it was extraordinarily beautiful. He couldn't clearly discern the nature of it, but it seemed, somehow, that it had a serpent's shape with lots of things (*cosas*) on it shining like eyes, but which were not in fact eyes. The sight of it gave him great pleasure and consolation, and when it disappeared he found he was very sad.

After a period of affective instability during which he fluctuated between serenity and depression, Loyola goes through a period of obsessional scrupulosity alternating with great disgust toward the ascetic life he is leading, disgust that gives rise to compulsive ideas of suicide. Later he finds a name that allows him to identify the enigmatic and seductive "thing" that appeared to him: the devil.

Loyola, then, had seen something near him; it appeared to be suspended in the air and was therefore situated in his spatiotemporal field, but as in all hallucination, it is not of the order of ordinary spatiality that would allow the object to be explored. Since, however, we have no evidence of hallucinatory delirium, can we regard this hallucination as a return of the repressed? The hysterical structure of Loyola's experience is undeniable. A number of characteristics point to it: reveries lasting for hours without his awareness of time passed; a romantic idealization of women and later of the saints he wants to imitate; countless dreams about accomplishing dazzling exploits; floods of tears, shed in sometimes pleasant, sometimes bitter moods. Nevertheless, nothing here suggests an actual hysterical neurosis. And even if the "thing" happens to concentrate a number of unconscious memories [16] (as is always the case in dreams or imaginary productions), the hallucinatory character of the vision cannot be understood simply as the return of the repressed in reality.

Loyola's hallucination can only be explained within its religious context. The "thing" is the sign of the brilliant and glorious life he had renounced, which still exercises a power of seduction over him and exercises it with a more powerful attractive force in proportion to the extreme and instinctual renunciations he imposes upon himself. To any convert this "thing" must necessarily appear as a form of temptation.

Moreover, in a milieu where temptation is necessarily the work of the tempter, Loyola invariably perceives his yearning for the worldly life he left behind as something induced by the devil. The text goes on to recount how "he reacted with great energy to a suggestion he sees as proceeding from the enemy: 'You there, give me some sort of note in which you'll guarantee me at least another day of life, and I, I'll change my way of living.' "[17] Then, in keeping with a notion prevalent in his age, he proposes a pact with the devil; but convinced beforehand that he will never obtain the promise he demands, and as a strategy to convince himself that the thing is only a mirage, he acts out this drawing of a pact in his imagination. Later, while he is standing before the cross, "he understands very clearly and with the full knowledge of his will, that it was indeed the devil," and as this devil continues to appear to him often, "he used to chase him off with a cane he always carried around with him."[18] I might add that at this point Loyola willfully identifies the vision as a mirage conjured by the antagonist of the God in whom he decidedly wishes to believe.

This hallucination exemplifies some of the more striking imaginary psychic processes involved in nonpsychotic cases. In Loyola's case, when certain repressed representations began to emerge they were condensed into a symbolic figure that became the thing he saw, and the same fascination he felt with regard to the repressed material was transferred onto the figure. It is also probable that the figure thus reconstructed was based on biblical accounts and Christian emblems. At the beginning of this hallucinatory episode the thought of the seductive life Loyola missed was in fact a fleeting vehicle of expression for the desires he was repressing, desires that had been present in all the daydreams he had entertained, at the margins of a consciousness scarcely aware of itself. This kind of thought that acts as the seed of a hallucination is comparable to the dream-thought, except that the former comes into consciousness as if it were a thought coming from outside consciousness. This is also the thought that becomes visually figured in the hallucination; the thought delegates its re-presentation to the imaginary figure but only on the condition that the represented figure appear to the subject as something foreign to him.

This enigmatic "thing" thus takes Loyola by surprise, especially since he had refused any recognition of its corresponding idea, taking it to be utterly foreign to his present identity. The affective memories he was brutally repressing would not be so easily tamed, and even his current dreams of religious heroism served to keep them intact by acting as a substitute for his previous narcissistic ideal. As we have seen earlier, the characteristic of affectivity is that it derealizes the ordinary world, so it is not surprising that representations that have been repressed and have received an especially high affective charge will make their way back into the field of the subject's perception as if they did not belong to the ordinary, present world. In some corner of the psyche hidden from him, the subject continues to hold and believe in these representations, and consequently finds he is incapable of fully believing the reality he wishes and chooses to believe in. The eruption of a hallucinatory image imposes upon him a belief that conflicts with the belief he professes. It would be difficult to understand this belief in the hallucination if a negative moment were not involved, corresponding to the negative hallucination that first causes the breach in reality into which the positive hallucinatory delirium inserts itself. In fact, as they emerge, the representations of repressed desires disrupt the world as Loyola had reorganized it after his conversion. But the fascinating form his repressed desires have taken also puts him in a state of conscious doubt. The negative moment does not precede the hallucination but coexists with it. In Loyola's narrative, we do not actually perceive the moment of the negative hallucination by itself; this is the moment that, in actually pathological cases, indicates the fact that a kernel of delirium had lodged itself in the subject's consciousness. The subject on the verge of a psychosis feels with great anxiety and perplexity that his habitual world is collapsing under the pressure of the delirium he is trying to ward off.

Loyola's relatively conscious belief in the pleasures proffered him by his repressed representations would not in itself have enough power to grant his figure of temptation the density of a visible thing. Even the paradoxical consciousness that accompanies the mythic imaginings of hysteria does not cause mental images to take concrete shape in the field of the hysteric's spatial perception. It is, in fact, Loyola's belief in the devil and in his visible manifestations that gives his unconscious belief the power of conviction, which in turn triggers the passage from a phantasmic visualization of the figure to an apparition that becomes visible to him. Any religious faith that stirs man's most ardent interests is capable of adding this coefficient of visible reality to the representations of belief, especially considering that faith affirms the supernatural as more luminously real than the reality we ordinarily see.

Psychotic hallucination, however, whether it is religious or not, has a radically different structure. As Freud's work has shown,[19] in schizophrenia the "thing-representation" has been abolished by an early and repeated disinvestment of it because when the thing first entered the field of consciousness it was too traumatizing to the subject to be retained or even repressed and preserved in the unconscious. From this world that has been partially banished, the only thing left behind is a language consisting of an ensemble of signs devoid of their significance because the subject never appropriated them to begin with. In an effort to restore the content of reality to a language emptied of meaning, the subject tries, through hallucination, to give these words the things they lack. In neurosis, on the other hand, the repressed representations of things try to speak out in a language whose aim is to bring to light what is concealed.

The psychotic hallucination, therefore, makes its appearance in the real precisely at the point where the real has ceased to exist for the subject.[20] Here the subject finds himself invoked by the oracular power of language to posit another reality over the one he has abolished, but the reality he derives from these purified words is nothing more than a simulacrum of the real. Moreover, the connections between words and things are not made according to the movement that normally flows between these two poles in meaning. In schizophrenia, for example, the perception of a thing is reduced to insignificance because the investment (or cathexis) that normally draws it into the act of signification has been withdrawn from the thing. At this point perception can no longer regulate the subject's belief in the real, which has thus been loosened from any anchorage it had in actual circumstances. The hallucination is produced precisely at the point where the word, acting now like an erratic sign, alights on some perceptual representation that—because of some resemblance it has with the abolished piece of reality—presents itself as the signified of the word in an attempt to give it the concrete body it lacks. Hence the Wolf-Man hallucinates that his finger is cut because he cannot otherwise conceive or signify any representation of castration.[21]

It might be said that in psychotic hallucinations the word subjugates the spirit and transmits its own certitude to the perceptual representations that the word has seized upon. A subject submitted to the violence of such a word finds himself dispossessed of the capacity to signify things by words and he is incapable of anchoring signifiers by things. The space of freedom necessary to the act of consenting to a belief is missing here. He does, in a certain sense, "believe" in his hallucinations, but only according to a mode of certitude that does violence to him. And yet often, at the same time, he does not believe it because he senses that the free play of the signifier has been preestablished, the dice already loaded here, and he simply submits to the game—without taking part in it, however, for he does not have the freedom to use its rules strategically.

On the other hand, in the visions we discussed above, no piece of reality has been actually abolished by a radical withdrawal of cathexis. When they emerge in hysterical neurosis or some other affective rupture due to some type of neurotic conflict, the representations of desire will reappear in the real in the form of hallucinations. These representations are disinvested of their cathexis by a violent repression, and as a means of mobilizing against these representations a counterinvestment of other representations takes place. It might be useful to mention here Freud's determined stance against Jung when the latter sought to equate the libidinal disinvestment of the ascetes with psychotic forms of introversion.[22] The two types of cases differ in that in the former the counter-investment remains in the range of the subject's suppressed pleasures and desires. Thus the new reality in which both Loyola and Marie Alacoque have reinvested strongly recalls the one it has displaced, and their counterinvestment revives previous desires. Since the work of sublimation that was brought to bear upon deeper hysterical processes was not accomplished, their desires were refused but not really transformed. As a result the new object of desire takes on the splendid aspect and seductive habits of the object for which it is a substitute. However, the former personage, only partially shed, now comes out from behind the scenes, and, taking its place in the foreground, finds itself on a stage that has now been converted into a universe of supernatural forces. This old personage is now more than the spellbinding figure of the subject's own hidden desire, and the stage is more than his own imaginary theater; the figure now becomes transformed into the emissary of powerful demoniacal forces—the deceitful antithesis of the living God—and the subject's belief in the active interference of the devil transforms the imaginary figure into a hallucinated reality.

The Mystic's Visions and Words

It is not an accident that visions, which are properly speaking ecstatic phenomena, and mystical ecstasies are frequently confused. It is very easy to yield to the naive and tempting mythology that presents mystical ecstasy as a physical or affective ravishment that erupts irrationally and invades one's spontaneous feelings or fulfills one's obscure yearnings. The mystics, however, have declared themselves the enemies of the predilection for this crude sort of mysticism. For them, true ecstasy consists in a permanent union with the divine, a union that goes beyond visions and physical raptures. This aim can be attained only after one has accomplished the long and complex path charted out by the critical exigencies of faith and by a close examination of man's faculties: sensation, imagination, affectivity, will, and conceptual knowledge.

As the iconoclasts of imagery propagated by popular religion, mystics practice a suspension of the forms of imagination that always attempt to produce visible signs of the divine manifestations. They are every bit as subversive toward theological systematizations that, because of their systematic aims, attempt to seize God in the intelligibility of conceptual relations. Mystics attempt to go beyond this; by placing themselves under the guidance of the word that reveals itself in the visible world and the spoken enunciation, they aim to bring about a union with the divine presence that manifests and announces itself to them. This opens up a space of belief where visions and words can become both the remnants of perceptual experiences or surpassed imaginative productions and premonitions of the union they anticipate and desire. The texts leave us no doubt that this is the significance mystics themselves bestow on ecstatic phenomena. This being said, however, the psychological problem regarding these hallucinatory phenomena is not so easily resolved, for if psychology aims for scientific method in these matters it must take account of the particular status these various phenomena have within the mystic endeavor.

In order to outline the phenomenal nature of visions and words spoken to the subject in mystical experience, we must first rigorously analyze a number of its representative texts. Teresa of Avila explicitly states that she never had an external physical vision, only visions of the imagination.[23] Moreover, she is convinced, for theological reasons, that after his ascension, Jesus Christ never visibly manifested himself on earth. St. John of the Cross allows for the possibility of "external physical visions" but he judges that they are less perfect than "supernatural interior visions" because in the latter the imagination is at a more advanced stage of the mystical way than any form of perception through the senses.[24] Corporeal visions—even "supposing that some of them come from God"—are in any case "obstacles to faith. . . . It is more fitting for the saint to push them away with closed eyes, without examining where they come from."[25]

In his exposition on the meditative life, John of the Cross treats first "the apprehensions which the soul can receive within itself by natural means, and whereon the fancy and the imagination can work by means of reflection"; then he treats "the supernatural apprehensions, which are called imaginary visions, which likewise belong to these senses, since they come within the category of images, forms, and figures, exactly as do the natural apprehensions . . . ; all the apprehensions . . . which, through the fine bodily senses, are represented to the soul and dwell within it after a natural manner, may likewise occur in the soul after a supernatural manner."[26] Even though they are supernatural, these visions are no less ambiguous because although these images are mediators of a divine presence, they risk drawing all our attention and may thus stop all further progress. One must look away from these forms of apprehension and then "these visions will profit the soul substantially, in respect of faith, when it is able to completely renounce the sensible and intelligible part of them."[27]

Mystical visions, then, are not called visions because they contain new information, for their only religious content is one of faith. As for their figurative representations, these are derived from natural perceptions. They are visions, however, because they are not the result of the active work of the imagination upon perceptual data or memory. Visions are given to those who have already reached an advanced stage of the mystical way and have gone beyond the active discourse of the imagination and the understanding—to those, in other words, who put themselves in a state of mind receptive to a distant presence. The decentering of the self by a process of ascesis furthers the renunciation of the febrile activities of reasoning and imagination and their attempts to seize the divine presence. Because these visions are gifts and because they have clear effect on the contemplative progression, they are interpreted as supernatural visions emanating from a divine activity. They are sent to console and encourage those who seek God when they find themselves in an affective desert, or those who, after prolonged bouts with the negative activity of the understanding, find themselves in the "horrible night of contemplation."[28]

Audible visions are of the same order as these imaginary visions. St. John of the Cross does not even call them voices but says they are an interior, spiritual understanding of words. Precisely because they are interior and because they belong to spiritual understanding, these audible words form part of the comprehensive category of visions: "for we call the understanding of the soul also its sight."[29] Such words are perceived as audible because they are not enunciations produced by a subject in active discourse. Their supernatural character is not, however, a guaranteed fact. Even though he considers them to be essential moments in the mystical ascent, St. John is even more distrustful of these than he is of imaginary visions. "In the shrewdness and stupidity of their small understanding"[30] many people in fact are talking to themselves without hearing it, "as if there were in fact two people."[31] The word of God's revelation can, however, be heard in one's interior being; at a certain moment, those who have fashioned their lives with the aim of listening to God's word will hear it, not simply as an object of their studious appropriation, but as actually spoken by the Other.

Though brief, this discussion has shown at least that the accounts given by the mystics of their ecstatic experiences are very subtle and highly articulated. If we suspend the divine causality posited by the mystics and refuse to settle for a rudimentary notion of hallucination, the psychological analysis of belief is the most natural method of elucidating this phenomenon. The mystics believe that through sound and vision words not simply produced by men can be given to them, and it is this that gives these words the character of a vision, a vision of superior quality if it is not a physical one.

This does not mean, however, that visions are a sign of the privileged election of the one who receives them; the vision simply constitutes a logical part of the mystical way. But although they are accepted as gifts from God, visions are nevertheless marked by a profound ambiguity: they reveal God, but they also conceal him. The "forms, images and figures" are only the outer clothing of true "spiritual communications,"[32] and it is only their invisible "substance" that is important, so it is not the visions as such that mysticism tends to believe.

St. Teresa, for example, does not consider that the refusal to grant any faith to words given in a spiritual form of apprehension is wrong,[33] but, like St. John of the Cross, she herself will believe in them when she sees that the words actually effect in the subject the transformations they announce. Sometimes mystics suspect that instead of manifesting God, certain visions may be an attempt to deceive them, visible forms being capable of having a diabolical as well as a divine substance. Moreover, says St. Teresa, certain natural weaknesses can also cause fake raptures. In order for visions and raptures to be true the soul must be able to "understand those secrets of which it is the object."[34]

These visions are undoubtedly of a very particular nature. Two different elements determine their status as visions: the fact that they emerge spontaneously, and the subject's belief in them. They are given to those who can attain a frame of mind in which all the faculties are gathered together and in repose. God can be found through imagination, which works with symbolic representations of divinity, as well as through understanding, which works with discursive concepts, but the mystic, knowing that God is not immanent in these signs, concentrates on the space between words and images and places himself in a state of receptive silence. This is not, however, a purely passive state; faith acts as an intentional arc that magnetizes the mystic's being toward God. When images or words emerge in this dark room of faith, it is the understanding of faith that judges their authenticity and provenance; then, by attending to the symbolic form in which these images or words appear, the mystic penetrates to the very substance that is intimated.

The spontaneous emergence of these visions is no more enigmatic than dreams or poetic inspiration. When the constructive activities of reason and the imagination cease, the thoughts of faith cast themselves in the same symbolic images that enkindled that faith to begin with. Having been progressively stripped down to its bare essential, faith again takes on a perceptible form, but this time in the consciousness that it is only a symbolic form. The return of repressed material favors this passage into a symbolic form, for it is unthinkable that any affective form of attachment to visible signs can be completely divorced from the subject's deeper psychic formations. With regard to psychology these visions are unquestionably a particular type of hallucinatory phenomenon. The mystics themselves, as if aware of this, warn against the pursuit of these visionary pleasures. If the mystics see these visions as a divine gift and for this reason call them visions, it is because they believe God is at work anywhere there is progress in faith. Without necessarily excluding a religious interpretation, psychology can reconstitute the process operating in visions and thereby account for them. In this way, too, psychology demystifies the miraculous halo that mystical discourse has conferred upon these visions, whose fascination, however, their own critical discourse also curtails.

Visions, therefore, are a hallucinatory phenomenon; they are, in short, thoughts whose content is disassociated from an actual perception, taking on a subjective, internally perceivable form, or sometimes, but more rarely, an exterior physical visibility. It appears that in this case, too, it is the subject's belief in their supernatural causality that supports his adhesion to these images as if they are realistic perceptions of visible scenes.

In order to dissipate any trace of confusion we can compare the different hallucinatory forms. In both delirious hallucination and mystical visions the subject tries to fill in pure words with a real perceptual content. With the mystics, however, no imaginary representation proceeding as if from the external world has to be substituted for a missing piece of reality, because in their case there is no hole in reality. There is, of course, as Teresa of Avila explains, some degree of derealization: "Life becomes a kind of dream; when I see things, I nearly always seem to be dreaming them."[35] Unlike the negative hallucination, there is no uncanny quality here to indicate that, in regard to the world the subject shares with others, his reality has shifted. Close, perhaps, to the dim state of consciousness typical of the hysteric, the mystic's derealization is nevertheless different from the hysteric's in that the mystic does not wind up becoming completely absorbed by vague daydreams. Similar to an amorous or poetic experience, this intense consent to another reality renders everyday things nearly insignificant, unreal like a dream. In this case, a new light tends to dissolve the visible contours of things, to such an extent that everyday objects and events now illuminated by this new reality themselves become the living symbols of this reality. The psychotic cannot believe in the reality of certain perceptual data and finds himself compelled to believe in his hallucination. In contrast, the mystic does not wish to believe that what he perceives is the divine reality itself now become visible, but his belief in the divine visibility of his visions remains free and critical. Both the neurotic hallucination and the mystical vision present the same process for spontaneously transforming thoughts into an imaginary form. The radical difference between them is that in the case of the mystic, conscious thought overrides the imaginary material, keeping a check on the fascination it arouses in the subject, whereas in neurotic hallucination repressed thoughts hide behind imaginary substitutes that reemerge in consciousness only to confuse the subject and take him by surprise. The neurotic is subjected to the violence of being compelled to hallucinate, whereas the mystic is in harmony with the visions his conscious belief unconsciously produces.

Visions and Words in Popular Religion

The Context

Outside the austere path of the mystics, apparitions, visions, and voices also flourished among the larger body of the Christian faithful. An artless realism characterized these visions, in which saints and other holy personages impart secret, prophetic, or historical information—sometimes information of a bizarre nature, such as the adventures of the holy foreskin. Bernadette Soubirous says, with complete assurance: "I saw it with my own eyes." And Joan of Arc, at her trial testified that "at the age of thirteen, she received a revelation from Our Lord, by a voice that taught her to govern herself."

> And she said that this same voice came again at noon, in the summer, while she was in her father's garden, on a day of fast, and she said that this same voice came from her right [the side of good] from near the church. And she said that this voice was rarely without a spot of light which was always on the same side as the voice. She also said that after she heard it three times she knew that this voice was the voice of an angel. And added too that the voice has always protected her well.[36]

It is clear that these phenomena do not have the same significance as the mystical vision, as is shown by the uncritical realism that accompanies them and frequently by the individual's ambition to be the bearer of a revelation. These features indicate that in popular visions a religious interest prevails that is different from those that motivate the mystical schools, the theological masters, or the ecclesiastical hierarchy. It is evident from their whole demeanor that these visions belong to popular religions—even if certain visionaries have played an important role in the government of the Church, and even if some apparitions have been granted official recognition by the Church (after a considerable period of precautionary distrust). To be properly understood, these phenomena must be situated within their cultural context. Seen from a psychological point of view, they belong to the socioreligious structure that determines them, which they in turn foster and confirm. As vague and variable as the sociological notion of popular religion may be, there are a number of oppositions inherent in the domain of religion that can give us an idea of the phenomena designated by this collective term. I should note that by "opposition" I imply those differences of interest and differences between expressive forms of ideal models that actualize the various possibilities contained in religion and in the human psyche. This concept, I may add, implies neither a disdain for nor an excessive valorization of popular religion.

In contrast to the almost iconoclastic austerity of the great mystical traditions, popular religion clearly adheres to the most visible signs that establish a psychical contact between man and the supernatural universe. Here the saints, acting as mediators between man and God, take on a special importance. Whereas God may remain distant and beyond all representation, the saints can be known, the stories of their lives recounted, their virtues and acts represented by an eloquent system of iconography. They are idealized, endowed with quasi-divine powers, and the most human of prayers, needs, can be addressed to them.[37] This more external form of religiosity fosters another side of faith; it emphasizes a more direct and affective expression of it by linking the everyday tribulations and doubts, joys and pleasures, to the aims of faith.

Theology, in contrast, assumes a critical role in the religious community; it discredits the less intellectual, more affective representations of popular religion because they remain far removed from its own elaborate speculations. For their part, ecclesiastical authorities mistrust any spontaneous form of popular devotion because it often takes a marginal position with regard to the sacramental practices sanctioned by the church and because it is too easily prone to cult-worship and other beliefs redolent of paganism. Most of the time these differences correspond to the opposition between those in power and those who are poor, between those who live in the city and those who live in the country. But not all these oppositions are as simple as all that, for a certain dialectical movement periodically inverts the simplicity of these rapports. Then, as a reaction against the deviations that threaten their own role, the authorities, powers, and intellectuals of the church may exalt the virtues of a childlike religiosity, or the beliefs of the simple folk, or blessings visited upon the poor; then the church emphasizes the gift of divine election as it is bestowed upon the "little ones" of its community. In this way, popular religion receives a special esteem and even sees some of its models officially consecrated. This recognition then legitimates the notion of ecstatic experiences and incites popular religion to produce more examples of them.

The Voices of Joan of Arc

To my knowledge, no in-depth psychological analysis of these texts has yet been made, and since I have not myself undertaken this laborious and demanding task, I can offer here only a few interpretive suggestions by way of hypothesis and as an outline for a comparative study of various ecstatic experiences. Competent historians who have studied the documents no longer regard Joan of Arc as a pious impostor, or an enlightened idiot, or as a witch or madwoman.[38] Those clinicians who would still pronounce hers a case of hallucinatory delirium would be simply betraying their own psychiatric incompetency and the general arrogance of the normalizing attitude.

If we apply the criteria developed above, it is evident that the voices Joan heard have nothing in common with hallucinatory delirium or hysterical neurosis. Having discarded such principles of explanation as gross prejudice, however, I would not choose, on the other hand, to approach the enigma of her destiny by simply introducing a principle of supernatural causality that would act through the vicissitudes of ordinary human realities, thus completely closing the gap between the religious phenomenon and its psychological explanation. Only by adjusting various correlations can we approach the secret principle operating in those hallucinatory voices and visions that do not fall within the range of pathology. Nor is it a matter here of explaining the phenomenon in its entirety, but rather of understanding how it becomes possible.

Quite a lot is known about Joan of Arc's personality. She was undoubtedly an exceptionally gifted child, an orthodox Catholic, illiterate but nevertheless well instructed by the Franciscan missionaries. Everything indicates that she was particularly sensitive to the political upheaval of her times and the prolonged suffering of her people. In the matter of ideas and behavior she was tenacious, compromising with no one and nothing, and perhaps matching in this only Antigone's dramatic intransigence.

We read that the first voice she hears "instructed her to govern herself," and this, for her, is an experience of capital importance. If we focus our attention exclusively on the voices that dictate her politico-military project, we are likely to be misled by facts and events that take on an irrational phantasmagoric quality only because they have been divorced from the latent principles that motivate them. "The basic model of the 'national Christian monarchy' dominant in her age was 'The English in England; the French in France; the legitimate, sacred king in Reims, as the lieutenant of God, the true king.' "[39] In this principle governing the society of her time Joan discovered the equivalent of one of the basic rules that governed her life as a Christian: to govern one's own self in obedience to God's throne.

If we consider her among the cohort of visionaries and prophets that proliferated in the Middle Ages, we can only be struck by the sobriety of the messages she reports. All the essential elements of the Christian conception of her milieu can be found concentrated in these messages. It cannot be said that their content shows any indication of mental disturbance. Nor can it be said that her visions reveal anything other than the representations of saints and angels she saw on the friezes and carvings in the churches. If the content of these visions is neither a delirium nor a return of the repressed, then no psychopathological process, properly speaking, can explain the phenomenon. The enigma takes on more precise contours: on the one hand, it is a matter of explaining how these voices and visions appear as phenomena she actually perceives in reality; on the other hand, it is a matter of understanding how a young peasant girl felt herself called to undertake so extravagant a course of action. The two questions, as we shall soon see, are interrelated.

Let us return to our point of departure: a supernatural voice exhorts Joan to "govern herself." The voice imparts no other message or mission to her. It simply gives a command that concentrates all the Christian education she has received. It is not, moreover, the strangeness of the message that arouses her fear but the fact that it is an utterance she hears in her field of perception. She soon identifies the speaker: an angel—in other words, according to tradition, a messenger from God. The voices come from her right, which, according to the popular Christian archetypes of her age, was where the guardian angel—that celestial double whose role is to instill in the child the idea of the good and the right— could always be found. For this child, the "voice of conscience" becomes God's voice, spoken in her ear by the tutelary angel. In this way, the performative force inherent in any speech act that utters a moral or religious command is explicitly attributed to the person who the subject believes enunciates it, and consequently the enunciation is actually perceived. There is no sign of a transference of desire here, as in the mystical quest; no displacement of desire either, as in religious hysteria; no anxiety of conscience, as in obsession. All we can say is that a particularly keen and vigilant religious conscience becomes subject to a divine and sovereign speech act that enunciates its sovereignty and nothing else.

Her perception of the voice as an audible one draws it hallucinatory force primarily from an intense, precocious identification of the voice of conscience with God's enunciation of the commandments. "I is an Other"[40] here, not in the mode of the imaginary identifications prevailing in hysteria, nor according to the substitution of subjects characteristic of religious deliria, but according to the structural relations established during the development of the subject's religious and moral conscience.

This structure of the religious interlocution, in the context of a religion based on the personal revelation of God, cannot of itself produce an audible hallucination, but it does lay the ground on which audible hallucination can occur, as it concretely occurred in Joan of Arc's case, in the form of a speech act whose content is simply the expression of its own sovereign divinity. In addition to this we have to assume, in this thirteen-year-old girl, the presence of an intense religious attentiveness and a strong poetic imagination capable of transposing the representations she had affectively invested into perceptible realities. If such nonpathological transpositions of the imagination into reality can be found in certain dreams, or in people who have recently lost someone they love, or in the distracted reveries of a lover, it is a fortiori possible in a young girl for whom the inspirational presence of a guardian angel is an evident reality.

Between the first voice she heard and the others that later imparted to her the fantastic mission she was to accomplish there is a big step, but not an insuperable abyss. From the pertinent documents it becomes evident that for Joan what had to be done was in the nature of an incontrovertible obligation. The compounded messages exhorting her to establish order according to God's will are the same as the first audible injunction exhorting her to rule herself according to his order of things. What has to be done is a command from God that specifically concerns her, and this command reaches her in the form of a spoken word.

Joan of Arc does not show any sign of the giddy, exalted feeling—so striking in religious delirium—that she was compelled to accomplish some particularly brilliant feat. She always remains subject to the word of command that pronounces itself by virtue of a universal symbolic order and that also happens to concern her personally because she wishes to act in obedience to God's sovereignty. During her trial she answers questions with the same authority she exercised while urging the king and his men to restore a divine order. Her hallucinatory experiences basically remain those voices whose commands she hears, encouraging and informing her as to the mission she must accomplish and reassuring her by giving strategic predictions. It is noteworthy that the visions recounted in the documents remain a secondary motif whose purpose seems to be primarily one of giving the speakers of the various voices some concrete feature identifiable within Christian iconography. The subsequent voices that command her mission are articulated over the first voice she heard: the circumstances surrounding her become so chaotic that her personal governance in obedience to God's order must be extended to the broader political and national domain. The fact that disembodied voices guided her in her obligation to the mission's fulfillment would not have been the least bit surprising for her since, like her contemporaries, she was as used to hearing about visions, voices, and prophetic inspirations as she was to hearing about the appearance of fairies and demons.

Has the enigma been explained? We can say that we have taken seriously certain historical information concerning a specific religious phenomenon; then, finding ourselves obliged to discard a strictly psychopathological explanation, we have developed as far as possible a psychological explanation that also takes into account the religious and cultural context of the epoch. Finally, we can only conclude that the phenomenon is certainly possible according to the laws of the psychology of language and religious belief. That such a phenomenon took place must remain a mystery of an exceptional personality. If it is impossible to elucidate entirely the therapeutic efficacy of the interlocutionary word, and if the secret of artistic creation ultimately evades our psychological understanding and explanations, why should we be surprised that Joan of Arc also remains a mystery?

Counterpoint: The Visions and Stigmata of Theresa Neumann

Many visionaries have taken their own dreams as supernatural visions prophesying the future or as revelations concerning unknown events in the lives of saints or as disclosures of theological or dogmatic "truths." These hallucinatory visions are full of contradictions and theological and historical errors. The contrast between them and the voices reported by Joan of Arc is striking. Nothing in the structure of religious language or of faith supports the oracular force of a voice that predicts (wrongly) someone's death, or one that announces the next coming of the Antichrist, or one that claims to have been present at the death of the mother of Christ in a little house in Ephesus. We may well suspect these to be the result, on the one hand, of an overflow of affective fantasies into religious discourse and, on the other, of an intensified narcissism that compels the subject to assert that he has been singled out by God to be the recipient of his private communications. We sense, in short, that we stand before the marvels of a religious hysteria. Still, such an interpretation may be too facile; in cases that have been carefully checked it has been found that the entire personality of the individual in question cannot be reduced to a psychopathological category.

I will apply the hypothesis developed in the previous section to a case that has been thoroughly documented, the case of Theresa Neumann. Although the foregoing interpretation is not automatically valid for other cases, the obvious similarity between various visionary revelations allows us to draw certain conclusions that enable us to posit the same general psychological approach.

Theresa Neumann's early medical history is well known.[41] At twenty she began to have paralytic seizures and contractions after taking a severe fall while working for several hours to extinguish a fire. She had several additional falls that left her severely injured and paralyzed and triggered the onset of sharp cramps and blackouts. She consequently lost her eyesight and had difficulty hearing. Her condition grew so critical that her doctors despaired for her life. Four years later, on the day of Theresa of Lisieux's beatification, upon applying one of Theresa's relics to her eyes she regained her eyesight. But another fall brought on such severe contraction, swelling, and infection in her left leg that the leg had to be amputated. On the day of Theresa of Lisieux's canonization, Theresa Neumann, suffering and bedridden for the previous six years, got up and moved about. A short time later she heard St. Theresa's voice, and the following day she could walk normally again.

She then began her "mystical calvary." In Lent of 1926, bedridden and ailing again, she had her first vision of Christ's agony in the olive grove. During her ecstatic identification with his agony stigmata appeared on her chest, hands, and feet. Later, wounds resembling the crown of thorns appeared around her forehead and a bruise appeared on her right shoulder, on the spot where the cross was supposed to have wounded Christ. Outside of these ecstasies she remained pretty much what she had been before her physical trials began, a simple, lively, charitable, sincerely Christian country girl with sound judgment.

The physical symptoms triggered by the first fall, the repetition of these falls, and her "miraculous" cures all lead us to suppose that we are dealing with a case of conversion hysteria triggered by a traumatic experience. This was also her family doctor's opinion long before she started having ecstasies—a diagnosis, by the way, that became the center of bitter contention. If we believe subsequent declarations made by the same doctor we can deduce that even if the organic lesions (a vertebral dislocation, for example) were partially responsible for the onset of her symptoms, a hysterical neurosis, facilitated by a certain somatic complicity (according to Freud's formulation), introduced itself, using the lesion as a springboard.

It would be astonishing indeed if Theresa's visions and stigmata had no relation to the hysterical neurosis from which she almost certainly suffered. Other mysterious episodes, attested to by credible witnesses, such as her speaking in tongues or her intuitive knowledge of what was "hidden" in the hearts of others, may call for a parapsychological explanation, and their possible links with hysteria are not known; but such episodes are by no means proof of supernatural interventions.

The discretion with which Theresa Neumann used her particular gifts—with the sole aim of helping along their religious journey those who sought her out—simply confirms the straightforward rectitude of her religious convictions. The absence of any theatrical ostentation seems to have struck her most skeptical visitors. She was not the kind of hysteric who likes to seduce others to her own mythomania.

We should consider the phenomena of stigmata in more depth. H. Thurston, the English Jesuit, concludes his excellent study on stigmatization with a thesis I would certainly endorse: it is "the result of what I will venture to call a 'crucifixion complex' working itself out in subjects whose abnormal suggestibility may be inferred from the unmistakable symptoms of hysteria which they had previously exhibited."[42] It was St. Francis, as a matter of fact, who first created this "complex." "It became a pious obsession; so much so that in a few exceptionally sensitive individuals the idea conceived in the mind was realized in the flesh."[43] "I venture to say that there is hardly a single case in which there is not evidence of the previous existence of a complication of nervous disorders before the stigmata developed."[44] The context makes it quite clear that the only exception Thurston acknowledges is St. Francis, who later became the identificatory model for all sorts of "autosuggestive" imitations. The fact that among the huge number of stigmatists only two men have worn the external marks of the five wounds confirms Thurston's belief that the stigmata can be explained as hysterical autosuggestion. Does it follow, however, that stigmata are only, as Corraze states, "the result of a series of pathological manifestations of which they are the apex"?[45] And is it true that "those who received stigmata are the ones who most dramatically express the masochistic dimension in Christianity"?[46] It is certain that hysterical stigmatization contains an element of masochism, but this is not simply an intentional masochism. Moreover, if it is neurotic, we must decipher its particular significance and its mechanisms. To equate masochistic perversion, neurosis, and the spiritual ascesis whose aim is to participate in Christ's passion is a futile and simplistic form of psychologism.

I will limit myself to pointing out four factors that contribute to the production of stigmata and determine their significance. First, the desire to identify oneself with Christ's suffering: this is a form of participating in the life of someone the subject loves, who is here posited as the model of religious love. Second, in the individual who wants to bring about a decentering of his ego and a religious sublimation of his erotic desires, this identificatory compassion for Christ allows the subject to fight against the desires he wishes to renounce. Third, to accomplish this sublimation the shortest psychological path is taken: the subject identifies himself on an imaginary and affective level with the suffering of his model. This kind of affective and imaginary identification has always characterized popular religion, as is evident from the cult of Mary the Mother of Sorrows and the cult of Ecce Homo. Francis of Assisi, who initiated the setting up of the local missions, was remarkably attuned to the character of the simple people, who because of their own trials were more immediately sensitive to Christ's suffering and would readily seize upon any visible representation of him who had died for love of them. Fourth, in this spiritual climate the process of hysterical identification is pushed to such a degree that the body appropriates the physical signs of mystical wounds.

The narcissistic desire to be especially and publicly chosen is clearly not absent from most of these cases, but this is not sufficient to trigger the appearance of mystical wounds. In order for the signs of suffering to become inscribed in the body, a powerful affective and imaginary identification with the model must take place. After Francis of Assisi's identification experience with the crucifixion, the model becomes doubled. Along with the desire to be identified with Christ, a lateral desire to equal publicly the human paradigm of piety is also introduced. This is one of the meanings that motivates what Thurston calls the "crucifixion complex." The fact that the reknown of one stigmatist quickly sparks the stigmatization of several contemporaries shows that the phenomenon is produced by a kind of contagion. This affective imaginary appropriation of an exemplary object of admiration is completely characteristic of the structure of hysteria. The process of autosuggestion is far more complex than Thurston believes; no individual, for example, can simply will an autosuggestive effect.

Like hysterical symptoms, stigmata are a form of body language, but do they, like symptoms, also serve to express, conceal, and sustain the repression of unconscious representations? Because of the absence of an extensive therapeutic analysis of stigmatization, one can only infer a number of hypotheses on the basis of information gathered from hysterical fantasies. These are fantasies that generally structure the feminine unconscious, but in hysterical neurosis they intercede in and perturb the subject's relationships—particularly sexual relationships. Now, one of the most basic of these fantasies is that of the physical wound of love received by the subject as a mark and seal of special election. The idea of an absolute sacrificial gesture can also magnify the force of this fantasy; like the initiation wound described above, this sacrificial gift symbolizes—in the imaginary domain of how the subject perceives and experiences his body—the assumption of his own sex in relation to an other who is the object of his desire. What specifically perturbs hysterics is the oscillation between the erotic imaginings that depict this fantasy and the accompanying anxiety and revulsion that cause them to reject it. All the horror of these sacrificial scenes, whose content is so powerful as to cause the subject to rebel, becomes concentrated in the "vaginal wound."

It may be supposed, then, that lodged in the desire for stigmatization we find the desire for this wound, this seal with which love marks the body of its choice. The mystical wound, then, could be seen as the realization—in religious terms—of an initiating wound that is itself the sign of a feminine desire that has been assumed by the subject. It can also be supposed that the displacement of the wound onto the body as it is portrayed in Christian iconography is the result of a hysterical repression of a feminine fantasy. But only a more thorough and precise understanding of the imaginary structure that determines the way these stigmatists experience their sexuality could instruct us on this point. In any case, stigmatization represents more than just one symptom of conversion, because the conscious representation of the symbolic significance of the wounds is too dominant. Without doubt, too, the overdetermination of this phenomenon varies from one subject to another. It is worth noting that someone with an imagination and affectivity as lively as that of Teresa of Avila, who also participated intensely in Christ's agony as a matter of spiritual practice, never bore the print of the stigmata. This rather confirms the interpretation outlined above concerning her mystical sublimation.

The foregoing considerations confirm and elaborate our preceding diagnosis of Theresa Neumann's physical symptoms as hysterical manifestations. But let us now examine her ecstatic visions. Each week, with the exception of Christmas, Easter, and other Christian feast-days, from Thursday noon until Friday at 1:00 P.M., Theresa fell into an ecstatic state. Her visions lasted anywhere from ten to fifteen minutes, alternating with periods of "ecstatic repose." During these visions she usually remained sitting up in bed, her arms extended outward, miming in lively gestures whatever she happened to be experiencing. Sometimes, as if completely absorbed in watching some distant spectacle, she would see one of the scenes of Christ's Passion. She would then awaken exhausted as if from a dream, and yawning and stretching she would lean back on her pillow in an ecstatic, peaceful union with Christ. Then a sort of psychic blockage seemed to establish itself. She could answer questions addressed to her, communicating various sorts of information to those around her, but in doing so she spoke as if she were a child and expressed herself, much to her surprise, as if she had just seen the vision for the first and only time. During these moments of ecstatic repose she also appeared to have forgotten completely the whole sequence of events, so that, for example, when she sees Judas kiss Jesus in the olive grove she cannot bring herself to believe he has betrayed Jesus, or when she sees

Jesus carrying the cross she has the wild hope that he might still escape. Moreover, though she feels herself participating in Jesus' holy omniscience, she cannot recognize the apostles Peter or John; she no longer knows what the word *pope* means. She believes she can recognize holy objects, but after one mistake the parish priest refuses to go on with the test. Nevertheless, she could still repeat a number of phrases pertaining to the passion that specialists later interpreted as Aramic. When she returned to her ordinary state, Theresa had no memory of these revelations or of the ensuing exchanges. On Christian feast-days, Theresa continued to have ecstasies, but on these days they were not accompanied by tears, and instead of the Passion she saw other episodes in the lives of Jesus, Mary, or one of the saints.

We can radically rule out the possibility that Theresa's behavior was deceitful or her stigmata fraudulent. And we will certainly not fall back on the term *histrionics*—a key word, in the old psychiatries of accusation, whose explanatory and scientific value is on the order of the *virtus dormitiva* used to explain why sleeping potions had the power to induce sleep. What Theresa Neumann manifests are the same events and scenes she herself sees, but at such a level of intensity that they absorb and exhaust her whole being, causing her body itself to reproduce the spectacles she has seen. Does the medium-like intensity of her visions indicate that their inspirational force has a divine origin? It is difficult to imagine the Holy Spirit acting like a mother with a five-year-old and turning one by one the pages of an illustrated version of Christ's Passion. In their modalities and effects, these ecstasies certainly correspond to hysterical crises. Nevertheless, their imaginary force and rhythm are disconcerting. In this particular case, one has the impression that only religious representations could have shaped, directed, and organized Theresa's crises as we observe them and that these same representations were capable of grafting onto the crises a meaning and finality that a believer as sincere as she could consider worth experiencing. But let us try to verify this hypothesis.

The prodromes to the visions, first of all, are symptoms announcing the return of a neurosis. As Lent began, a year after her miraculous healing by her patron saint, Theresa began to grow sicker and weaker, and although no one could diagnose the disease, she wound up bedridden again. She grew progressively weaker as Holy Week drew near, and during Holy Week she had her first visions. There can be no doubt that her physical ailments were a repetition of her previous hysterical paralysis. Having been miraculously healed, Theresa must at any cost prevent herself, unconsciously of course, from falling ill again for fear of discrediting her miraculous cure. Now a miraculous ailment, reproducing Christ's suffering, gave satisfaction to the demands of her neurosis, transforming it into another miracle, and in this way somewhat matching the life of the patron saint she so admired, Theresa of Lisieux. We should not suppose that Theresa invented this happy compromise; only the unconscious is clever enough to bring about this ingenious solution.

The ecstasies, punctuated by a series of visions and periods of rest, can be compared to those hysterical crises in which we also find a succession of paroxysmal and recuperative phases. These crises, regulated as they are by the series of episodes from the Passion, are not exactly typical, but what crisis is typical? We do, however, find here the succession of tonic and resolutive phases characteristic of hysteria. In these phases, as in other crises of nonreligious sorts, the subject, speaking from a semiconscious state of mind, will attempt to relate the ecstatic or frightening nature of his representations or sometimes, in this light state, will make highly personal comments about those around him. In Theresa's case these declarations consisted of revelations about their private lives (what is called "cardiognosis").

As she watched the evolving succession of scenes given through visions, Theresa was completely captivated by each spectacle before her. In these visions she was both a spectator and an actress miming through gestures her participation in her hero's life. But she behaved exactly like a little girl enacting a mystery play for the first time in her life; she placed herself completely in her hero's circumstances. With the transitivity typical in a mirrored, specular relationship, she transfers onto him all her own childish wishes and feelings. Judas' kiss, for example, is plain proof of his sincerity, and on the way of the cross she is certain that Jesus will be clever enough to flee from his executioners. This imaginary identification with Jesus moves in both directions that constitute the structure of projection: she projects herself into the other (heteroprojection), and she identifies herself with the other (introprojection or autoidentification). Moreover, the regressive psychological state activated by her crises is undeniable; it explains the strange forms of behavior observed in her durings these crises, which the spectators called "a curious amnesia."

These visions during a critical state of consciousness, the evident regression, the specific content of the visions, and their symptomatic antecedents—all these factors must be taken together, and it is only by a study of the concealed connections between them that we may find an explanation of the significance of the visions. What benefit did they procure for Theresa? We may leave aside any secondary benefits that she might unconsciously have sought, for they are really only supplementary considerations that afford little understanding of the fundamental processes at work. What excessively traumatic representation or memory is being repressed here? And what is the symbolic link between the imaginary constructions she entertained at the time of her visions and her unconscious fantasies? These are the questions that should orient our interpretations, and the answers to them may together give a key to the enigma.

Theresa Neumann's compassion for the rejected and tortured figure of Christ clearly caused her to suffer too. It is evident that she found in this suffering a great source of pleasure. To label it simply a form of masochism is to cut short the question by appealing mechanically to a scientific word. If we apply our earlier propositions concerning stigmatization and, with reference to Teresa of Avila, sublimation, we see that by participating in Christ's suffering Theresa Neumann raises her condition to another plane, the universal mystery in the struggle between good and evil. The mystical aim obviously operative here transforms her crisis into a work of sublimation. Nevertheless, the appeal to sublimation in this case leaves too much unexplained. Because of its regressive character, this rather astonishing mystical fireworks too obviously presents its symptomatic character. The combination of pain and pleasure does not specifically gratify any perverse erotic pleasure, but it evidently repeats, through condensation and displacement onto a more noble representation, some underlying traumatic experience in which pleasure and suffering were intimately connected. The essential psychological benefit yielded by visions is that they provide the scenario in which symptoms can perform their twofold task: they repeat and express a traumatic experience with all the affective charge they once had; and they repress the experience by the same repetitive expression provided by the symptom.

The facts are well known. Theresa, born into a poor family, was working for a farmer when a fire broke out in a neighboring farm. "At the sight of the burning hay and falling loft crashing down around me, I began to tremble with fear, as children do when they meet Saint Nicholas."[47] A childhood full of hardship and privations during which she had been subjected to heavy chores, her brutal treatment at the hands of her employer, the mixture of fascination and terror aroused in her by the fire, her exhausted efforts to fight the fire—all these elements must have gathered together to form a complex scenario that she experienced as both a fascination and a terrifying attack upon her psyche. This pattern left its inscription in her psyche.

In the midst of the battle against the fire, Theresa dropped a bucket full of water and, slipping off the ladder, fell backward. Later, when she began to show all the classic symptoms of hysteria, she frequently repeated this backward fall, often taking a severe blow on the head as she did so. These events converged to form the picture of a hysterical neurosis organized around the nucleus of a hysterico-epileptic attack. She reproduced the gist of this experience in subsequent attacks: her fascination and terror when confronted with the violence of the fire and of her employer's behavior toward her. The traumatic experience with the fire probably revived older childhood memories, because one is immediately struck by her association between the traumatic scene and her childhood memory of the terror and fascination aroused by the figure of St. Nicholas.

An analogy between the thematic content of her traumatic experience and the Passion establishes a bridge between the two: the terrifying violence, the aggressive attack and rejection. By invading her body with paralysis and convulsions, her hysterical symptoms also materialized the effects of both the aggression she experienced and her defensive retreat from it (her repeated falls backward). Her visionary participation in Christ's Passion allowed her to combine both her passive and her active impulses; in this way a subject can, by vividly imagining it, actively reproduce an aggression and a rejection that were once only passively experienced. Anyone with a smattering of clinical understanding can see that this way of actively repeating a traumatic experience has a partially curative effect on the subject.

To the infantile chronological regression we have previously noted corresponds another, topical regression that gives fuller significance to the first. Here, as in all neurotic regression, it is obvious that the subject does not actually become a child again. Those standing around her are surprised at the contradiction between Theresa's infantile way of expressing herself and the simultaneous use of her normal intellectual capacities. The regression is selective; it only touches those psychic elements that are associated with the past events of specific unconscious representations. The infantilism of her voice, her habit of counting those around her ("there are one, two, three people here"), her enraptured wonder before each episode of the Passion—all these were staged with the aim of representing a scene: certain infantile memories rose to the surface, and without knowing it, Theresa acted them out as any medium might do. At certain moments, moreover, she split and doubled herself: Theresa, the adult, talked about herself as if she were Theresa, the child. Once, for example, when a visitor importuned her with a question, she answered: "You can't talk to Resa now, she's sleeping."[48] Some people, more devout than perspicacious, took these words as if Christ himself had spoken them.

From a clinical point of view, this chronological and topical regression becomes perfectly intelligible. Experience has sufficiently demonstrated that an adult neurosis always renews an infantile neurosis that may have been brief and might have even passed unnoticed. If, as I claimed earlier, visions do exercise a cathartic and partially therapeutic effect, it follows that by reason of the transferential regression visions activate, they also unleash the traumatic experience that took place in childhood.

Once we are aware of the subtleties involved in unconscious connections and representations, we can also conclude that her identification with her patron saint, Theresa of Lisieux, also contributed to Theresa Neumann's strange destiny. During this epoch, Theresa of Lisieux represented the exalted ideal of sanctity attained through acceptance of suffering, illness, and untimely death. Theresa Neumann was healed by her patron; her participation in Christ's passion and death offered an additional way of attaining the same sanctity. Theresa of Lisieux's insistence on a childlike spirituality undoubtedly evoked echoes in Theresa Neumann, and if one also recognizes the hysteric's penchant to identify with and act out an infantile ideal, it is not surprising to see these various factors converge in the active dramatization, for example, of her "ecstatic repose." Her feeling of peaceful union with Christ and of participating in his omniscience also materialized the dream of an idealized childhood lived in proximity to a father who was also the ideal friend.

The foregoing analysis inevitably raises a question inherent in the psychology of hysteria, that of the relation between hysterical neurosis and sexuality. Nothing in the documents at our disposal contains the slightest clue to the nature of Theresa Neumann's relationship to sexuality. Nevertheless, generalizing from experience, one can suppose that the neurosis itself constitutes an attempt to evade sexuality. If such is in fact the case, Theresa's hysterical-mystical crises must have involved an element of erotic gratification, a paradoxical gratification because it is partially sublimated. Some of the racier comments she made during her ecstatic trances can certainly be interpreted this way. For example, once when an image of the Sacred Heart was placed against her chest she was heard to sigh, "Dear Saviour, you prick me so much that I'm burning up."[49] It seems that the spectacle of the Passion, substituted for her experience with the fire, inflamed in her an interior fire sparked off by Christ's touch.

I might add, in conclusion, that the ecclesiastical authorities' refusal to grant supernatural status to Theresa Neumann's "mystical" experiences testifies to the lucidity of those who, rather less enlightened by psychology than by theology, clearly perceived the rather baroque and phantasmagoric character of her visionary revelations and behavior. I must, however, call attention once more to the fact that aside from her ecstatic moments Theresa Neumann was a simple, straightforward, affable, hard-working Christian, with few traces of self-exalted nonsense. During her neurosis she became depressive, unmanageable, and intolerable to her family; yet after her ecstasies she resumed her previous open and agreeable manner. Her crises, therefore, had a clearly therapeutic effect on her. In the same way that the maenad's occasional Dionysiac outburst, governed by a mythological calendar, allowed the Greek city-state to maintain an orderly life during the intervals, these ritualized eruptions of hysterical fantasies on a sublimated level gave Theresa Neumann a frame of serenity, so that her normal personality could expand itself between her moments of concentrated passion. It is difficult to see how nonreligious representations could have had the same symbolic efficacity. Christ's Passion afforded her the scene by which she could give shape and figure to her traumatized and repressed passions, thus enabling her to move beyond them onto a more universal and liberating plane. For Theresa really did live according to the mystical idea of contributing, for her sake and humanity's, as St. Paul said, to the fulfillment of what was missing in Christ's Passion. The hallucinatory mode in which she lived the mystical idea, however, is a combination of three elements: the repetition of a traumatic experience, a cathartic gratification of repressed desires, and the repeated labor involved in the sublimation of her hysteria.

The case of Madeleine Le Bouc ("The Goat"), whose choice of this name for herself is clearly significant, calls for a similar analytic approach. Janet dedicated a celebrated descriptive study to her case; his poverty of interpretation is redeemed only by his copious documentation and accurate description.[50] I would propose a diagnosis of hysterical psychosis. Although there is in this case a blend of mental illness, "mystical ecstasies," and sincere religious devotion analogous to Theresa Neumann's, here the pathological features of religious hysteria are more exaggerated. It is worth noting, however, that here too the same religious representations that have been distorted in being used and monopolized by her illness and that confirm it also create the symbolic space through which a partial cure can be marked out.

Is it possible to infer, on the basis of an analysis of one case, that the same lines of interpretation can be applied to all other mystical visionaries? According to all the evidence, the visions of the great mystics are very different from the ones I have just examined. Joan of Arc is a rather exceptional phenomenon; she has remained such an enigma that countless efforts have been made through the centuries to reduce her— against all historical evidence—to more manageable dimensions. But what are we to think of the whole cohort of individuals who have received, through visions, all sorts of privileged communications from God, or who have witnessed *de visu* episodes in the life of Christ, Mary, or the saints? I have already pointed out how popular religion can act as a fertile soil for such hallucinatory experiences. I do think, however, that generally, if not always, these phenomena occur in people who are disturbed and who reach a relatively successful resolution of their troubles by transposing their experiences onto somewhat mystical aims and concerns. The examples just examined are related to a desire of a specifically religious order, and they belong to the category of hysterical manifestation, but other kinds of visions, such as those of prophetic intent, correspond rather to the paranoid personality.

Apparitions

Although I cannot undertake here an in-depth study of the copious material on apparitions, I do not wish to avoid entirely the psychological and clinical problems they pose. Those first sparks that took place in Lourdes subsequently ignited a conflagration of apparitions in various parts of the world. Of all these, the Vatican (Pius XII) recognized only one, that of Fátima. This means that by the authority of the pope, the Church decided, in a manner affirmed as fallible, on the authenticity of the apparition that took place there and subsequently authorized it as a place of worship. The Vatican did not recognize the apparitions claimed in Beauraing and Banneux (Belgium), but it did authorize the bishops of those districts to authorize them as places of worship. The Catholic church proceeds on these issues with a reticence it only rarely countermands; it judges only the actual effects of religious conversion and events deemed miraculous, inferring from these effects the probable authenticity of the apparitions. The Church limits its psychological examination of these phenomena to a psychiatric evaluation of the equilibrium, integrity, morality, and authenticity of faith attributed to the beneficiaries of the apparition. It sometimes happens that in a precipitation of piety, those who are responsible for this judgment may deceive themselves, as some experts believe occurred in Beauraing and probably in Banneux as well.

The term *evidence* here must be understood in the same sense it has in expert psychiatric evaluation. More specifically, it refers here to the observable signs of doubt the visionary might have concerning the reality of his visual and auditory perceptions. Cases of fraud can be detected easily, but although some of these cases have been denounced by religious authorities, some false apparitions have nevertheless mobilized enormous masses of people whose aspirations have found in them a common chord. When there is no evidence of fraud, a psychological examination of those who have seen the apparition becomes a more delicate matter, and any conclusion must remain necessarily hypothetical. There are, however, certain signs that may indicate to the trained observer whether the "seer" in question—albeit sincerely believing in his apparition—may or may not have some oblique awareness of the irreality of his perception, in which case we know that we are observing the oscillation between belief and unbelief so frequently found in both infantile and delirious hallucination.

In light of these considerations, it follows that a completely guileless belief that is strenuously maintained when it is put to the test, and one that produces consequences in the life of the "seer" (as was apparently the case with Bernadette of Lourdes), gives us no concrete sign on the basis of which a psychological examination might conclude that it is a case of hallucination. After having verified the religious effects produced by the apparition at Lourdes and by its message, the believer can conclude as to the probability or, indeed, the authenticity of these apparitions—an inference that the principles of faith cannot really support or ground, but that certain theological convictions can. After all, one can always ask, why couldn't Christ or the Virgin manifest themselves as more generally visible, and why not communicate something that could clarify an element of faith more fully adapted to present needs?

No psychological analysis can either prove or disprove this inference as to the authenticity of an apparition, but it does keep the freedom to propose hypothetically that such an apparition could be a hallucination of the same kind as Joan of Arc's voices. Any Christian deciding to adopt this explanation finds himself in good company. Didn't Teresa of Avila claim that Christ has not manifested himself physically since his Ascension? According to St. John of the Cross, God stirs up vision in man's inner, spiritual eye with the aim of encouraging those who seek him; but St. John refuses to consider physical visions seriously even for a second because, even supposing they do come from God, they are finally obstacles to faith. The psychologist might reply, however, that a child who wants so much to see divine beings, invisible and yet still wondrous to him, is surely not capable of distinguishing spiritual from physical visions.

The conflagration of apparitions and the massive procession of pilgrims they have launched in the Catholic countries of the Western hemisphere should be watched with a certain vigilance, but they do not deserve our scorn. Apparitions and mass pilgrimages may testify to the populace's thirst for marvelous events, but they also show how the Christian religion, thus caught up in the metamorphosis of culture, has tremendous difficulty in capturing adequate imaginary forms that would allow the supernatural to show forth in man's ordinary life.

The media populates our imaginary life with constantly changing images. The imagination of the Middle Ages was undoubtedly no less populated. Our images, of course, are present in our homes, our newspapers, our TV sets; whereas their images, religious images, were gathered in their churches. But compared to their places of pilgrimage and those great cathedrals, the most dazzling cinemascopic fiction projected onto our largest screen becomes merely infantile, mainly because it is only a game, *a pastime*.[51]

By means of apparitions the religious imagination creates the external signs of a divine visibility. One can always denounce their fabulatory function, for God, after all, is not a puppeteer—but one should also consider the austerity of the Christian faith. This faith harks back to a holy revelation that is constantly receding farther and farther back into time, and like our technological civilization, Christian faith has progressively stripped and impoverished itself, both on an affective and imaginary level, of nature's symbolic resonance. The ancient universe of mediating figures has now been relegated to the museums visited by cultivated tourists. Is it surprising then that people should try to listen and capture God's voice through the mouth of some Pythian seer? The place the Eastern orthodox tradition has given to the icon in its worship and cultural forms provides a good example of how man's thirst for an exemplary visibility and mediating forms can be satisfied in a way that does not yield to psychological illusion, in a way that is authentically Christian.[52]

9 • The Figures of the Devil

For our purposes it is of little importance whether one believes that demons are only the products of man's imagination or real beings of a supernatural order. By the simple fact that they are granted religious belief, they obviously belong to the psychic reality of certain populations. The proliferation of legends surrounding them should not, moreover, conceal what demons—in light of man's different experiences of them and the variety of beliefs concerning them—may actually symbolize and what functions they bring into play in man's psychic life. The most disturbing of these experiences, demonic possession, will claim most of my attention.

The very notion of possession first requires some elucidation of the relationship between the ecstatic possession prevalent in some religions and the diabolic possession more specific to the Christian religion. Later it will be necessary to see what light psychology has cast upon this phenomenon; for psychopathology has taken the religious category of possession to designate a psychological paroxysmal tension that has, even in the absence of the subject's belief in demons, a marked affinity to this religious phenomenon. A study of demonic possession may also shed some light on the various elements of psychological possession, making it more comprehensible to us.

Ecstatic Possession and Diabolical Possession

Many religions grant specific privileges to a subject who is possessed by a god or spirit. In biblical religion, however, God does not possess man, he lives among his chosen people. God's spirit establishes his dwelling place in the man who chooses to unite himself with him. It is in light of God's inhabitation in man that biblical religion conceives of possession as something opposed, as something that subverts God's dwelling within man's spirit. Man can only be possessed by a principle contrary to God, so it is not accurate to say, as some have, that mysticism is the symmetrical inversion of diabolical possession. In both cases there is a decentering of the subject, and in both another space and level of experience are opened up to man. In the case of the mystic, however, the subject decenters himself in order to recenter himself, whereas the possessed individual, as the term itself suggests, finds his being and identity stolen from him, finds himself alienated by a force that is in him but not present before him, a force that speaks through him but not to him.

The God of the monotheistic revelation does not possess but "inhabits" man. Not being a chthonian power, this God does not occupy man's spirit by sucking him down toward a primordial abyss, nor does he possess man in a rapture that eclipses man's consciousness of himself. Even when they bring about an overflow of joy or pleasure, the ravishments of mystical ecstasies cannot be considered possession because they are a union sought by the subject to which God also freely consents. Through ravishments the mystic participates in God's presence without experiencing the kind of violence that leaves him torn asunder, as in possessions. With this transposition of ecstatic union into a profoundly different form and level of experience, Christianity brings about a modification in the concept and experience of possession. Whereas in other cultures the possessing demon is either an ancestral or a divine being, in Christianity he definitely belongs to the dominion of God's antagonist. In this way, the Christian faith that determines the values and modalities of ecstasy also determines the experience and significance of possession. The possessed is the captive victim of derangement; he is seen as someone who is pleading for God's intervening power to liberate him from his captor. With a clarity that decisively distinguishes them from those engaged in demoniacal mysticism, Christians proclaim that Christ conquered the forces of evil because God has raised him.[1]

First, let me clarify my point of view. I will not discuss questions concerning belief or disbelief in the devil. It is not within the scope of psychology to decide whether this belief (which is not mentioned in the Christian credo) is an essential part of Christian faith or one of the various mythological schemes through which Christianity has thought the history of salvation. In the past, especially during the Renaissance, exorcisms had an apologetic and demonstrative function: the devil was forced, on the public forum, to avow both his iniquitous acts and his final defeat. Through the advances of psychopathology, these diabolical manifestations have taken on a human face. Any trained observer who, for theological reasons, believes in the devil will nevertheless see in these phenomena pathological manifestations that have taken on a diabolical mask. The possessing agency (or demon) then absents himself from our direct observation by hiding behind a pathological formation. Drawing from sources other than the direct perception of visible diabolical subversions, this theological stance can then maintain that the devil's strategy is, as Bernanos said, to get people to forget his existence. Because it is impossible to catch him in the act, it is then legitimate to recognize that the devil acts through the intermediary of hidden powers in the world— ideological and sociological powers, for instance. From this point of view, Satan's work hides behind what clinical psychology accurately interprets as pseudodiabolical possessions and demonopathic psychoses.[2] This interpretation converges with an old Judaic tradition according to which Satan is an evil force working through man; consequently the Talmud distinguishes Satan from demons of other origins, such as spirits without bodies or the souls of wicked men punished by God, all of whom exercise their power as external to man.[3]

Looking now at Jung's psychology, we find that it does not really distinguish between theological and psychological perspectives. Jung puts psychology at the service of theology, but, thinking that psychology states more clearly what theology intends to say, he nevertheless winds up making theology subservient to psychology. He gives belief in the devil a central position in his psychology. He sees the devil as situated at the very heart of the godhead itself, making of him a Satanic fourth instance. In doing this Jung believes he is completing the evolution of dogma by transforming the trinity into a "quaternity."[4] According to Jung, then, the problem of evil, held by the Christian tradition to be one of the most unfathomable mysteries of existence, would be finally "explained" by this theory. Jung's refusal to maintain a dualistic perspective between theology and psychology results in the remythologization of both perspectives: psychology reverts to mythological theology, and faith becomes a primitive sort of gnosticism.

Of course, not all of Jung's disciples agree with these speculations. They usually suspend the issue of the devil's theological status and simply identify him as the symbolic expression of an archetype—in other words, a "spiritual" reality residing within man.[5] I do not see what intelligibility this concept of archetype is supposed to provide, so I will leave it aside and concentrate instead on various psychological characteristics of possession.

Although it brackets the question of the devil's actual existence and action in the world, psychology cannot evict the question of the devil's significance. Confusing these two inquiries, psychology often loses itself in inconsistent theoretical explanations, trying, for example, to explain away belief in the devil by a vague concept of projection, as if one could reduce an ancient and multifarious belief to some elementary mechanism of individual psychology. My own ambitions are more limited. My procedure will be similar to the one I used in studying the psychopathological forms of religion and the psychology of mysticism. That is, I take the subject's beliefs into account and try to understand them by situating them in their cultural frame of reference.

The subject's beliefs and the belief systems of his milieu both exercise a decisive influence on the possible demonopathic forms pathology may take. A certain personal predisposition and cultural context naturally provide favorable conditions for belief in the devil, and it is the task of psychology as well as history and sociology to examine the various currents that determine the specific significance of this belief in various historical contexts. But it is the existence of this signifier, available through the religious tradition, that finally allows this belief to take shape; it is also this signifier that prescribes the various meanings the belief assumes.

Shamanistic possession, which can be found in religions where ecstatic possession prevails, provides a good illustration of the specific differences between ecstatic possession and forms of possession in the Christian context. The contrast between them shows how by reducing ecstasy, possession, and mysticism to the same sort of transgressive experiences, one merely surrenders to a romantic myth based upon facile intercultural comparison.[6]

I. M. Lewis, one of the best specialists in the subject, tells us that during his initiation the shaman goes through a number of crises of possession, during which he experiences moments of mental disorder.[7] According to Lewis, the terrifying voyages the shaman takes to the other world are similar to states of depersonalization and psychotic delirium. A number of Western observers who have addressed this phenomenon have also concluded that shamans suffer from profound personality disorders of hysterical, epileptic, or even psychotic character.[8] Thus, P. Radin, G. Devereux, N. Cohn, L. Laugness, J. Silvermann, M. Mead, and G. Bateson perceive shamans as schizoid personalities who would be considered marginals in our society but whom other cultures have succeeded in tolerating and integrating into their social structure. Other observers, better informed and more attentive to different cultural forms, claim, on the basis of thorough investigation, that although some shamans may indeed be insane, most are in perfect psychic health. A. Métraux, for example, insists that it is not legitimate to equate Haitian voodoo practices with pathological forms, and E. Stambrook shows how the probationary period of the Candomble rite in Bahia actually eliminates potential psychotics. Lewis summarizes his observations in this way: "Where spirit possession is a regular explanation of disease, the fact that certain forms of insanity and epilepsy may also be regarded as manifestations of possession does not necessarily mean that the people concerned are unable to differentiate between them and other forms of possession."[9] Lewis does not entirely exclude the presence of a psychological predisposition in the choice of shamanic vocation, but he finds it necessary to go beyond a reductive psychologistic or psychiatric explanation. Eliade tries to reconcile these contradictory views on shamanism; he describes the shaman as a medicine man who, through an assumption of his psychological troubles into his vocation, manages to master them. Leopold Szondi calls this process sublimation and socialization by operotropism.

Lewis, however, does not find this interpretation entirely satisfactory, for the significance of shamanism is not limited or reducible to an individual private experience attributable to a psychopathological predisposition. The whole symbolic structure set in motion in shamanic possession is a public structure sanctioned by the culture, and seriously disturbed individuals could neither observe the rules of the ritual nor follow through its cathartic initiation. Those called to the shamanic vocation must be capable of sustaining the experience of disorder induced by the ritual. In cults where the fullest and most authentic expression of shamanic possession can be found, we see that the shaman must expose himself to the most dangerous forces of the cosmos. He transgresses the limits of the ordered world and forgoes the protections that govern normal social existence; in this way he learns how to master the powers of darkness that form the basis of the social order but threaten it nonetheless. "But this symbolic wound [the disorder that marks the shaman with the seal of his encounter with transcendental powers] which asserts the supremacy of the gods as the arbiters of both disorder and of order ... is a necessary but not a sufficient condition for the assumption of the shamanistic calling. The observer is not the slave but the master of anomaly and chaos." "Out of the agony of affliction and the dark night of the soul comes literally the ecstasy of spiritual victory ... that reasserts his mastery of the universe and affirms his control of destiny and fate." "If by incarnating spirits he embodies the most profound intrusion of the gods into the realm of human society, his mastering of these powers dramatically asserts man's claim to control his spiritual environment and to treat with the gods on terms of equality."[10] The metaphor of marriage expresses well the shamanistic relation: "If the shaman is contractually bound as moral partner to a divinity, that deity is equally tied to its human spouse. Both are inseparably conjoined: each possesses the other."[11]

By using the formal procedures of structural analysis one can look at shamanistic ecstasies and possession in comparison with those of Christianity, and by examining each in light of certain themes applicable to both, one can outline the various points of correspondence and displacement between them. In both cases we find a recurrence of the same formal themes: the subject tested by an experience of disorder, possession, spiritual triumph, conjugal union with the divinity—all these testify to a commonly shared universal problematic. When situated within the intentional pattern that specifically determines their significance, the contents of these themes reveal what a profound change Christianity has brought about in them.

In the Christian tradition there are two clearly differentiated figures that correspond to the single figure of the shaman: the mystic and the exorcist. Let us look first at the exorcist, since it is he who, according to all the evidence, serves a function analogous to that of the shaman.

As confused as the boundary between sorcery and possession often was during times of widespread obsession with the devil, the two types of phenomena were nevertheless considered distinct from each other. History records the terror Satanism inspired, which, exploding into massive collective hysteria in the fifteenth and sixteenth centuries, caused thousands to be burned at the stake. Society sought to purge itself by fire, concentrating particularly on the eradication of those who, because of a secret and perverse malevolence, were supposed to have linked up with the devil in the aim of injuring their neighbors and destroying the established Christian social order. These sorcerers and sorceresses were not possessed, but they were considered capable of manipulating the subversive powers of the devil with whom they had allied themselves. The uproar the devil caused in his possessed victims was seen in opposition to the secret signs by which his allies betrayed their agency of his malevolent power. Any social isolation of somewhat savage character—a paralysis of some kind, a partial anesthetization of part of the body, a momentary muteness, or psychopathological conduct of a socially deviant nature—could be construed as the devil's print, left on the body consequent to intimate commerce with him. It was believed that the pact by which Satan's tool delivered over his soul was remunerated by the pleasures reaped from fornicating with the infernal power. Sometimes, sorcerers and sorceresses themselves hallucinated that they had participated in diabolical bacchanals, imagining that they had use of magical powers after they had been initiated into the Satanic cult.[12] This twofold distinction of diabolical forms as sorcery or possession corresponds to two of the devil's characteristics and to the distribution of his functional roles in the world of demons. On the one hand, the infernal deflagration spreads the sound and fury of the social, religious, and psychic ruin it wreaks upon the world; on the other hand, Satan remains the hidden master who hides his insidious games because he needs men and women to accomplish his subversive work.

Sorcerers and sorceresses were clearly of sound mind, and yet, because of some physical abnormality, social marginality, or other particular influence, they drew the mistrust of their neighbors upon themselves. In the absence of any obvious form of insanity, Satan's radical malignity was attributed to them, the malignity of the "Cunning One," both maleficent and sly. The spectacular crises of the possessed, on the other hand, were taken as evidence that the subject was in the grip of demonic powers. These madmen and madwomen were clearly not masters of their own being; since they were not in possession of themselves they were possessed by spirits. Because they vociferously performed unnatural obscenities and sacrileges, they could only be the prisoners of foul spirits. It was for these spirits, who greatly outnumbered the sorcerers, that exorcism was reserved.

The famous story of the convent of Loudun in seventeenth-century France exemplifies this distinction.[13] The prestige and charm of the parish priest, Urbain Grandier, an influential and highly orthodox preacher, captivate Mother Jean of the Angels and excite her erotic fantasies. The whole convent is drawn into her diabolical furors. At the trial she accuses the priest of casting a spell on her. The judges, convinced that the obscene monstrosities and sacrileges in the convent were of diabolical origin, impute them to the maleficent powers of the priest; the judges declare him a sorcerer and burn him alive at the stake. Mother Jean, the "victim," is cured by exorcism. Her deliverance is so manifest that she is invited all over France to show her miraculous healing to the king and all the nobles, bishops, and dignitaries of the country, and she subsequently becomes the most consulted prioress of her times.

Exorcists can heal the possessed by virtue of the power vested in them over the forces of evil. A clear analogy can be drawn between the functions and qualifications of the shaman and those of the exorcist and the psychoanalyst. Because of their particular initiation, all three are capable of liberating the victims of hidden forces from their captivity. Nevertheless, the concepts used to identify these forces, and, consequently, the forms alienation may take and the procedures of liberation that will be used are fundamentally different in all three cases. For the shaman and the exorcist certain disturbances of the spirit have as their origin the intervention of harmful spirits. Both the shaman and the exorcist have power over these spirits, and both are themselves immune to contagion from them. Their society authenticates their being qualified for this work and officially confers the power of healing upon them.

The cultural and religious systems of reference, however, are not the same for the exorcist and the shaman. The gods of the shaman are responsible for both the order and the disorder in the world of man. In the case of the exorcist and his "patients," on the other hand, two antagonistic poles are the structuring forces of the universe; the activity of the exorcist actually participates in the apocalyptic struggle between these two poles. The exorcist interprets the signs of possession in the light of his faith and his theological tradition, whereas the shaman is initiated into his function by an experience of possession that takes place under the aegis of his mythology. Having passed through this initiatory experience, the shaman acquires a personal power over the gods. The exorcist, on the other hand, receives his divine power through the ecclesiastical body, which in turn inherited it from the victorious power of its founder.

By interpreting the various signs by which spirits mark their hold over their captive subjects, the shaman and the exorcist have in fact prepared for the advent of the science of psychopathology, and their practice of healing by means of the word paved the way for psychotherapy. As Dr. Ferdière has shown in his commentary on the first chapter of an exorcist's manual, because the Church considered the mentally disturbed to be possessed, it did not cut them off from the community and did not refuse them the sacraments.[14] According to Ferdière, it was this attitude that showed psychiatrists the course they should follow. Although he says he is not a believer, Ferdière adds that in this age of the clinical interpretation of insanity, the psychiatrist should not fail to recognize that mental illness touches upon spiritual values and consequently should not underestimate the help and consolation the chaplain or the theologian can bring to the sick.

If we translate the state of possession into psychiatric or psychoanalytic terms, we can understand and articulate the efficacy of the shaman and the exorcist in their practices. The exorcist's manual, for example, clearly has a clinical significance. In the hermeneutic of the various physical and psychical symptoms it outlines, the manual develops a sort of differential diagnosis. Moreover, the personal qualities required of the exorcist are very similar to those of the therapist. Claude Lévi-Strauss calls the shaman's efficacy "symbolic,"[15] and I would extend this term to the practice of the exorcist as well. An important part of the rite of exorcism, as a matter of fact, consists in the identification and naming of the spirits that possess their victim.[16] Using the language of theological beliefs, the exorcist and the possessed assign names to the voices crying out from the mouth of the possessed and to the forces that agitate and overpower his body. (I will discuss the meaning of this process of deliverance later, when I analyze the various significations of posses- sion.) Exorcism, however, is not a strictly verbal process; it is a ritual whose gestures and imperative language express an actual conflict between two forces. Both the exorcist and the possessed believe that the struggle must be a violent one, but they also know that a divine power will triumph if the exorcist can mobilize it by his ascesis and his prayers and if the possessed can sustain the desire to be delivered and the effort necessary for his conversion.

The interpretation of possession in the language of the human sciences can in some measure account for the meaning of possession as well as ground the effectiveness of the rite on the work of man's reason. And yet, by declaring this efficacity to be symbolic, the psychological interpretation also demythologizes it and subsequently tends to efface its properly symbolic dimension. The religious references functioning in possession and exorcism are not simply the metaphorical manifesta- tions of a mental illness; the symptoms of the illness also intimately incorporate the metaphors of a spiritual combat. The psychological inter- pretation of possession often empties possession of the religious and existential dimensions of its suffering. As justified as this psychological discourse may be, a simplistically causal application of it carries the dan- ger of regarding possession as only a surface manifestation of a psychic cause without ethical or religious experience behind it. In this case, the symbolic interpretation, by reducing the very experience of the symbolic to a strictly psychical level, paradoxically strips the psychic dimension of its symbolic forms and content and thus abolishes it. This leads to a naturalistic reduction analogous to the one described by Foucault in his analysis of the scientific interpretation of madness: "It may happen some- times that certain concepts or certain pretensions of understanding will cover this primary dispersion [of the experience of madness] in a su- perficial manner: witness, for example, the efforts taken in the modern world to speak of *madness* only in the most serene and objective of terms as *mental illness*, in an attempt to obliterate all the values of *pathos* in the variety of meanings implicit in the term *pathology* or in that of *philan- thropy*."[17] We can see how, reacting against this obliteration of the sym- bolic, a demonologic interpretation makes its obstinate return in the present, at a time when the disciplines of psychiatry and psychoanalysis had thought they had definitively triumphed over this mythology. It is not the purpose of this work to judge such beliefs, but the light that modern psychological interpretation has cast on the phenomenon of possession must be taken into consideration here. In so doing, however, we must remain attentive to the various implications of translating this phenomenon into a psychological language whose task is to deploy the symbolic aims of a pathological form by analyzing its imaginary modes of representation.

The Interpretation of Forms of Possession

There where demonology thought it recognized a supernatural current running counter to nature, clinical psychology discovered the manifestations of our psychical nature. Clinical psychology eliminated ancestral rites and substituted less lyrical but more efficacious procedures. Although it demythologizes the belief in diabolical possession, clinical psychology nevertheless leaves the space open for belief in the work of the devil, while depriving that belief of any visible support. Just as, according to Freud, the death instinct never openly shows its face but insinuates and conceals itself inside the manifestations of Eros, the devil, supposing that he is at work in the horrors and sufferings of man, will also never show his face by obviously detectable signs. As a matter of principle, clinical psychology consigns his voice to silence. As inexplicable as pathological phenomena can fundamentally remain, no supernatural power can be posited as acting within the folds of psychology. Consequently, nothing authorizes the distinction that has been made between possession and pseudopossession.[18] This artificial distinction testifies to a confusion of perspective and an incapacity to assume the consequences of such confusion. If psychopathology has shown that perturbations of a demonopathic character derive from definable psychic structures and processes, then illness and "true possession" must be tightly bound to the same web, and it is no longer possible to posit this distinction between psychic and diabolical causes. To maintain exorcism as a special rite for the deliverance of cases of "true possession" is just to maintain a relic of a prepsychological culture.

Experience is pitiless; it has relentlessly taught us that each time one pushes the analysis of a case of possession as far as possible, one finally reaches an insurpassable limit: the age-old belief in the devil that makes him *exist* for the subject. As much as one tries to exclude him from reality and bury him in some chapter on psychopathology, one must finally admit that he makes a place for himself in the world by virtue of his presence in the religious discourse on evil. In cases such as these, the explanation of possession by psychopathology has as its counterpart the partial explanation of pathology by the discourse of belief.

The clinical interpretation of possession is situated within two interlocking regions: that of the coordinates of the culture, and that of the psychic reality which, finding a specific affinity with the culture, adopts them for itself. There are, as a matter of fact, some striking coincidences between the images of the devil and certain significations latent to pathology. The devil always represents the subject's shadow, something that manifests itself as strange or foreign to him. The idea of possession can become implanted in pathologies only where processes of defense against this stranger present in the self consist of a doubling, or splitting, through which the stranger becomes another that is both inside and outside the subject. Both hysteria and the splitting of the ego in psychosis conform to these conditions.

There are three striking exceptions to the resemblance between certain images of the devil and the attributes he manifests in cases of possession. In the Judeo-Christian tradition,[19] Satan is the prince of pride, the father of lies, and the accuser of man before God. These roles, however, which define his essential perversity and the substance of his subversive function, are attributes of a lucid state of mind and are thus by their very nature unsuited to being diffused into the dense sense of pathos present in states of possession. There is a contradiction between the exercise of a radical evil and this sort of deranged enslavement to an abusive power.

Using the analytic method, we can first see possession as a hallucination that depicts the realization of repressed desires whose frenzied character bursts out through the possession. We can therefore hypothesize that the violence of these desires converges with a belief in the devil to give rise to a hallucination. If we take into account the subject's resistance against these desires, we would say that he manages to lift this repression by delegating the realization of his desires to the other, the devil, in him. The two types of structure and resistance that we have already distinguished present two differentiated modes of possession-hallucination. Either the possessed delegates his desires to another personage that represents his unconscious ego, as in the case of hysteria, or he ejects them from his unconscious, in which case they make their return from the outside in the form of demonic assaults, as in the demonopathic delirium of the split personality witnessed in psychosis.

The reader may be surprised to find that I exclude guilt neuroses from the category of possession even though several authors have derived certain forms of possession from the guilt complex.[20] It is true that guilt always weighs heavily on unavowed desires, yet possession is not a system of defense against the presence of guilt; it is rather a hallucinatory strategy that leaves no room for a guilt neurosis. Possession does not consist of an active defense against a fault, for the fault is not itself present in the unconscious subject because guilty instinctual movements have been projected onto a figure foreign to the subject's self. And yet, by taking control of the subject whose secret desires he assumes, this diabolical stranger sets in motion other psychic forces besides the subject's desires.

Hysterical or Antimystical Possession

The literature on this subject is abundant, and the cases recorded in diocesan or municipal archives correspond in kind to those encountered by contemporary psychiatrists. In this day and age they are, of course, quite rare, but in earlier ages the belief in possession served to invite it, and the publicity given to the "admirable accounts" of the exorcists' victories over demons became the models for odd and extravagant displays of hysteria. Later, the Victorian era, under whose influence women were successfully restricted to the family circle and their bodies securely covered up, gave rise to the celebrated crises that came to correspond to the medical model of the female nervous crisis. As a matter of fact, it is characteristic of hysteria to seek out firmly established cultural patterns into which it can cast the fantasies of the subject's repressed desires.

Possession was, and is still, generally the prerogative of women, just as sorcery was most commonly found among women. There are two reasons for this, one sociological, the other psychological. Social and cultural repression bears more harshly on women than men, and ritualized power over demons was the specific privilege of the male. Lewis, for example, observes that "clandestine ecstatic cults have always attracted followers among the weak and oppressed, and particularly among women in male-dominated societies."[21] The psychological reason for this is linked up with a sociological condition. The idea of possession itself suggests something that overflows and bursts out in a crisis, and this something is the saturated libido of the seduced and frustrated body. Now, it cannot be denied that the female libido, not having an organ that might visibly polarize it in the subject's imaginary construct, is generally more diffuse in women's interior experience of their bodies than in men's, and correlatively, this libido tends to manifest itself on the surface of a body arrayed in libidinal emblems. The old image that connected hysteria with the migration of the womb (*hustera*) through the body prefigured the mystery that psychoanalysis would later unveil.

Since I do not know of any psychoanalytic study of a case of possession, I will examine an old case that has been fairly well described. The "Discours admirable et véritable des choses advenues en la ville de Mons en Hainaut, à l'endroit d'une Religieuse possessée, et depuis délivrée"[22] (The admirable and true account of the things that occurred in the city of Mons in Hainaut, concerning a nun who was possessed and then delivered) is a paradigm of its genre. Published in Louvain in 1586, shortly after Sister Jeanne de Ferry's demonic tribulations (1584–85; she died in 1620), this narrative includes the confessions of the possessed, who related the events with considerable apologetic candor.

When she was four years old, Jeanne, the daughter of a violent and alcoholic father, was "handed over to the devil's power" by her father after he came home from a tavern. "[I] was seduced by the devil's suggestion, who presented himself to me as a handsome young man asking to be my father and giving me a piece of apple and a bit of white bread." This devil subsequently multiplied into various devils who gave her all sorts of sweets and anything else she wanted to eat but in return extorted various renewals of written pacts from her, some of which she was forced to swallow with an orange, among other things. The demons kept copies of these pacts, whose hiding place Jeanne revealed during her exorcism. The demons then incited her to give herself over to worldly pleasures. They became strongly authoritarian, threatening to torture her if she refused to obey them. They tormented her violently in order to make her refuse communion and launch blasphemies at the sacred host. They forced her to look with horror upon the religion of "a false God ... hung like a criminal on a cross."

At fourteen, however, she entered the convent of the Black Sisters in Mons; she completed the novitiate and took her vows at the age of sixteen. In the meantime no one noticed that "I had given them [the demons] full power and authority over my soul and my body." She continued to blaspheme, to desecrate the host, and to let herself be transported by a demon named Magical Art, who took her "day or night, wherever I wanted to be." A whole litany of devils seized her—the Wicked Traitor, Heresy, Turks, Pagans, Saracens, Blasphemers; they came into all the parts of her body and all her senses, "and I became completely transmuted from a creature into a devil." They made her take off her religious garb and they smeared her body with "a very excellent oil." She was forced to eat meat on days of abstinence and to spit it out on feast days. In her confessions Jeanne does not explicitly indicate what erotic adventures she had with the devils, but she does relate how one day a demon named Bloodthirsty, "carrying a sharp knife, came into my body and carried me to a table, and as I screamed in great pain, he carved a piece of flesh out of my body." This happened three times, and it was in her "precious parts" that Bloodthirsty made his incisions.

As the mood of these demons progressively deteriorated, they pushed Jeanne to despair and finally made an attempt upon her life. Her physical exhaustion and her alternating crises between arrogance and anguish eventually alert the community. Several priests are consulted. On discovering her secret life, they submit her to repeated sessions of exorcism during a period of a year and a half, but the devils put up a strong resistance. She has a number of relapses and goes through convulsive crises, bouts of screaming, respiration blockages, epileptic rigidity of the body, nocturnal flights, and attempts at suicide. When Cornau (the Horned One), the devil-father of her first seduction, is finally expelled, Jeanne is consoled by taking the canon who exorcised her as her father, with his consent. Jeanne's exorcists had already been considerably impressed by her phases of amnesia and aphasia, which they had taken as signs of the supernatural nature of her possession, but their stupefaction is unbounded when, after having been adopted by the canon, "the nun reverts to the simplicity of a child, ignorant of everything she once knew about God and his creatures, and is incapable of speaking any words other than 'Father John' (the canon) and 'Pretty Mary' (Magdalene)."

After having taken St. Mary Magdalene as her new mother, Jeanne played with a painted image of the saint as if it were a doll, "holding it to her breast, as if she wanted to give it suck." One day she called the bishop "grandfather" and promptly relapsed into a convulsion, followed by a crisis of anorexia, until "grandfather" took her into his palace in order to watch over her physical and spiritual welfare. In the meantime, Jeanne experienced a series of ecstatic revelations in which Mary Magdalene appeared to her surrounded by a bright light and gave her the directives that would insure her salvation. Because of the spreading rumors about the bishop, however, Mary Magdalene convinced her to leave the episcopal palace and return to the convent. In memory of the happy turn in Jeanne's fortunes, the people of Mons gave their bishop the nicely equivocal epithet of "the good devil of the black sisters."

Jeanne de Ferry's "admirable" history seems to have perplexed P. Debongnie, who concludes his commentary with a question: "Which of the two sides wins the day in this story? Is it a mystery of diabolical guile? A mystery of feminine psychology? Or is it perhaps both of these together?"[23] And yet confessions such as this one, where the possessed parades so frankly all the devilry of hysterical neurosis, are quite rare. The story of Jeanne's childhood possession brings out two basic elements: a hallucinatory substitution of an ideal father in the place of her own shameless father and the imaginary seduction she experienced as a child at the Oedipal age. Even if these memories were only a personal myth constructed after the fact, they are such a manifest mise-en-scène of hysterical fantasies that they are surely transpositions of Jeanne's unconscious representations. And even supposing that she fabricated this childhood fable after the pattern of the popular tales she had heard, it is undeniable that as an adult, she believed she recognized her own childhood in this portrait of a little girl that she herself was not, so much does this figure reveal to her a past she was confusedly trying to reconstitute.

These two inaugural fantasies, which realize on an imaginary level two fundamental female fantasies, later engendered the great myth of a possession elaborated in the shadow of a mystical orientation. The fact that Jeanne followed both these paths at the same time shows that they were in some way parallel, both responding to the same desires. And yet they were also mutually contradictory insofar as her possession was an attempt to satisfy these desires by archaic imaginary constructions, whereas the religious path requires a transformation of this archaic imagery by sublimation.

Her hallucination of the first devil, who was both an ideal father and an attractive young seducer, was linked to her desire to be seduced and passively given over to a splendid being who could take possession of her body and soul. In contrast to this fascinating seductivity, the Christian religion, presenting for her adoration a wounded and humiliated Christ—a figure who is figuratively castrated—appeared repulsive to her. Religion, however, still held a powerful attraction for her, and particularly that mysterious part of it enveloped by the halo of the marvelous, the Body of Christ given under the species of white bread. It is surely no accident that during her adolescence, Jeanne, a "lively spirit drawn toward the higher things," had shown a passionate interest in questions concerning the Eucharist; nor is it surprising that the abuses and blasphemies the demons provoked her to perform were generally directed toward the host. It was her original seducer, as a matter of fact, who was the first to offer her the white bread.

The litany of demons that consequently possessed her satisfied Jeanne's intense orality by the meals they offered her in her dreams. And when she reverted to the "simple-mindedness of an infant," she suckled the image of her adoptive mother, who was in fact her own double in this interplay of mirror-images. After a series of successful exorcisms she then had a relapse, particularly marked by anorexia, until her "grandfather," the bishop, took her to his home and provided for her like a good father. During her possession at the convent, her orality also became the domain of these inversions between the mystical and the diabolical paths: she ate meat on penitential days and fasted on feast days. There is no doubt that a prevailing oral position determined these two parallel paths, both of which search for plenitude by the incorporation of an absolute. She even eats the pacts that constitute her attachment to those who represent all kinds of magical delights for her; by so doing, she accomplishes in an inverted way the command written in the Book of the Apocalypse—to eat the book of life.

Considering the extent of the oral register, I am inclined to believe that possession by the devil is basically a possession of the devil. Through a regressive invitation of her dominant orality, the Oedipal seduction finally leads to her incorporation of the seducer. Whenever there is true possession, the devil is always *in* the body; he possesses from within. In any case, the image of the devil corresponds to the fantasy of incorporating the other. "The one who is possessed represents the devil who inhabits him as having a body smaller than his own,"[24] an image frequently confirmed by the small devils carved on cathedral walls. This case illustrates some of the similarities and differences between possession and mysticism. Whereas God inhabits the subject in the manner of a guest, the devil inhabits him like a desired but terrifying tyrant who takes possession of him. With the devil there can be no face-to-face exchange, no interlocution; the devil screams through the mouth of the possessed, and the subject cannot recognize himself in this altered language. Because this ventriloquist's voice does not declare his identity, the possessed himself must try to identify him, and he can usually succeed in doing so only in the course of therapy by exorcism.

But let us push this analysis further in the direction of analytic interpretation as such. The multiplying devils who inhabit Jeanne's body provoke spasms and convulsions; either they make her howl or they make her mute; they give her nausea, cause her to vomit, burn her, torture her. We cannot fail to see here the fantasy of the incorporated imaginary phallus. If we consider the ancient image of the womb migrating through the body, we can say that it now symbolizes the imaginary phallus. In possession, the devil gives this phallus a figuration borrowed from the dangerous and seductive power of the idealized Oedipal father. Is it just an accident that Jeanne's first devil, representing the seducing father, is also the last one, named Cornau, from which she finally detached herself after months of exorcism? Through the "cunning devilry of the signifier," this name condenses the fantasies of her possession. *Cornau* combines two French words, "cornu" (horned beast) and "beau" (beautiful)—thus, the horned father-devil who presents himself as a beautiful young man. Note that of all the names of her devils, Cornau is the only one that has no immediate signification. The second devil who entered Jeanne's body was called Garga, a name obviously derived from the word *gargoyle*, a frequent figure for a demon. Jeanne did not identify by name these first two diabolical guests, Cornau and Garga, until the end of the exorcism. Cornau would later reveal the profound significance of the possession, whereas Garga provided the image for her hallucinations.

It is not surprising that the possession triggered other fantasies in her besides oral fantasies. The devil in the body bedevils all the desires of the body. The paternal devil-phallus in her body demands confirmation and reinforcement by sexual penetration. Consequently, after a long series of magical ravishments, Bloodthirsty appears armed with a blade and cuts into her "precious parts" three times, taking out pieces of her bloody flesh. The hysterical desire for—and terror of—the vaginal wound is here accomplished by a penetration that brings about a feminine castration; the body opened and its seal scored into the flesh. This castration, however, cannot remain on an imaginary level: instead of giving the phallus, with bloody violence, the possessor takes his pound of flesh. The last of her parade of devils, Bloodthirsty, closes off the regressive cycle and the return of the Oedipal fantasy. Until the day Jeanne begins her catharsis, she has no alternative but to exhaust herself in these fantasies that consume her.

Jeanne's confession, like those of all the possessed, is a long account of her sins. Her exorcism naturally brings about the reversal of her private pleasures into guilt. But her narrative reveals consciousness of the evil with which she was plagued. It is not easy to get a clear grip on this consciousness of evil because it is of a truly paradoxical nature. Aside from the names of the first two devils and the last, all the names spring from popular appelations of Christ's traditional enemies: the Great Traitor (Judas), Heresy, Magic Art, Turks, Pagans, Saracens, Blasphemers. She chooses her visitors well; she delegates her revolt against religion to their dominion. Is is out of guilt, then, that she allows these inhabitants to scream out her abuse and perform her acts of blasphemy? The paradox here, one typical of hysteria, consists in avoiding any confrontation with guilt by allowing herself to be unconsciously dominated by the passions that had been awakened in her. Without being explicitly aware of it and yet having some oblique consciousness of it, Jeanne, like Glendower in Shakespeare's *Henry IV*, calls forth "the spirits from the vasty deep." It sometimes happens, in other cases, that guilt triggers a hallucination of possession, like the one produced in the case of Achilles.[25] But the possession in this case remains an unconscious strategy used to eliminate the distance that a consciousness of guilt implies and, through a process of doubling characteristic of the imaginary identification, to cling to the internal force of desires and revolts, which, after having been initially banished, return to invade the unwary subject.

Like the hallucinatory phenomena previously analyzed, Jeanne's fantasies are conditioned by the widespread belief in the possibility of possession. The possessing devil assumes charge of her wildest dreams and magical fabulations. Insofar as he is God's antagonist, he gives her repressed desires the proportions of an antimystical absolute. Even though it is a modality of hysterical neurosis, possession also has its own specific aims, aims that should not be misunderstood by supposing that hysteria is simply the same neurosis under a sequence of changing masks.

A diversity of cultural discourses each time mobilizes specific processes that leave their own print on hysteria, just as they do upon any other psychic figuration. Of course, both orality and the fantasy of the incorporated paternal phallus constitute a basic and universal thread of the hysteric's unconscious, but diverse cultural references then fill up this symbolic network in the unconscious with their specific existential content.

Possession may have its moments of intoxicating fantasy, but it does not remain the happy excursion into the garden of wild desires so ardently dreamt of by those who yearn for a transgressive madness. The furies of possession betray something more than the insurrection of repressed desires, and it is naive to suppose that possession is the hallucinated realization of desire, comparable to the mise-en-scène found in dreams. Possession is as full of nightmares as the dreams of neurotics. Its furor is the outcry of the trauma undergone by the hysteric who has been passively seduced, at least in fantasy, and who repeatedly experiences an imaginary but aggressive assault. She remains attached to it by a passion as powerful as love, but all forms of joy or pleasure are finally perverted into a masochism devoid of pleasure. This does not contradict the fantasy of the incorporated paternal phallus, because the phallus here incorporated represents a sanguinary violence. Having once incorporated it, the hysteric is then possessed by it and suffers internally the outbursts of a brutal violence that tortures and dismembers her. The same phallus that possesses her propels her toward a similarly destructive violence. Because it comes into her through copulation, it can only be experienced as a violation. One of the fantasies common to hysteria, that of finally appeasing the phallic fury by completely surrendering oneself in a last act of self-sacrifice, alternates with the fantasy of a savage and destructive explosion. Possession illustrates rather clearly the links between hysteria and psychogenic epilepsy; the relationship between the two should be understood in light of their common fantasy, the unexpected seduction exercised by the paternal phallus over a subject whose desire is strongly fixated in the oral position. The fantasy of incorporation reproduces the seduction by means of oral representations. It is not only the satisfaction of the desire to be possessed, it is an active repetition of the traumatic violence that the subject suffered.

According to Françoise Dolto, the child's image of the devil corresponds to certain aspects of possession.[26] In contrast to wild animals, who kill out of a vital necessity, without moral regulations, the devil is perceived not as amoral but as immoral: "For the child the devil is synonymous with his own disappearance as a social being. If he consorts with him, the child enters into a world without social norms, beyond all rule." The devil, then, is the figure of the disorder that threatens every-thing that lives. He is the contrary of a "metaphysical transcendent."

Demonic possession can also be compared to Dionysian possession. There are certain features showed by these two that differentiate them from shamanic possession. When Dionysus makes his presence felt among the faithful, "his coming is an irruption, his action is passion. When the god is there, his follower *is no longer there*. Like the god, he is outside himself. Man does not have hold of himself in his presence to the god, he is held." "Possession by the god is a dismemberment. The god brings everywhere the contradiction that he is."[27] His invasion ter-rifies his adherents by a mutism that projects them suddenly into the grip of a savage cruelty. What happens in these possessions? The myth of Dionysus that governs them gives them a symbolic content of their own. Dionysus is the figure of an internal contradiction between the emergence of form and its aspiration toward the dark ocean that lies at its genesis. In contrast to Dionysus, the biblical demon represents an inversion of the symbolic order whose structure was given by the mono-theistic message. In all these forms of representation, specific cultural signifiers mobilize different dynamic schemes in the unconscious. Be-cause they have been ritualized and integrated into the rhythms of a diastolic pathos and a systolic social context, these Dionysian possessions apparently do not bring on the dissociation of personality found in demonic possessions.

Demonopathy in the Psychotic Doubling

I will limit myself here to differentiating this form of pathology from the kind of possession I have just analyzed. It falls under delirious psy-choses, and any in-depth study of it should find a legitimate place in a comparative study of various forms of religious deliria.

The particular case observed and schematically described by Lher-mitte is an exemplary one.[28] The case concerns a man "haunted by the problem of sex since his childhood, . . . who tends to indulge in solitary practices, with a certain inclination to homosexuality." When he married he was "so continuously assailed and tormented by obsessions that he increasingly found himself forced to take refuge in prayer, concerted control of his thoughts, and remorse. He then began to feel an increas-ingly violent compulsion to pray, until one day he felt a strange trans-formation take place inside him, and everything that took place around him became a symbol for him" of either good or evil spirits. In this "frenzied symbolization" we can recognize what Groddeck called the compulsion to symbolization. It points to the violent irruption of unconscious representations that are imposing themselves with an almost hallucinatory force upon the subject's perceptions. This man's possession becomes established on the occasion of a frankly hallucinatory episode. One day, as he was walking in the Bois de Boulogne in Paris, "he thinks someone is calling him, and hears words" that Lhermitte does not care to repeat but whose content can be surmised given the place and the patient's fear of homosexuality. Terrified, he runs home and says to his wife: "This time the devil is with me; I'm possessed." Subsequently, "he constantly feels the devil's inopportune presence, continuously talking to him, launching abuses and the vilest obscenities at him. . . . He often taunts and orders him about, reminding him of all his past faults. . . . The evil spirit not only assails him with filthy remarks and repeats his own thoughts to him in order to irritate him, but he also presents to his view the most bewildering pictures of lewdness. . . . These lustful scenes, greater in beauty than any the sons of men could possibly represent, are given an even sharper attraction by the brazen character of the homosexuality depicted in them."

A certain element of lucidity accompanies this delirium. As he describes it later, the subject writes that "the thought that knows it is being thought" gives the devil the means by which he acts upon the mind. Lhermitte unfortunately does not report the subject's exact formulations. Nevertheless, it seems to me that this delirium is comparable to that of Perceval,[29] who also stated after his cure that in some corner of his mind he was conscious of being delirious. Here again we find that paradox of consciousness that must adhere to the belief in its delirium, even as it knows that it is mentally deranged. Because of this paradoxical consciousness, this kind of possession is both more invasive and less possessive than hysterical possessions are. In this case the distance between the subject and the devil is at once nonexistent and infinite. The devil does not inhabit the body, he possesses the subject in the manner of being *with* him. He assails the subject from without, remaining always the fascinating tempter, the grimacing menace, the double who accuses the subject of the very faults to which he incites him. The devil acts as a spokesman here, assuming all the sordid representations that the subject ejects from consciousness and thus effecting return from without in the form of the devil who constantly accompanies him.

The fact that homosexuality constitutes the nucleus of the material that has been projected outside the subject agrees with Freud's analysis of paranoia. Here, however, the paranoiac projection is not founded on any of the three possible inversions of the statement "I (a man) love him."[30] We are not dealing here with erotomania, delusions of persecution, or jealousy; this form of demonopathic paranoia avails itself of a religious signifier in order to transpose a repressed homosexuality onto the outside world. In this case, too, it is a religious signifier that permits the emergence of a pathology whose problematic can be avowed only indirectly, in which case the demonopathy reported here very probably spared the sick man a more serious and irreversible form of paranoia.

The Experience of Dereliction

After two centuries of a triumphant demystification of superstition, a new wave of occultism is sweeping the Western World. Works on the occult become best-sellers; astrology, cartomancy, and spiritualism are cropping up all over, offering their services to the anxious citizens of the age of reason. Is the occult a substitute for faith, as *Time* magazine claimed?[31] Perhaps the most somber fact in this resurgence of the occult is the return of Satan. In the United States, Blatter's novel *The Exorcist* was on the best-seller list for fifty-two weeks. When the film version was shown in the United States and parts of Europe, these countries were swept by fascination with the Satanic. Are all these enterprises successful because they satisfy some thirst for strong emotion experienced through fear? This is certainly the case, and in this sense they are a counterpart to the pornographic films that have become a part of the contemporary imagination. There is a correspondence between the anxiety-ridden nightmares stirring beneath the ground of man's reason and the idyllic innocence of his wildest dreams of pleasure that brings to mind the highly contrasting images in Hieronymus Bosch's paintings. It would nevertheless be a form of psychological quackery to reduce these phenomena strictly to a sort of emotional blandishment looking for ways to escape the monotonies of a way of life constrained by technology and disenchanted by the consolations of reason. These phenomena manifest and disguise some of the most essential rifts and fissures in human existence, even if they do take these absurd and wretched forms. Motivation psychology and that form of sociology that defines itself in reaction to the oppressive power establishment can both try in vain to restore the peaceful sleep of reason that Satan's return has recently disturbed.

Earlier I analyzed the pathology of possession with relation to the determinant biblical signifier that gives a symptomatic form to concealed desires and buried traumas, but the roots of possession cannot be understood unless one specifies its relationship to basic experiences that, although not pathological in themselves, find a means of expression in reference to the figure of evil. I should mention once again that this analysis does not imply a position either for or against Satan's actual existence. And yet I have found that the positive belief in the devil articulates and is grounded in the experience of a dark abyss; this is the case both when this belief clings to popular superstitions and when it rejects them for fear of appearing ridiculous. It is into this abyss that pathological possession has cast its gaze—even if it has only glanced for the space of a second, it remains haunted by the memory of the abyss, and the pathology builds itself over it in an effort to forget what it has seen. For every symptom is, after all, just an aborted attempt at healing.

Let us begin with the old and naive story of possession and exorcism told about Haitzmann the painter and recounted by Freud in "A Seventeenth-Century Demonological Neurosis."[32] The neurosis was a common one during the epoch that Freud calls the "dark times" of the Middle Ages. Freud thought that it revealed its secret as clearly as any infantile neurosis precisely because both were neuroses of a "primitive" age. The plot of the story is relatively simple. After his father's death, Haitzmann, having become profoundly depressed, falls into a condition of wretched poverty and decides to sign a pact with the devil, who appears to him in the guise of an honorable bourgeois. There is no point in following the complicated conditions of the two pacts; suffice it to say that the essential agreement is written in the painter's blood as follows: "I sign a bond with this Satan, to be his bounden son and in the ninth year to belong to him body and soul." Things did not go well for this "poor devil" of a painter; convulsive crises, paralysis of his legs— both typical in the parade of afflictions that follows possession—little was spared him. But when the date of the pact's fulfillment approaches Haitzmann has himself exorcised and claims back his pacts. He then enters the order of the Brothers of Mercy and goes on to lead a peaceful life with them, tempted to renew his pact with the devil only when he has drunk a bit too much wine. It is evident, says Freud, that the devil is a substitute for the father (a *Vaterersatz*), a duplicate (*Nach-bild*, a copy that came later to replace the father). Later the religious community replaces the father-provider and provides security in the life of this painter, who had been abandoned without recourse. He therefore "vows" himself to religion in the same way that he first "vowed" himself to the devil. This sleight of hand works the therapeutic effect: the neurosis of possession with its hallucinations and convulsions ceases to afflict him.

But why exactly was there a therapeutic effect if it was simply a matter of replacing one copy of the father by another copy? Is it only because the last is a father figure who effectively provides for him, even if it is at the price of a somewhat austere life? Or is it because it is socially more legitimate to enter the religious life than to draw up a pact with the devil? Freud would never have explained the cure of any of his own patients by the mere promise of a bit of well-being or some other sort of secondary benefit. This particular work is marked by some of Freud's most profound observations on the pre-Oedipal condensation of paternal and maternal figures into the figure of a devil endowed with both a penis and breasts; it also contains his comments on the ambivalence of the devil-god; all the same, his analysis of this case ends with an analytic quid pro quo that turns the pathos of a whole libidinal economy into a utilitarian comedy of an exchange of goods. Underlying this analytic romance, however, we find one of Freud's fundamental themes, the longing for the father. Unfortunately its intensity is lost in a conceptual fog in which all fathers become the same, much like the celebrated cows that all look black at night. If all these fathers can become indifferently duplicated figures, why should the substitution of one father for another effectuate the passage from neurosis to its resolution? We confront at this point one of the basic difficulties implicit in the theoretical formulations of psychoanalysis, one that has prompted epigones to apply psychoanalytic concepts rhetorically to any issue at hand.

We know little about Haitzmann, a man formerly possessed who eventually found his peace in religious life. We do know that during a period of distress in his life he gave his body and soul to the devil, who in turn promised to fulfill his desires and even, after a period of nine years, to become a father to him. All this strangely resembles the pact of ownership Jeanne de Ferry drew up with her seductive young man. When Haitzmann's horned devil exposes his breasts we recognize that the figure harks back to some profoundly primordial attachment. It is clear that Haitzmann must have undergone not simply poverty but profound dereliction. His father's death opened up a gulf of solitude and impotence. The devil, then, to whom the painter gives his soul is surely something more than a substitute for his dead father. The popular image of the bourgeois devil's apparent respectability provides the association with the father, and the traditional representation of diabolical images calls forth some of Haitzmann's deepest desires. Following the path laid down by these images, Haitzmann gives himself to an all-powerful, magical father whose figure manages to fulfill all the archaic fantasies that his mortal father had disappointed.

Analytic experience has often shown us how mourning for the father can plunge the subject into grief when the unconscious representation of the father armed with omnipotence and immortality dissolves; this is the ideal father whose idealization sustains the subject in his own narcissism. I have tried to show elsewhere how depression is the collapse of a narcissism built on a fragile and idealizing identification.[33] This type of idealization can be traced back to its primary source in the oral stage. I spoke of the need for the absolute that goads it. I also noted how this kind of orality, fixated onto a compulsive avidity (*Süchtigkeit*), can generate the quest for drug-induced visions, intense visions of supernaturally saturated colors or such intimate contact with things that the subject no longer experiences distance or loneliness. Is it possible that drug-induced ecstasies have taken the place of the splendid visions once promised by pacts with the devil?

The experience of dereliction often feeds a hatred of life and of the world. In melancholic forms of mourning, the subject's complaints scarcely conceal the reproaches launched against the deceased for the betrayal of having disappeared. The subject's disappointment in himself, which is but the echo of the exasperated expectations he addresses to his parents, finally holds up for derision the love with which they sought to give a life but which has only produced refuse. One need only consider the mute hatred that can become directed toward the Creator when religious faith places him as the father figure at the origin of existence and at the heart of the subject's greatest hopes; man's praise may turn to disappointment. The devil is also the symbolic figure for this profound hatred.

The buffoonery surrounding the devil turns into irony an idea that can be traced back to the depths of a dereliction that would inspire too much terror were one to dwell on it. This is also the basis of the idea of the dark god who has wormed himself into the depths of being, a god who sometimes reveals himself through the cracks in the world that the din of life hastens to conceal. At moments like these, the God of love and glory proffered by the Christian message seems like an execrable fraud. The words Mallarmé used to describe the universe's divine principle, of which he wishes to rid himself, concisely express the substance and reality laid bare by the experience of religious hatred: "This old and spiteful plumage, crushed, happily, God."[34] At moments like these religious lyricism seems like a dark and voluntary illusion. The rage for demystification that seems to consume some people finds in the figure of Satan its most fantastic emblem. This does not imply any positive belief in Satan, however. It is rare to find people, outside any explicit engagement with the Christian faith, who will push their demystifying hatred to the point of positing Satan as their avowed principle of the world. But the occult fascination with Satan can play upon the imagination in search of symbols.

I venture to say that this experience of dereliction and hatred constitutes the much denied and ill-recognized ground of the pathology of possession, a ground whose essence becomes apparent in the alternation between phantasmagoric delights and a fury that convulses the human face, twists the body, and hurls blasphemies. This ambivalence of the god-devil figure is in fact one that decomposes the figure of God insofar as he remains the object of an infinitely magnified attachment, a phantasmic condensation of idealized parents. The wounds that reality then inflicts upon the subject split this God into an ambivalent power.

Certain biblical signifiers further guide the decomposition of this representation: the archaic fantasies of the oral stage and the subsequent fear of being devoured are transferred onto the devil. The hatred of an impotent God who has become monstrous in his deception and his empty promises finds both a spokesman and a symbolic support in the figure of the devil. In this way the figure of the devil becomes more complex than the figure of God. He comes to represent all the essential contradictions; he is the central nothingness opposed to everything that is experienced as religious mystification. But he also represents the magical power to which the subject clings in order to transfigure, on an imaginary level, the misery of existence. Once deceived, this attachment unleashes a hatred that proclaims the non-sense of life and seeks to bring it into realization by means of destruction. This hatred scorns the world, but, beast that it is, it also clings to the body to torture and devour it.

The same sorts of ideas generally flash through the state of mind that accompanies suicidal impulses. In colder, more objective moments, these ideas appear like a fixed notion knowledgeably reasoned out and justified by philosophical argumentation. They are as obstinate as obsessions and will not let themselves be moved by any consideration. If the subject is not caught defenseless and swept into the act in a moment of giddy impulse, he may defer the execution of it by setting himself some apparently harmless conditions for the conclusive act. He must first accomplish some task, for example. But whenever the sense of dereliction is renewed, the suicidal individual is plunged again into an atmosphere where day and night, hate and the longing for an absolute reconciliation, a fierce destructiveness and the dream of returning to a past abundance, all coexist. These suicidal crises, which are similar to hysterico-epileptic ones, are also analogous to neuroses of demonic possession. I propose the hypothesis that the existence of the cultural representation of possession allows the subject to substitute it for suicide. It is worth noting that suicidal attempts often occur after the possessed has been ritually freed from the demon inhabiting him.

In mysticism, the figure of Satan has all the features we have just analyzed, yet its status is radically different. For mystics, the devil assumes the substantial density of a reality because he is not confused with the fantastical features often attributed to him but rather is identified as their ultimate cause. In the occult, the fascination Satan exerts is emblematic—he is but a vague reference for a universal principle of evil; in the neurosis of possession he is the signifier onto which the subject attaches his fantasies. To the mystic, however, Satan becomes real as the mystifying antagonist of God. Those mystics for whom God is the most lucid reality are also those who most lucidly believe in the reality of the devil.

For John of the Cross[35] the devil is basically the prince of mystification, and here we are outside the field of psychology as such. In the works of John of the Cross, the devil is not so much a given fact that we can experience but rather a force both interior and exterior to the psyche. In possession, as we have seen, the devil is a psychic reality that is an internal and affective principle, a principle of pathos, but also, because it is an obscure and disturbing reality, one that is represented as an external invasion that holds the subject captive. The critical lucidity—reinforced by anthropological analysis—that John of the Cross brings to bear on the experience and knowledge of faith unmasks the Satanic mystification as a form of self-deception. His anthropology, integrated in the principles of faith, constitutes a coherent theory that identifies two basic domains where "the father of lies" can capture the believer by making use of his own tendencies.

The devil first "subtly lies in wait in that passage from the senses to the spirit." The faculties of the senses, especially the internal ones of imagination and memory, become the marketplace where the devil makes his first bargains. He baits the imagination by making "false things seem true, and true things seem false." By applying a relentless dialectic, John of the Cross dismantles the secret complacencies that lure men into the blindness and self-duplicity through which they surrender to the devil's wiles. He denounces especially the insidious manner in which the devil insinuates himself in those relations to God where men and women rely on visions and emotions. But the most subtle trap the devil lays in the path of man's ascent to God is that of religious pride. Like a dangerous animal lying in wait in the shadow of man's way to faith, the devil profits from man's all-too-human inclination to exalt himself; those souls prone to grandeur, he dazzles in their search for God, capturing them in their own self-satisfaction. In the work of John of the Cross, the devil is similar to that image of madness represented in the moral fables of the latter Middle Ages, an image that first seduces man, then leads him to ruin. In St. John's works, however, madness no longer has a moralistic significance; it is rather defined as a form of enslavement to something revealed as nonessential, as nonbeing, in the light of faith. Only after the spirit reaches its transformation in the process of liberating itself from all its attachments can it rediscover, without becoming ensnared in it, the beauty of the world as a metaphor of God.

I do not think that either psychology or psychoanalysis can bring anything to bear on St. John's belief in the devil. On the contrary, as a process of disillusionment and of the liberation of meanings latent or captive in men, psychoanalysis rather finds an ally in this belief. For John of the Cross, the concept of the devil as God's contrary is actually a diacritical figure that allows one to penetrate the fog of duplicity. If we take one of Lacan's formulations, we can say that the devil is that absence or disorder of being that fills and disrupts man's existence with its imaginary constructions. There is, however, a radical difference between disillusionment in psychoanalysis and in mysticism: for John of the Cross the ultimate form of self-enclosure is that form of self-sufficiency incapable of the abandon that would permit the subject to let himself be freely conquered by God, and find joy in such an exchange.

Teresa of Avila was no less adamant in tracking down the imaginary inversion proffered by him she called "the Liar," "the hypocrite," "the sinister one." But being somewhat more imaginative and spontaneous in her affective moments, she knew from experience the human tendency to attribute to the devil what in fact stems "from our own imagination and our own bad humors, especially if one is melancholy." She warns against such facile resignations. There are two basic types of experiences in which she perceives the devil actively at work. If certain ideas ("words one has heard") appear to be good but are experienced with an accompanying sense of disquiet or "uneasiness whose cause remains undiscernable . . . I then ask myself if it is not a case of one spirit feeling out another one." Convinced as she is by her faith and experience that God is light and that he brings peace, this troubling of the spirit is a warning to Teresa that the mind does not judge rightly. The spirit, though susceptible to delusion in judgment, preserves an intuitive sense that can distinguish truth from error; it is the effect thought has on affectivity that serves one here. In this case the devil truly acts as the cunning genie who blinds the spirit in such a way that reasoning can no longer offer a guarantee of its veracity. The sense of an inner freedom nevertheless preserves a more distinct and inalienable criterion as a basis for judgment.

There is, however, a second kind of experience that is more redoubtable than the uneasiness of spirit described above—the experience of guilt, which, following a conversion, can erode the subject's confidence in faith. The doubt disseminated by the devil in this case does not concern the possibility of deceiving oneself; instead it attacks the very desire which, now demystified, takes wing in mystical desire. Teresa confirms her self-doubts in the name of God himself—her desires are so great that they appear presumptuous. At certain moments she borders on melancholic delirium and sees her own faults as the cause of all the world's evils. In this despair, however, she recognizes the devil working at the destruction of her confidence and faith, and she consequently chooses to cling to the conviction of her own faith that God, who is more powerful, will lead her to victory.

The contrast in the forms the devil takes in mysticism and possession is perhaps a strange one. They both exist in the same cultural epoch and they share a common feature: in the same Christian context, the devil is always the seducer who insinuates himself into the subject's imaginary constructs and desires in order to deceive and disrupt him from within. The devil can possess the subject only by virtue of a pact, or only with some complicity on the subject's part. In the context of Christian belief the devil represents a point of reference, contrasted to God, that allows one to disengage truth from falsification. The subject, faced with these two paired references, can thus recognize his own naked truth, as a being divided between the unreasoned desires that can disrupt his existence and the clarity that can liberate him. As they articulate his existence along a vertical mode, these two points of reference make man attentive to the precariousness of his existence. And they also save him from a sense of his fundamental dereliction. Here lies the essential difference between this determination of Christian faith and the fascination with Satanism found in certain contemporary mythological representations. As an emblematic figure of nonmeaning, of the deception and violence lodged in all human endeavors, Satan becomes the sign of a quasi-metaphysical reality. This remythologizing of Satan perverts the original meaning of the belief in him. There are certain Christian traditions that legitimize a profound pessimism about the world, given its domination by the spirit of evil; thus Luther, for example, was believed to have likened man to a piece of waste spawned by the devil. But Luther warns against the kind of melancholy that leaves man prey to the devil's temptations; he relies on his faith to unmask melancholy as a form of allegiance with the devil and to transform his sense of helplessness into hope.

It is significant that the same type of belief concerning the way the devil works reappears particularly in groups of mystical bent such as the "charismatic" or the "pentecostal" movements. From the small amount of information available on the subject, I am inclined to think that in these milieus the insistence on the reality of the spirit of evil is meant basically to liberate man from the doubt and sense of dereliction that assail him when he finds himself implicated in questions of faith. From the accounts reported to me it is the moment when a serene and complacent attitude of faith, with neither problems nor fervor, becomes profoundly shaken, not by intellectual doubts or a general disenchantment but by a certain call of faith itself—after, in other words, an experience of "conversion"—that the spirit of evil takes on a very real immediacy for the subject in question. Two experiential themes that had once seemed shamefully superstitious now give reality to belief in the devil: the difficulty of overcoming the feeling of hatred by forgiveness and the sometimes anguished resistance to abandoning oneself confidently to faith. These themes converge, constituting together the experience of dereliction.

The idea of possession, proceeding from ancient times, crept progressively into the biblical idea of Satan; the theme of the power of evil that haunts man is carried over to the register of unconscious imagery and is given its specific signifier. Consequently, although he is identified as the victim of an alien force, the possessed does not find himself cast outside a community that believes it holds a victorious power over the enemy. Possession, however, is not purely exterior to the victim; the rite of exorcism evokes the participation of his own word in order to name and identify the spirit that has alienated him, and the repetitive duration of the ritual leads him to untie the mirages, anxieties, and hatred that have captivated him. In the final analysis, possession and its cure are the realization, at the level of unconscious imagery, of the same themes that mystics, with their critical vigilance, denounce and elucidate throughout their spiritual journey. Because the imagery of possession is now little more than the carbonized memory left from an ancient culture, the neurosis has taken other forms and therapeutic techniques have replaced the rite of exorcism. Nevertheless, there still remains the matter of knowing whether a discourse on the unconscious can recoup all the ancient significations of possession. Certain experiences of evil and dereliction find difficult expression in a discourse other than religious. Is it simply the illusory wish for some reconciliation with existence? Or the wish for death in its undisguised truth? These questions, put to faith, also arise from faith; faith either drowns in them or is reborn to its truth.

• Suspense and Repetition

 Through these analyses it has become clear that however stable its conviction, faith is nevertheless discontinuous in its practice. Faith lives, it has its own life, and like all life, it has its mutations. Born of an encounter between a God who exceeds man's reason and a psychic life that exceeds his conscious intentions, the experience of faith goes beyond the limits of the intelligible universe and walks with little assurance in it. Signs of the divine come to us from our immemorial depths, from which they derive their instinctual density. To the theoretical gaze, the signifiers of religious language constitute an ordered ensemble that seems to participate in the immutability of the eternal, like a vast heaven woven with constellations. But faith is not the contemplation of theoretical truth external to our flesh and substance. According to the biblical sense of the word, "knowledge" of God is an intimate commerce comparable to the physical and affective knowledge shared by a man and a woman who give themselves to one another. Insofar as it is a consent to a living God, faith makes this God come into man's psychic reality and carries this reality toward signs of the divine. By this effective encounter, the destiny of a life is woven, destiny in which the thoughts and desires of man and God seek each other out, are exchanged, and sometimes clash with each other.

By engaging man at a level beyond the lucidity of his reason, faith also becomes filled with the same obscure forces and veiled words that inhabit the psychic body of men and women. In this way the vicissitudes of the psyche and those of faith become intertwined. Consequently, an understanding of faith must pass through an elucidation of man's psychic dramas, and considerations of the order of faith will clarify the laws and events of the psyche.

In this analysis I have taken this twofold approach, and it has allowed me to circumscribe some of the major disturbances that threaten a religious life. Visible symptoms are the signposts by which we are warned of the psyche's more wayward paths. In identifying the neurotic forms of religion, however, we have had to recognize that these signposts never mark out a straight course: these errant paths are not at the periphery, but at the very heart of our being. Both psychic health and the religious view seek and accomplish each other by working also with what is deficient in us. Notions of an untroubled state of mental health or of an unclouded religious authenticity are phantasms of omnipotence. It is true that in neurosis man's energy becomes drained and fixated and his religious life mutilated. Although religion aims to save man, to promote his integrity, liberate his essential resources, and expand his existence, a debased or falsified religion has the dangerous power of confirming the sick man in his neurotic self-destruction. But it can also provide him with the vital forces necessary to sustain a collapsing psyche.

An explanation of the processes at work in neurosis also makes the boundaries that separate sanity from pathology considerably more flexible. After having finished the course of these analyses one may perhaps find oneself with an uncertain sense of expectation, left as it were in suspense with the feeling that once well-worn trails have become confused, that darkness and light merge into one another, that man finally dwells and travels falteringly through a hazy twilight as an exile from the full light of day. Once one is caught up in the play of motives and intentions that are not altogether entrapments or constant values, the temptation is great to demand neat formulas and clear outlines.

Let us evoke Dante, "the pilgrim of the Holy Face,"[1] who, midway in the path of his life, found himself in a dark and savage wood "where the sun itself fell silent." After he emerged from the wood and climbed a hill with heavy steps, a being appears to him, a being who after a long silence still seems indeterminate in contour, with a presence clearer than that of a shadow but less so than a living man. Virgil, sent as a guide to help Dante along his way, is himself left "in suspense" between the certitudes of reason and his incapacity to transcend the limits to which his vision takes him.

Whether we call them psychoanalysts, philosophers, or theologians, these guides to whom we address the questions that truly concern our innermost personal life can never give us the ultimately sovereign answer through which the question itself would find its refuge and end. Various models can provide various directions, just as an analysis of man's experiences, both wretched and joyful, can help to elucidate some of the unavoidable phases and vicissitudes of religious experience. These models cannot be reused and reissued without their somehow turning into secondhand facsimiles, and even if we were to try to use them so, the destiny of an individual cannot flow entirely along the tracks marked out by another. "No one can build for you the bridges you alone must pass to cross the river of life, no one but you, no one but you alone.... In all the world there is but one path that you alone can travel. Where does it lead? Do not ask this: follow it."[2]

• Notes

PREFACE

1. M. Merleau-Ponty, *Résumés des cours 1953–1960* (Paris: Annuaire du Collège de France, n.d.), p. 169.

CHAPTER 1. RELIGION AND PATHOLOGY

1. Among the abundant literature on the subject see in particular J. Pouillon, "Malade et médecin: le même et ou l'autre? Remarques ethnologiques," in *Incidences de la psychanalyse. Nouvelle Revue de Psychanalyse* 1 (1970): 76–98.
2. See, for example, Mark 1:23–27, 5:1ff., 9:14–17; Matthew 7:28ff., 12:44; Luke 4:39, 13:11–16.
3. See, for example, E. Corin and G. Bibeau, "De la forme culturelle au vécu des troubles psychiques en Afrique. Propositions méthodologiques pour une étude interculturelle du champ des maladies mentales," in *Africa. Journal of the International African Institute* 45 (1975): 280–315.
4. M. de Certeau, *L'Écriture de l'histoire* (Paris: Gallimard, 1975), pp. 249–50, 298.
5. This perspective is clearly maintained in the first chapter of the *Traumdeutung*, which opposes a science of dreams and their "interpretation." In German the title of the work emphasizes this.
6. S. Freud, *Obsessive Actions and Religious Practices*, in *The Standard Edition of the Complete Psychological Works of Sigmund Freud*, ed. James Strachey (London: Hogarth Press and the Institute of Psycho-Analysis, 1953–74), IX, p. 119. Subsequent citations will be to *S.E.* volume and page.
7. "Devout believers are safeguarded in a high degree against the risk of certain neurotic

illnesses; their acceptance of the universal neurosis spares them the task of constructing a personal one." Freud, *The Future of an Illusion*, S.E. XXI, p. 44.

8. See, for example, the letter to Putnam (8. VII, 1915), quoted in E. Jones, *The Life and Work of Sigmund Freud*, vol. 2 (New York: Basic Books, 1955), pp. 416–18.

9. A. E. Maeder, *Studien über Kurzpsychotherapie* (Stuttgart: E. Klett, 1963), pp. 146–47.

10. N. O. Brown, *Life against Death* (London: Routledge and Kegan Paul, 1959), pp. 3–76.

11. R. Laing, *The Politics of Experience and the Bird of Paradise* (Harmondsworth: Penguin, 1967), pp. 108–19: see also C. Delacampagne, *Antipsychiatrie. Les Voies du Sacré* (Paris: Grasset, 1974).

12. A. Maslow, "Self-Actualizing People: A Study of Psychological Health," in E. Clark, *Self-Explorations in Personal Growth* (New York: Van Nostrand, 1956), and *Toward a Psychology of Being* (New York: Van Nostrand, 1962).

13. For a typical example see R. Masters and J. Houston, *Mind Games* (New York: Dell, 1972).

14. For a discussion of various themes regarding this question see H. Fortmann, *Als ziende de Onzienlijke*, vol. 3b, *Religie en geestelijke gezondheid* (Hilversum: P. Brand, 1968).

15. F. Duyckaerts offers an excellent critical analysis of concepts like integration, autonomy, adaptation, and the normal man; see *La Notion de normal en psychologie clinique* (Paris: Vrin, 1954).

16. Duyckaerts, ibid., pp. 139ff.

17. Freud, S.E. XIX, pp. 69–108.

18. See L. de Heusch, "Cultes de possession et religions initiatiques de salut en Afrique," in *Religions de salut* (Bruxelles: Université libre de Bruxelles, 1962).

19. Ruth Benedict particularly insists upon the cultural relativity of representations of the "normal"; see *The Writings of Ruth Benedict: An Anthropologist at Work* (London: Secker and Warburg, 1959), pp. 262–83.

20. 2 Corinthians 12:2–4.

21. See the examples given in M.-C. and E. Ortigues, *L'Oedipe africain* (Paris: Plon, 1973), p. 180.

22. W. James, *The Varieties of Religious Experience* (New York: New American Library, 1958), p. 34.

23. Mark 3:20–31.

24. T. Szasz, *The Myth of Mental Illness: A Critical Assessment of the Freudian Approach* (London: Secker and Warburg, 1962).

25. Using the notion of *Gestalt*, K. Goldstein characterizes pathology essentially as some form of catastrophically disoriented behavior. See "The Organism," in G. Lindzey and C. S. Hall, eds., *Theories of Personality* (New York: Wiley, 1966), pp. 275–90.

26. We can turn to Freud's work for comments bearing on this subject. "The patient's incapacity for love, resulting from his extensive repressions, naturally stands in the way of a therapeutic plan of this kind—i.e., being healed by love—" (*On Narcissism: An Introduction*, S.E. XIV, p. 101). "The distinction between nervous health and neurosis is thus reduced to a practical question and is decided by the outcome—by whether the subject is left with a sufficient capacity for enjoyment and efficiency" (*Introductory Lectures on Psychoanalysis*, S.E. XVI, p. 457. It is only in reference to normal activities that Freud distinguishes health from morbid behavior, and the more technical observations he makes examine only the psychological conditions of these. In *The Unconscious* he accordingly advances the thesis that "as long as the system's Cs. controls affectivity and mobility, the mental condition of the person in question is spoken of as normal" (S.E. XIV, p. 179; also S.E. XIV, p. 194). We will find the same point of

view in Szondi's work. The "everyday" man who attains a balanced but only slightly creative form of existence is not proposed as the model of normality. Szondi refers to a concept of the "humanized" existence in his *Schicksalanalytische Therapie* (Bern: H. Huber, 1963), p. 113). He then goes on to analyze the alliance of instinctual tendencies that most frequently accompany this form of existence.

27. Consider the lament of the courtly poet Jaufré Rudel: "I am spurred by this love to such a point that when I hasten to her it seems to me that I run backwards toward myself while she flies away from me."

28. Freud, *Instincts and Their Vicissitudes*, S.E. XIV, p. 137.

29. On the basis of clinical studies P. Castoriadis-Aulagnier has forcefully demonstrated in a book of remarkable theoretical insight that the experience of pleasure is a necessary condition for an object to be invested with psychic interest (in other words, for an object to acquire existential status for the psyche); for example, a "pleasure in thinking" must precede the "will to think" or the "desire to think." See *La Violence de l'interprétation. Du pictogramme à l'énoncé* (Paris: Presses Universitaires de France, 1975), p. 71.

30. "We can only be satisfied if we assert that the process of civilization is a modification which the vital process experiences under the influence of a task that is set by Eros and instigated by Ananke—by the exigencies of reality; and that this task is one of uniting separate individuals into a community bound together by libidinal ties." Freud, *Civilization and Its Discontents*, S.E. XXI, p. 139.

31. Freud, *The Dynamics of Transference*, S.E. XII, pp. 99–100.

32. 2 Thessalonians 3:6.

33. 1 Corinthians 14:14.

34. Galatians 5:22.

35. A. T. Boisen initiated a movement of pastoral training for the care of psychiatric patients. He holds that therapy must be carried out through primarily religious counseling. His well-known mistrust of religiously neutral therapies, especially those inspired by Freud, is related to his own seriously disturbed past, which has been frequently disrupted by religious delusion. See Boisen, *Religion in Crisis and Custom: A Sociological and Psychological Study* (New York: Harper, 1955) and *Out of Depths* (New York: Harper, 1960).

36. W. Daim, *Depth Psychology and Salvation* (New York: Ungar, 1963); *Umwertung der Psychoanalyse* (Wien: Verlag Herold, 1951). I. A. Caruso, *Existential Psychology* (New York: Herder and Herder, 1964). V. Frankl, *Aerztliche Seelsorge* (Wien: Fr. Deuticke, 1946); *Der unbedingte Mensch* (Wien: Fr, Deuticke, 1949). V. von Gebsattel rightly emphasizes the danger of this logotherapy: the therapist who wants to do pastoral work (*Seelsorger*) becomes an obstacle to the healing process precisely because he seeks to mobilize the patient's will; see *Prolegomena einer medizinischen Anthropologie* (Berlin: Springer, 1954), pp. 350–51.

37. V. W. Turner, an anthropologist, analyzes in detail the type of exchange between the instincts in the psyche and cultural signifiers, an exchange carried out through ritual symbols; see *The Forest of Symbols: Aspects of Ndembu Ritual* (Ithaca: Cornell University Press, 1967), pp. 29–30.

38. Freud, *Infantile Neurosis*, S.E. XVII, pp. 114–15.

39. Ibid., p. 68.

40. E. Jones, "Psychoanalysis and the Christian Religion," in *Essays in Psychoanalysis*, vol. 2 (New York: International Universities Press, 1964), pp. 198–211.

41. A notion developed by V. Lanternari in *Les Mouvements religieux des peuples opprimés* (Paris: Maspero, 1962).

42. When the poet B. Goetz consulted him for therapeutic purposes, Freud replied that

the poet's creative work should be sufficient to overcome his problems. "Souvenirs sur S. Freud" in *La Psychanalyse. Recherches et enseignement freudiens de la Société française de psychanalyse*, vol. 5 (Paris: Presses Universitaires de France, 1959).

43. C. Lévi-Strauss, *Structural Anthropology* (London: Penguin, 1973).
44. P. Woollcott, "The Psychiatric Patient's Religion," *Journal of Religion and Health* 1 (1962): 337–49.
45. L. Binswanger, from his illuminating study *Erfahren, Verstehen, Deuten in der Psychoanalyse. Ausgewählte Vorträge und Aufsätze*, vol. 2 (Berlin: Franke Verlag, 1955), pp. 67–80.

INTRODUCTION TO PART II

1. G. W. F. Hegel, *Philosophy of Right* (Oxford: Clarendon Press, 1952), pp. 24, 83–84.
2. Freud, *Civilization and Its Discontents*, S.E. XXI, p. 126.

CHAPTER 2 . THE RELIGIOUS NEUROSIS OF CULPABILITY

1. In *Civilization and Its Discontents* (S.E. XXI) as in other texts, Freud affirms that the feeling of guilt in obsessional neurosis imposes itself violently upon consciousness. I have become convinced that we are dealing not with a conscious feeling of guilt but with behavior whose aim is to avoid guilt and make amends for a fault of which the subject is really not aware. We may wonder whether Freud's interpretation of religion as a collective neurosis does not blur the distinction between a consciousness of guilt and obsession. According to my findings, the representation of the particular fault is repressed in obsession, while the affective conscious content of guilt, incapable of finding a permissible representational form, is transformed into a sense of obsessive obligation.
2. J. Lacan, *Écrits* (Paris: Seuil, 1966), pp. 800–01; translated into English by A. Sheridan (London: Tavistock, 1977), pp. 289–99.
3. H. Bergson, *The Two Sources of Morality and Religion* (London: Macmillan, 1935), p. 9.
4. See J. Laplanche, *Vie et mort en psychanalyse* (Paris: Flammarion, 1970), pp. 17–43.
5. Freud, letter to Fliess, 31 May 1897.
6. F. W. Nietzsche, *The Birth of Tragedy and the Genealogy of Morals* (New York: Doubleday, 1956), p. 277.
7. G. Deleuze, *Présentation de Sacher-Masoch. Le Froid et le cruel* (Paris: Minuit, 1972), p. 89.
8. L. Szondi, *Triebpathologie*, vol. 1 (Bern: H. Huber, 1952), pp. 375–76.
9. Freud, *An Infantile Neurosis*, S.E. XVII.
10. M. Foucault, *The History of Sexuality*, vol. 1 (New York: Pantheon, 1978), p. 68.
11. See V. E. von Gebsattel, *Prolegomena einer medizinischen Anthropologie* (Berlin: Springer, 1954) pp. 74 ff, on "the world of the obsessional," and E. Strauss, *On Obsession* (New York: Coolidge Foundation, 1948) pp. 10–15.

CHAPTER 3 . THE COLLECTIVE NEUROSIS OF CULPABILITY

1. In my opinion, Gregory Bateson's analysis of the double bind, offered as a theory to explain schizophrenia, is also applicable to the paradoxical conflict that binds neurosis.

I have drawn on P. Watslawick, J. Helmick-Beavin, and D. Jackson, *Pragmatics of Human Communication* (New York: Norton, 1967).

2. See Foucault, *The History of Sexuality*, vol. 1 (New York: Pantheon, 1978), pp. 17–21.

3. The studies made by N. Elias on rules of etiquette have shown that since the Renaissance, man has progressively introduced a greater distance between himself and his body's instinctual expressions. The restraints imposed by this process of social refinement became interiorized as internal restraints. See *La Civilisation des moeurs* (Paris: Calmann-Lévy, 1973).

4. See F. Dolto's "Comment on crée chez l'enfant une fausse culpabilité," in *Trouble et lumière. Etudes Carmélitaines* (Paris-Bruges: Desclée De Brouwer, 1949), pp. 43–56.

5. Discussing the origins of guilt, Freud takes the position that only the obstacles to the aggressive instincts will entail "an aggravation of the feeling of guilt" (*Civilization and Its Discontents*, S.E. XXI, p. 134). It is indisputable that when libidinal instincts conflict with the limitations imposed by interdicts or by reality, they always excite the aggressive instincts. In this context, I adhere to part of Szondi's theory of affect as instinctual violence (the factor "e")—the violence at the source of guilt itself. See *Triebpathologie*, vol. 1 (Bern: H. Huber, 1952), pp. 81–90; *Moses Antwort auf Kain* (Bern: H. Huber, 1973), pp. 148–49.

6. The story of Helen Keller illustrates this admirably. See the discussion between J.-B. Pontalis and F. Dolto, in Pontalis, *Après Freud* (Paris: R. Julliard, 1965), pp. 349–66.

7. P. Ricoeur gives an excellent analysis of various philosophical reflections on the amoral or immoral aspect of the passions in *The Symbolism of Evil* (Boston: Beacon Press, 1972), pp. 126–50.

8. Freud, *Civilization and Its Discontents*, S.E. XXI, p. 122.

9. *Moses and Monotheism*, S.E. XXIII, chapter 3, part 2, section C, describes "the progress in spirituality" represented by the Judaic faith in one God and the interdict against any image of him. This progress is paid for by the "renunciation of the instincts" discussed on pp. 116–21.

10. Freud, *Civilization and Its Discontents*, p. 85.

11. Ibid., p. 102.

12. Ibid., p. 111.

13. Matthew 13:24–30, the parable of the darnel.

14. Luke 16:1–13, the parable of the crafty steward.

15. Matthew 5:44–48; compare Luke 6:32–36.

16. P. Klossowski, *Un destin si funeste* (Paris: Gallimard, 1963), pp. 220–21.

17. Lacan, *Écrits* (Paris: Seuil, 1966), pp. 93–100 (pp. 1–7 in Sheridan translation). On this subject see also A. De Waelhens, *Schizophrenia: A Philosophical Reflection on Lacan's Structuralist Interpretation* (Pittsburgh: Duquesne University Press, 1978), pp. 66–81.

18. Lacan has amply discussed and illustrated the psychological effects of the subject's entry into the structured field of language. See *Écrits*, pp. 273–322, 799–806 (pp. 62–107, 297–304 in the Sheridan translation).

19. See J. Daniélou, *Platonisme et théologie mystique. Essai sur la doctrine spirituelle de saint Grégoire de Nysse* (Paris: Aubier, 1944), pp. 50–65: "Thus mortality, sexuality, and every other aspect of biological life is considered foreign to man's true 'nature' " (p. 61). "As a result of the fall (the soul) was clad with a variety of *pathè*"—in other words, everything about him that concerned animal life, birth, nutrition, generation, and psychologically speaking, all knowledge through the senses, desire, and so forth.

20. Genesis 1:27.

21. The reader can look to a variety of works for a detailed analysis of these symptoms and neurotic processes. An extensive analysis of the secondary processes often used

by obsessional defenses will be found in Freud's classic study of a case of obsessional neurosis: *The Rat-Man, S.E.* X.

22. See, for example, Luke 16:7–10.
23. A. Hesnard, *L'Univers morbide de la faute* (Paris: Presses Universitaires de France, 1949).
24. A. Hesnard, *Morale sans péché* (Paris: Presses Universitaires de France, 1954), p. 40.
25. Ibid., pp. 40–41.
26. See P. Kaufmann's excellent analysis of this problem in *L'Expérience émotionnelle de l'espace* (Paris: Vrin, 1969), pp. 17–18.
27. In *Moses and Monotheism* (*S.E.* XXIII) Freud interprets official Jewish tradition as recorded in Scripture as the manifestation of a latent traumatizing memory: the murder of Moses. The analogy posited between that and the repression of guilt in an individual neurosis constitutes the "postulate" that governs his interpretation of biblical texts. (This reference to Freud does not, of course, imply that I completely adhere to his interpretation of Judaism as a model of repressed guilt.)
28. Freud, *A Disturbance of Memory on the Acropolis, S.E.* XXII, p. 246.
29. Freud, *Civilization and Its Discontents, S.E.* XXI, pp. 125–26.
30. See Lacan, *Écrits*, pp. 101–24 (Sheridan translation, pp. 8–29), on the relation between the specular identification and aggressivity.
31. F. Dolto demonstrated this clearly in "Cas cliniques de régression," in *L'Évolution psychiatrique* 3 (1957): 427–72.
32. In the conclusion of *Totem and Taboo* (*S.E.* XIII) Freud rightly stresses that "what lie behind the sense of guilt of neurotics are always *psychical* realities and never *factual* ones" (p. 159). But he also affirms the importance of the infant's realizations of his wicked impulses (p. 161).
33. Matthew 5:21–28.
34. J. L. Austin, *How to Do Things with Words* (New York: Oxford University Press, 1962). D. D. Evans, *The Logic of Self-Involvement* (London: SCM Press, 1963).
35. Austin, *How to Do Things with Words.*
36. This theme is developed by S. Leclaire, in *On tue un enfant* (Paris: Seuil, 1975).

CHAPTER 4. RITUAL IMPURITY AND DEBT

1. E. Shils, "Ritual and Crisis," in J. Huxley, ed., *A Discussion on Ritualization of Behavior in Animals and Man* (Philosoph. Trans. Royal Soc., B n. 772, London, 1966), pp. 447–50.
2. Contemporary anthropologists no longer explain magic as a ritualistic superstition, although the popularized usage of the word retains this connotation, which was inherited from earlier "enlightened" anthropologists. E. E. Evans-Pritchard provides a good example of this shift in the meaning of the term: "To try to understand magic, as an idea in itself, what is the essence of it, as it were, is a hopeless task. It becomes more intelligible when it is viewed not only in relation to empirical activities but also in relation to other beliefs, as part of a system of thought; for it is certainly often the case that it is primarily not so much a means of controlling nature as of preventing witchcraft and other mystical forces operating against human endeavor by interfering with the empirical measures taken to attain an end"; see *Theories of Primitive Religion* (Oxford: Clarendon Press, 1967), p. 111.
3. J. Piaget, *The Moral Judgment of the Child* (London: Routledge and Kegan Paul, 1932), pp. 184–94.

4. Piaget, "The Child's Construction of Reality," in *Experiments in Visual Perception* (Harmondsworth: Penguin Books, 1966), pp. 423–30.

5. Freud, *Totem and Taboo*, S.E. XIII, pp. 75–99.

6. V. von Gebsattel, *Prolegomena einer medizinischen Anthropologie* (Berlin: Springer, 1954), p. 83.

7. M. Eliade, *Patterns in Comparative Religions* (New York: Sheed and Ward, 1958), pp. 14–15.

8. I have not examined the structuring effect that ritual brings about in social behavior—a point often raised by anthropologists. I do, however, recognize the importance of this dimension, as is apparent from my insistence on the collective cultural unconscious that is responsible for forms of classification in thought.

9. These are studied by M. Douglas in *Purity and Danger: An Analysis of Concepts of Pollution and Taboo* (London: Routledge and Kegan Paul, 1966), chap. 3, "The Abominations of Leviticus," pp. 41–57.

10. P. Ricoeur, *The Symbolism of Evil* (Boston: Beacon Press, 1967), p. 52.

11. Freud, *Moses and Monotheism*, S.E. XXIII, pp. 116–21.

12. My research on the subject appeared in "Regard du psychologue sur le symbolisme liturgique," in *La Maison-Dieu* 91 (1967): 129–51.

13. Freud, *The Interpretation of Dreams*, S.E. V, p. 484. The last words are in French in Freud's original text.

14. R. L. Rubenstein, *The Religious Imagination: A Study in Psychoanalysis and Jewish Theology* (Indianapolis: Bobbs Merrill, 1968, chaps. 4, 7).

15. R. Couffignal, *L'Epreuve d'Abraham. Bible et littérature* (Toulouse: Université de Toulouse-Le Mirail, 1976), vol. 30.

16. Freud, *Moses and Monotheism*, S.E. XXIII, p. 12. This theme has been explored by Marthe Robert in *D'Oedipe à Moïse: Freud et la conscience juive* (Paris: Calmann-Lévy, 1974), p. 222.

17. Lacan, *Écrits* (Paris: Seuil, 1966) p. 810 (p. 308 in Sheridan translation).

18. R. Bultmann, *Kerygma and Myth* (New York: Harper, 1961), pp. 34–38.

19. A. Malraux, *Le Miroir des limbes. Lazare* (Paris: Gallimard, 1974), p. 160.

CHAPTER 5. DESIRE: PSYCHOLOGICAL SOURCES AND CRITERIA

1. H. Bergson, *The Two Sources of Morality and Religion* (London: Macmillan, 1935), p. 273.

2. See B. R. Wilson, *Religious Sects* (New York: McGraw-Hill, 1970).

3. See L. Vercruysse's research in "The Meaning of God: A Factoranalytic Study" in *Social Compass* 19 (1972–73): 347–64.

4. See R. C. Zaehner, *Mysticism Sacred and Profane* (London: Oxford University Press, 1961); E. Underhill, *Mysticism* (London: Methuen, 1960).

5. These are contentions of J. H. Leuba, for example, in *The Psychology of Religious Mysticism* (London: Routledge and Kegan Paul, 1972).

6. See E. Panofsky, *Renaissance and Renascens in Western Art* (London: Paladin, 1970), pp. 190ff.

7. See A. De Waelhens, "Les Contradictions du désir," in *Savoir, faire, espérer: Les Limites de la raison*, vol. 2 (Brussels: Facultés Saint-Louis, 1976), pp. 441–56.

8. Freud, "On the Universal Tendency to Debasement in the Sphere of Love," *Contributions to the Psychology of Love*, II, S.E. XI, p. 181.

9. Text by Coventry Patmore quoted by E. Underhill in *Mysticism* (New York: Dutton, 1961), p. 2.
10. See D. W. Winnicott's wonderful article on the link between transitional objects and the space of culture, "The Location of Cultural Experience," in *Playing and Reality* (London: Tavistock, 1971), pp. 95ff.
11. Inspired by Hermann, L. Szondi developed the psychology of attachment, combining under the rubric of *Anklammerung* (the "m" factor) the two modes we might distinguish as attachment (linking) and adherence (clinging to). The latter term is generally adopted as the translation for *Anklammerung*.
12. Freud, *Notes upon a Case of Obsessional Neurosis, S.E.* X, p. 234.
13. Freud, *Moses and Monotheism, S.E.* XXIII, pp. 112–22.
14. See E. Benvéniste's study "Subjectivity in Language," in *Problems of General Linguistics* (Miami: University of Miami, 1973), pp. 206ff.
15. Those familiar with Leopold Szondi's work will perhaps see that I have availed myself of and reinterpreted the ideas he developed on the p factor, which is constitutive of the ego-vector. For Szondi, the p factor designates the power to be, designates language, participation in the life of the spirit, and the function of belief. See *Ichanalyse* (Bern: H. Huber, 1956).
16. I am opposed to the Lutheran dualism emphasized by A. Nygren in *Agape and Eros* (Chicago: University of Chicago Press, 1982). As we shall see with reference to the mystics, agape is a tendency arising from an identification with God, and it is animated by desire (eros).
17. See Leuba, *The Psychology of Religious Mysticism*, Chap. 5.
18. Ibid., p. 57, 154.
19. Ibid., p. 315.
20. Ibid., p. 299.
21. Ibid., pp. 191ff.
22. P. Janet, *De l'Angoisse à l'extase. Études sur les croyances et les sentiments*, 2 vols. (Paris: Alcan, 1926). I will come back to this work.
23. Benedictus XIV, *De Servorum Dei Beatificatione et Beatorum Canonizatione* [1734], 4 vols. (Patarii: Typis Seminarii, 1743), 3:481.
24. J. Lhermitte's *Mystiques et faux mystiques* (Paris: Bloud and Gay, 1952) provides a wide spectrum of personal and historical observations, although it is not well developed analytically.

CHAPTER 6. HYSTERIA

1. *Mémorial*, in *Oeuvres* (Paris: Gallimard, Pléiade, 1950), p. 338.
2. F. Perrier, "Structure hystérique et dialogue analytique" in *Confrontations psychiatriques* 1 (1968): 101–17.
3. Freud, *On Narcissism: An Introduction, S.E.* XIV, p. 94.
4. H. Davenson, *Les troubadours* (Paris: Seuil, 1961), pp. 157–70.
5. J. Leclercq, *Initiation aux auteurs monastiques du Moyen Age. L'Amour des lettres et le désir de Dieu* (Paris: Cerf, 1963).
6. See P. Kaufmann, *L'Expérience émotionnelle de l'espace* (Paris: Vrin, 1969), pp. 17–23.
7. Janet (*De l'Angoisse à l'extase*, vol. 2, p. 456) suspects this emotional disorder of being pathogenic.
8. Freud, *S.E.* I, p. 239, Letter 52.
9. Freud uses the term *Organsprache* to describe this.
10. Freud, *The Neuro-Psychoses of Defence, S.E.* III, p. 49.

11. A. Green, *L'Affect,*" in *Revue Française de psychanalyse* 34 (1970): 1057.
12. Freud's choice of words; see *On Narcissism: An Introduction, S.E.* XIV, p. 91.
13. According to J.-P. Sartre (*Being and Nothingness* [New York: Philosophical Library, 1956], pp. 558ff.), the mystical crises of an adolescent are in themselves devoid of significance, and it is not until later that they are shown to be either a first sign of a religious vocation or a fortuitous phase of puberty, according to the way it is valorized after the fact. To this Merleau-Ponty (*The Phenomenology of Perception*) [London: Routledge and Kegan Paul, 1970], pp. 378–79) answers that it already has a meaning because it is an attitude inserted in the context of fundamental relations with the world and others. Considered true in itself if it draws on all the subject's resources and concerns his whole being, it is like real love, one that can also end when the subject or the beloved changes. Even though I agree with Merleau-Ponty, I must nevertheless mention that he does not take into account the interweave between conscious and unconscious meanings. This study attempts to focus on the fact that the adolescent's mystical breakthrough, like love, also derives from the unconscious representations that inhabit the subject. If he changes, as he must, it is precisely as a result of the labor imposed on him by the mixed multiple meanings that constitute his experience.
14. For a comparison of this process with what takes place in the analytic transference, see P. Castoriadis-Aulagnier, "A propos de transfert: Le Risque d'excès et l'illusion mortifère," in *Savoir, faire, espérer: les limites de la raison*, vol. 2 (Brussels: Facultés Saint-Louis, 1975), pp. 426–32.
15. Lacan, *Écrits*, pp. 93–100 (pp. 1–7 in the Sheridan translation).

CHAPTER 7. ILLUSTRATION BY SOME VARIANTS

1. Janet, *De l'Angoisse à l'extase*, vol. 1, p. 464.
2. Ibid., p. 460
3. H. Lemesle, "La Transverbération de sainte Thérèse d'Avila," in *Revue de l'hypnotisme* 16 (1902): 78–87.
4. J. Maréchal especially elaborated this issue in *Studies in the Psychology of the Mystics* (London: Burns, Oates, and Washburne, 1927).
5. Teresa of Avila, *Book of Her Life*, X, 1, *The Way of Perfection*, XXV.
6. P. Valéry, *Oeuvres*, vol. 2 (Paris: Gallimard, Pléiade, 1957), pp. 96–97.
7. Teresa of Avila, *The Interior Castle*, Seventh Mansion, I, 7.
8. Bergson, *The Two Sources of Morality and Religion*, pp. 250–65.
9. Freud, *New Introductory Lectures on Psychoanalysis, S.E.* XXII, p. 97.
10. Freud, *Civilized Sexual Morality, S.E.* IX, p. 187.
11. In *The Phenomenology of Spirit* (Oxford: Clarendon Press, 1973), Hegel accurately identified the idea of utility as the fundamental concept of the Enlightenment.
12. S. Ferenczi, "Hysterical Materialization: Thoughts on the Conception of Hysterical Conversion and Symbolism," in *Further Contributions to the Theory and Technique of Psychoanalysis* (London: Hogarth, 1960), p. 96.
13. J. Laplanche, "Pour situer la sublimation," in *La Psychanalyse à l'Université* 1 (1976): 424.
14. A paper on sublimation was supposed to complete his series on metapsychology. It is thought that Freud wrote it and destroyed it.
15. See Freud, *Civilization and Its Discontents, S.E.* XXI, p. 79.
16. Freud, *The Ego and the Id, S.E.* XIX, pp. 44–45.

17. Freud, *On Narcissism: An Introduction*, S.E. XIV. The Freudian thesis of the joint constitution of the subject (the ego) and the object of love through narcissism shows, paradoxical as it may seem, that before it can become a morbid withdrawal in itself, narcissism is a fundamental process. This point concurs with what phenomenology and linguistics have elucidated at other levels of the subject's constitution. I dealt with this issue in my study "Le sujet en psychanalyse," in *Problèmes de psychanalyse* (Paris: Desclée De Brouwer, 1972).
18. Freud, *Instincts and Their Vicissitudes*, S.E. XIV, p. 137.
19. Freud, *On Narcissism*, S.E. XIV, p. 100.
20. Freud, *Civilized Sexual Morality*, S.E. IX, p. 189.
21. Freud, *On Narcissism*, S.E. XIV, p. 100.
22. See "pleasure principle," in J. Laplanche and J. B. Pontalis, *The Language of Psycho-analysis* (London: Hogarth, 1973).
23. M. Montrelay, *L'Ombre et le nom. Sur la féminité* (Paris: Minuit, 1977), pp. 77–81.
24. This is the concept of the imaginary developed by Lacan, which he distinguishes from the real and the symbolic. See his *Écrits*, pp. 808–10 (pp. 306–08 in the Sheridan translation).
25. Teresa of Avila, *Book of Her Life*, XXIX, 16–17.
26. As Dr. Lemesle contends in "La Transverbération de sainte Thérèse d'Avila."
27. G. Groddeck, *La Maladie, l'art et le symbole* (Paris: Gallimard, 1969), pp. 275–90.
28. Teresa of Avila, *Interior Castle*, Seventh Mansion, II, 3.
29. B. Bettelheim, *Symbolic Wounds, Puberty Rites and the Envious Male* (Glencoe, Ill.: Free Press, 1954).
30. Teresa of Avila, *Interior Castle*, Fifth Mansion, IV, 3.
31. Ibid., Seventh Mansion, II–III.
32. K. Shelderup, *Die Askese* (Berlin: W. de Gruyter, 1928), pp. 202–26.
33. See, for example, H. Moller, "Affective Mysticism in Western Civilization," in *Psychoanalytic Review* 52 (1965): 115–30.
34. Simone de Beauvoir, *Le Deuxième Sexe* (Paris: Gallimard, 1949), chap. 13. The author, however, praises Catherine of Sienna for her virile temperament.
35. *Venerabilis Agnetis Blannbekin quae ... Wiennae floruit, vita et revelationes ...*, published in Vienna in 1730 by Bernard Pez, librarian of the Abbey of Melk in Austria.
36. *Vita et revelationes*, chap. 37.
37. Ibid., chap. 78.
38. Montaigne, *Essays*, Book III.
39. D. Witny, "Mysticisme et érotisme," in *Revue de l'hypnotisme* 24 (1910).
40. See Freud's study of President Schreber, *Notes on a Case of Paranoia*, S.E. XII, pp. 63–64.
41. This concept is developed by Freud in *Three Essays on Sexuality*, S.E. VII, p. 178.
42. The documents in the autobiography of Margaret-Mary Alacoque are complex and controversial. Dr. Rouby (*Revue de l'hypnotisme* 18 [1902–03], nos. 4, 5, 6, 7, 12) states that after the first edition in 1739 by Languet de Gergy, the text was not only completed but also expurgated of certain expressions that were too obviously suspect. I had at my disposal only the new edition, released by the monastery of Paray-Le-Monial, of the text presented by Mgr. Gauthey: *Vie et oeuvres de sainte Marguerite-Marie Alacoque*, vol. 2 (Paris: V. de Gigord, 1920). The autobiographical section covers pages 29–119.

CHAPTER 8. VISIONS AND VOICES

1. H. Ey, *Traité des hallucinations*, 2 vols. (Paris: Masson, 1973); the definition given in the text is from vol. 2, p. 1441.

2. Ey, *Traité des hallucinations*, vol. 1, p. 27.
3. P. Guercy, "Théorie de la perception de l'image et l'hallucination chez Spinoza, Leibniz, Taine et Bergson," in *L'Hallucination* (Paris: Masson, 1930). Quoted by H. Ey, vol. 1, p. 68.
4. Ey, *Traité des hallucinations*, vol. 1, p. 46.
5. Ibid., p. 45.
6. Ibid., p. 1440.
7. Ibid., p. 741.
8. Ibid., p. 37.
9. J.-P. Sartre, *Imagination* (Ann Arbor: University of Michigan Press, 1972), p. 89.
10. Ey, *Traité des hallucinations*, pp. 41–42.
11. By the term *negative hallucination*, classic to the psychiatry of his time, Freud designates the absences of consciousness typical in hysteria and the hysterical subject's failure to recognize persons and objects. Thus a negative hallucination is the prelude to double or split consciousness. This notion is taken up and more fully elaborated in his remarks on the splitting of the personality. (See *Studies on Hysteria*, Anna O's inaugural case, in *S.E.* II.) The term comes back again in his study of Jensen's *Gradiva* (*S.E.* IX). According to the young lady's assertions, Harold has the gift of "negative hallucination," the art of not seeing or recognizing persons who are present.
12. I borrow this expression from Minkowski, who says that a third world emerges between the subject and the objective world; see "La réalité et les fonctions de l'irréel," in *L'Évolution psychiatrique* (1950), pp. 59–136.
13. Janet, *Névroses et idées fixes*, vol. 1 (Paris: Alcan, 1898), pp. 156–212, the case of Justine.
14. *Autobiography*, III, pp. 19–20, in *Obras completas de San Ignacio de Loyola* (Madrid: La Editorial Catolica, 1952), pp. 43–44.
15. Polanco, *De vita P. Ignatii et Societatis Jesu Initiis 1573, Fontes Narrativi*, vol. 2, p. 527, quoted by L. Beirnaert: "L'Expérience fondamentale d'Ignace de Loyola et l'expérience psychanalytique" in *La Psychanalyse* (Paris: Presses Universitaires de France, 1957), vol. 3, p. 115.
16. In the study previously cited, Beirnaert relates this "thing" to the imaginary (in Lacan's sense of the word) that worms its way into the different levels of the psyche's constitution. Although I approve this probable but nonetheless hypothetical interpretive construction, I consider it preferable to limit oneself to an interpretation of the precise text within its immediate context.
17. This particular phrase is not found in the autobiography but is reported in the *Fontes Narrativi*; Beirnaert ("Ignace de Loyola et l'expérience psychanalytique," p. 123*n*) considers it to be the more spontaneous form.
18. *Autobiography*, p. 75.
19. Freud, *The Unconscious, S.E.* XIV, p. 203.
20. Lacan's formulation in *Écrits*, p. 392.
21. Freud, *An Infantile Neurosis, S.E.* VIII, p. 85.
22. Freud, *On Narcissism, S.E.* XIV, pp. 79–81.
23. Teresa of Avila, *The Interior Castle*, Sixth Mansion, IX, 3.
24. St. John of the Cross, *Ascent of Mount Carmel*, II, xi, 2–4.
25. Ibid., II, xi, 7.
26. Ibid., II, xvi, 1–2.
27. Ibid.
28. St. John of the Cross, *The Dark Night of the Soul*, II, i.
29. St. John of the Cross, *Ascent of Mount Carmel*, II, xxiii, 2.
30. Ibid., II, xxix, 2.
31. Ibid., II, xxix, 1.

32. Ibid., II, xvi.
33. Teresa of Avila, *The Interior Castle*, The Sixth Mansion, III, 4–9.
34. Ibid., The Sixth Mansion, 4, 12.
35. Teresa of Avila, *Book of Her Life*, XL.
36. *Le Procès de Jeanne d'Arc*, presented by G. and A. Duby (Paris: Gallimard-Julliard, 1973), p. 30.
37. I have developed this theme in "Interprétation psychologique du 'phénomène Antonien,'" in *Il Santo* 16 (1976): 237–49.
38. See J. Le Goff, s.v. "Jeanne d'Arc," in *Encyclopedia Universalis* (Paris, 1968).
39. Ibid.
40. A. Rimbaud, in his letter of 1871 to Paul Demeny: "Je est un autre...," *Oeuvres complètes* (Paris: Gallimard, Pléiade, 1946), p. 254.
41. Fr. Gerlich, *Die stigmatisierte Therese Neumann von Konnersreuth* (München: Kösel, 1929); Gerlich adamantly defends the supernatural nature of both the stigmata and visions of Theresa Neumann.
42. H. Thurston, *The Physical Phenomena of Mysticism* (London: Burns and Oates, 1952), p. 122.
43. Ibid.
44. Ibid., p. 123.
45. J. Corraze, *De l'Hystérie aux pathomimies. Psychopathologie des simulations* (Paris: Durod, 1976), p. 243.
46. Ibid., 245.
47. Gerlich, *Die stigmatisierte Therese Neumann*, vol. 1, p. 18.
48. B. De Poray-Madeyski, *Le Cas de la visionnaire stigmatisée Thérèse Neumann de Konnersreuth* (Paris: Lethielleux, 1940), p. 89.
49. Ibid., p. 102.
50. Janet, *De l'Angoisse à l'extase*; refer also to the supplementary letters and unedited testimony in *Études carmélitaines* 16 (1931): 20–61.
51. A. Malraux, *L'Homme précaire et la littérature* (Paris: Gallimard, 1977), p. 22.
52. See P. Evdokimov's wonderful study, *L'Art de l'icône. Théologie de la beauté* (Paris: Desclée de Brouwer, 1970).

CHAPTER 9. THE FIGURES OF THE DEVIL

1. Ephesians, 1:21.
2. J. Gayral, *Les Délires de possession diabolique* (Toulouse: Presses Universitaires, 1944); J. de Tonquédec, "Quelques aspects de l'action de Satan en ce monde," in *Satan, Études carmélitaines* (Paris: Desclée de Brouwer, 1948), pp. 493–506.
3. See N. and H. W. Schnaper, "A Few Kinds Words for the Devil," in *Journal of Religion and Mental Health* 8 (1969): 107–22.
4. Jung, "Answer to Job," in *Collected Works of C. G. Jung*, vol. 11 (London: Routledge and Kegan Paul, 1952).
5. See G. Zacharias, *Satanskult und schwarze Messe. Ein Beitrag zur Phänomenologie der Religion* (Wiesbaden: Limes Verlag, 1964); R. S. Scharf-Kluger, *Satan in the Old Testament* (Evanston: Northwestern University Press, 1967).
6. C. Priault and L. Saghy make clear how the belief in spirit possession prevalent in West African traditions becomes transformed into diabolical possession when it comes under the influence of Christianity; see "Les confessions diaboliques," in *Prophétisme et thérapeutique* (Paris: Hermann, 1975), pp. 121–52.

7. I. M. Lewis, *Ecstatic Religion: An Anthropological Study of Spirit Possession and Shamanism* (Harmondsworth: Penguin, 1971).
8. See chap. 7 ("Possession and Psychiatry") in Lewis, *Ecstatic Religion*.
9. Ibid., p. 183.
10. Ibid., pp. 188–89.
11. Ibid., p. 190.
12. See the "Procès d'Anne de Chartraine (1620–1625)," reported in *Satan*, pp. 380–85. Referring to this case, Lhermitte (*Satan*, p. 472) makes the common mistake of confusing sorcery and possession, whereas the text of the trial shows clearly that the accusations brought against Anne de Chartraine were "crimes of casting spells."
13. M. de Certeau has dedicated an in-depth historical and sociological study to this issue in *La Possession de Loudun* (Paris: Julliard, 1970). In *L'Écriture de l'histoire* (Paris: Gallimard, 1975), chap. 6, he deals with the phenomenon of Loudun again in order to clarify certain questions he had left open.
14. G. Ferdière, "Le Diable et le psychiatre," in *Entretiens sur l'homme et le diable*, colloquium of Cérisy-la-Salle, 1964, directed by M. Milner (Paris-La Haye: Mouton, 1965), pp. 317–48.
15. C. Lévi-Strauss, *Structural Anthropology* (London: Penguin, 1969).
16. M. de Certeau gives particular attention to this aspect of possession in *L'Écriture de l'histoire*.
17. M. Foucault, *Histoire de la folie à l'âge classique* (Paris: Gallimard, 1972), pp. 181–82. Portions of this book have been translated into English under the title *Madness and Civilization* (New York: Random House, 1965).
18. This distinction was made by Lhermitte in "Les Pseudo-possessions diaboliques," in *Satan*, pp. 472–92.
19. See A. Frank-Duquesne's excellent study "Réflexions sur Satan en marge de la tradition judéo-chrétienne," in *Satan*, pp. 179–314.
20. Lhermitte, "Les Pseudo-possessions diaboliques"; Ey, *Traité des hallucinations*.
21. Lewis, *Ecstatic Religion*, the caption of an illustration facing p. 112.
22. Published in Louvain by Jean Bogart, reedited by Bourneville, a student of Charcot, in the *Bibliothèque infernale* (Paris, circa 1880).
23. P. Debongnie, "Les Confessions d'une possédée. Jeanne de Ferry," in *Satan*, pp. 386–419.
24. J. Vinchon, "Les Aspects du diable à travers divers états de possession," in *Satan*, pp. 465.
25. See Janet, *Névroses et idées fixes*, vol. 1, pp. 375–406.
26. F. Dolto, "Le Diable chez l'enfant," in *Satan*, pp. 429–41.
27. H. Maldiney, *Aîtres de la langue et demeures de la pensée* (Lausanne: L'Age d'homme, 1975), pp. 249–50.
28. Lhermitte, "Les Pseudo-possessions diaboliques," pp. 485–86.
29. *Perceval's Narrative (Autobiography of a Schizophrenic, 1830–1832)*, published by Gregory Bateson (Stanford: Stanford University Press, 1961).
30. This is the mechanism of paranoia analyzed by Freud in the last chapter of *President Schreber, S.E.* XII, p. 63.
31. "The Occult: A Substitute for Faith," in *Time*, 19 June 1972, pp. 38–48.
32. Freud, *A Seventeenth-Century Demonological Neurosis, S.E.* XIX, pp. 69–105.
33. A Vergote, "La Névrose dépressive," in *Topique* 17 (1976): 97–126.
34. S. Mallarmé, *Correspondance, 1862–1871*, ed. H. Mondor and J.-P. Richard (Paris: Gallimard, 1959), p. 241.
35. This discussion is based on P. Lucien-Marie de Sainte-Joseph, "Le Démon dans l'oeuvre de saint Jean de la Croix," in *Satan*, pp. 86–97.

1. The title of R. Dragonetti's work, *Dante pèlerin de la Sainte Face*, Romanica Gandensia XI (Ghent, 1968).
2. F. W. Nietzsche, *Unzeitgemässe Betrachtungen*, III, 1, in *Werke*, vol. 2 (Leipzig: Naumann Verlag, 1906), p. 214.

Index